THE GIRL FROM KATHMANDU

THE
GIRL FROM
KATHMANDU

Twelve Dead Men and a Woman's Quest for Justice

CAM SIMPSON

HARPER

An Imprint of HarperCollins*Publishers*

HarperCollins books may be purchased for educational, business, or sales promotional use. For information, please email the Special Markets Department at SPsales@harpercollins.com.

FIRST EDITION

Designed by Bonni Leon-Berman

Library of Congress Cataloging-in-Publication Data has been applied for.

ISBN 978-0-06-244971-9

18 19 20 21 22   LSC   10 9 8 7 6 5 4 3 2 1

For my late grandfather, Ben Arnold,
who gave me a joy for life; and my mother,
Judy Fagel, who gave me a love for stories

CONTENTS

ACKNOWLEDGMENTS

This book would not have been possible without the invaluable assistance of Dr. Minani Gurung, who guided me through Nepal in 2014 and 2016, and who translated so much beyond language. Her wisdom about culture, gender, and human nature made this work possible. Flynn McRoberts is one of my most valued friends and one of the best editors working today. I was incredibly lucky to have him lead the edit for the original investigation, published in the *Chicago Tribune*, and to get his input every step of the way during the many years I worked on this book. Abigail Fielding-Smith deserves special thanks for her priceless suggestions on the manuscript, as well as her personal support and patience. I am indebted to others who offered feedback and support, including the amazing Sascha Alper, Kim Barker, Tim Farnam, Dan Hagen, Jeremy Kahn, Quil Lawrence, Stryker McGuire, Jonathan Morrow, Sarah O'Connor, Evan Osnos, Ed Robinson, Vernon Silver, and Eric Westervelt. Special thanks go to Rima das Pradhan-Blach for her ideas and support in my original investigation.

I also want to thank George W. Papajohn of the *Chicago Tribune*, whose force of will helped make the original investigation possible; and the inimitable Michael Tackett, Jim O'Shea, Ann Marie Lipinski, and George de Lama. For their unwavering and more recent support, I wish to thank Reto Gregori, Bob

Blau, and Ellen Pollock. I am forever indebted to the absurdly talented Josh Tyrangiel, who, in league with Bryant Urstadt, helped me explore better ways to tell stories of consequence. Finally, thanks to Jonathan Jao for his remarkably thoughtful edit of this book, and to Larry Weissman and the legendary Claire Wachtel for believing in it.

AUTHOR'S NOTE

The Girl from Kathmandu is a work of nonfiction. All the events and people are real, and none of the names, places, or dates have been changed. The narrative is drawn from repeated interviews with the critical players and from more than thirty thousand pages of documents, most of which were generated during a decade of litigation. Further details can be found in the "Note on Sources" and "Notes" sections at the end of the book.

PART I

*"Give Us His Breath
or His Body"*

1

MARCH 2013
Washington, DC

Kamala Magar, heart racing, stomach rising, gathered herself by focusing on the little things her lawyers had told her to do. *Sit tall and straight in your chair. Interlace your fingers and place your hands on the table in front of you. Breathe.*

The long table's dark finish was so glossy she could see her hands and face reflected back in a kind of shimmer, as if she were looking into a still pool. A packet on the table marked "Exhibit 58" held her memories in photocopied snapshots: her husband posing alone in front of their farmhouse; her ten-year-old daughter beneath the endless blue of the Himalayan sky. Directly across the table from Kamala, a video camera fixed on a tripod stared her down. On either side of it sat defense lawyers, each representing one of the two companies she was blaming for her husband's death of almost a decade earlier, when she was not yet nineteen. The lens closed in on her face. Her breathing quickened.

She wore a royal-blue long-sleeve *kurti* top with embroidered lilac trim swirling across her chest. The shawl around her neck was tightly wrapped, more like a piece of armor than a scarf, but the weight of a lapel microphone pulled it low, exposing her throat to the chill of the conference room. Terrilyn Crowley, the court reporter, sat off to the side with her stenography machine. Crowley had come to Washington, DC, all the way from Houston for the deposition, chosen by the attorney seated to the left of the camera. He represented KBR Inc., formerly known as Kellogg Brown and Root, the $4.5 billion military and construction contractor that had generated so much controversy during the Iraq War for its Texas-based parent company, Halliburton. The conference room was home turf for KBR, even though it was far from Texas. They were in the heart of Washington's "K Street" neighborhood, on the top floor of a glass-sided building, where KBR's law firm resided. K Street's boulevards are canyons lined with office blocks, each building nearly equal in height and brimming with lawyers and lobbyists representing America's biggest companies.

Crowley administered an oath to Kamala. She swore to tell the truth.

Joseph Sarles's boyish face masked the sharpness of his cross-examination skills. His tone with Kamala as he began his interrogation lacked sting, but it also held no warmth. Filming a deposition tends to affect the conduct of lawyers and witnesses alike. If for some reason Kamala could not appear at trial, jurors might see this as her only testimony, hence her hands folded on the table, her back against the chair, her composed presentation. Sarles, too, needed to be careful, not just about what he said to the widow, but also about how he said it. Jurors might sympathize with Kamala even more if his questions came off as cruel or aggressive toward a young woman who had been through so much.

Sarles kept his voice at a steady, bloodless pitch, as if reading aloud from an accounting textbook. His tone barely changed when he began asking Kamala about four of the worst minutes of her life.

"Did you ever see any video, at any time, that related to your husband?" Sarles asked.

Kamala drew a deep breath and slumped forward. Tears welled behind her eyes, but she sat still, staring, lost, into the table's reflection for what seemed an eternity—five seconds of silence passed, and then ten, and then twenty. No one in the room made a sound. Kamala swiveled gently from side to side in the gray chair, as she did when she comforted her daughter, eyes still lost in the table's sheen. Slowly, she lifted her head. "Yes," she said, looking back at Sarles. "I have."

"Can you describe what video you've seen?" he asked.

Kamala dropped her gaze to the table again. This time it took only a few seconds for her to gather herself and look back toward her questioner. "I saw the one—the one in which they killed him," she said, almost in a whisper.

Virtually everyone in Kamala's life, nearly everyone she had ever met, nearly everyone in her homeland, had watched her husband die. Vendors had sold the execution video on DVD in the dusty streets of Kathmandu and even in the smaller towns. Some had hawked single viewings in curtained booths offered with a cup of tea for just a few pennies. Even the other widows in the ashram where she had lived after being rejected by her late husband's family knew how he had died, or had even viewed his murder. When she met people for the first time, she felt their knowing pass as a momentary silence, or saw it in an arrested expression on their faces once they realized who she was. After Kamala learned she might testify, she had yielded to a voice that told her she had to see, had to know, despite all her instincts in the almost nine years in which she had avoided those four minutes and five seconds.

"When did you see it?" Sarles asked her.

"After a long time," Kamala said.

"Who showed it to you?"

"I looked at it myself. I watched it on my own," she said.

"Where were you when you watched it? . . . Were you at your house, or were you someplace else?"

"At my house," Kamala said.

"How did you get a copy of the video?"

"Objection!" said Anthony DiCaprio, seated directly to Kamala's right. There was no judge in the room to rule on DiCaprio's objection, but objections in depositions are common, creating markers in the record that allow questions to be challenged and stricken later if warranted. They also give lawyers a tactical tool to emphasize a line of questioning that could be seen as unbecoming to jurors watching later on a big screen in the courtroom. Kamala's lead attorney, a decorated human rights lawyer named Agnieszka Fryszman, had brought DiCaprio into the case specifically for this purpose. "You'll be our pit bull," she had told him.

Fryszman looked drawn. The lids of her brown eyes drooped and she'd lost so much weight that her "lucky" outfit, a black pantsuit she'd worn for years to every court appearance, gave her the look of a child dressed in her mother's clothes. There didn't seem to be a limit to the resources KBR was piling into its defense. Its cadre of lawyers fought even some of the most mundane facets of the litigation to the extreme, burying Fryszman in so many paper salvos that she didn't have time to depose a single KBR employee, even as a trial date loomed on the court calendar. The defense had also made the fight personal, accusing Fryszman of misconduct in a raft of charges that might derail her career and hurt almost every lawyer who had helped her in the case. Her assistant counsel, an idealistic young woman with degrees from Harvard and Columbia, had resigned after skirting the edge of a nervous breakdown. Now, as Kamala suffered through her interrogation, Fryszman and her law firm had just one week left to respond to KBR's charges. A star witness had stumbled badly in an earlier deposition, giving KBR more fodder. If Kamala broke down under questioning, the defense could pounce again, dealing a potentially significant blow to the case at the worst possible moment.

There was cause to worry. Most people who are grilled by a lawyer for the first time have at least seen a cross-examination in the movies or on television, but Kamala had grown up in a mountain village where the only power came from a battery in the back of a transistor radio and the only running water poured down gullies or through a tap jutting from a stone wall built into the mountainside at the village well. Although she had moved to Kathmandu after her husband's murder, she had never flown on an airplane until the journey that brought her to Dulles International Airport three weeks before her testimony; nor had she ever seen snowfall except on the distant peaks of the world's highest mountain range, which dominated the horizon of her village in the subtropics of the Himalayas. Powder had covered the U.S. capital when Kamala arrived in February. She regarded the snow with wonder and wished her daughter could see it.

Despite her exhaustion coming off a ten-thousand-mile journey, Kamala had worried herself awake that first night at the Washington Plaza Hotel. She had never been apart from her daughter and could not escape her fear of what might befall the child if something happened to her on this trip. Everything in the hotel room seemed so foreign, reminding her of how far she was from home: the keyless electronic door, the coffeemaker she struggled to use, the bright white linens impossibly smooth across the surface of the bed. For years, Kamala had focused solely on returning to life and raising Kritika alone, keeping everything else in the shadows. But during that sleep-less night in the Washington hotel, memories of her husband were inescapable. Attesting to them was the reason she had found herself in such a strange place.

That night, she rose and moved to the small bathroom. There she stood in front of the vanity and the seamless mirror cover-ing the wall behind it, reading the lines of her face, looking into her own eyes. *I came here to fight for my husband*, she told herself, *but everything would be so different if he had come home as he'd promised. None of these things happening now would even have crossed my mind.* She saw herself crumple. After a moment, she opened the taps, leaned over the bathroom sink, and with cupped hands raised the water to her face.

In the days that followed her arrival, Fryszman and Di-Caprio tried to prepare Kamala for the cross-examination, with DiCaprio playing the bad guy in mock sessions, but he didn't always get far. Many attempts began or ended in tears. Fryszman had worried that moving forward with the case at all would be too much for the families of the dead. She had hoped for a quicker resolution, given that so many respectable modern American corporations customarily own up to the actions that take place along their supply chains, all the way to the most basic raw materials and services—the conditions on the farms that grow the cotton used to weave the denim sewn into blue jeans, the mining of the tin that goes into the solder holding together the components of an iPhone. Yet, for the signal case that had helped define human trafficking in the United States, Halliburton and its former subsidiary, KBR, had refused to ac-cept even a modicum of responsibility for their *human* supply chain—a supply chain, moreover, that in 2004 fell victim to the worst massacre of U.S. civilian personnel during the Iraq

War and that would make KBR Halliburton the biggest war-time contractor in American history. For the company's defense team, it was rather simple reasoning: admitting any responsibility or settling the case with these twelve families might result in thousands more suits against the company, given just how big that human supply chain was. Although she struggled, Kamala told Fryszman and DiCaprio that she wanted to get her testimony right, for her husband, for her daughter, and for the others who had also lost husbands, fathers, and sons in the four-minute video that Sarles would pick away at.

Now, following his objection to the question about how Kamala had come to see the video, DiCaprio turned to Kamala and told her it was okay to answer.

"It was in my phone's memory card," she said.

"How did you get a copy of it on your mobile phone?" Sarles asked.

"Objection!" DiCaprio said, then, calmly to Kamala: "You may answer."

"I downloaded it," Kamala said.

"You downloaded it from a website?"

"Yes."

"Do you remember the name of the website?"

"No."

"How did you learn about the video? . . . How did you find out that this video existed?" Sarles asked, seemingly oblivious to the fact that virtually every adult in her nation of twenty-seven million people knew of its existence.

"I don't remember specifically how I came to know," Kamala said.

Sarles peppered Kamala some more with questions that made little sense to her—Did you watch it on your phone, or someone else's? Did you watch it sometime recently? Is it possible you watched it for the first time in the last six months? Finally, he asked her the one question for which he already knew the answer: "Can you describe for me what you saw when you watched the video?"

Kamala sank back into the chair, coldness seeping into her. She had tried to push the images, the infernal sounds, out of her mind, but now there were flashes: a white blindfold wrapping a face; a hunting knife against a throat; young men, some just boys, lying facedown beneath the sky; the barrel of a rifle. Then the sounds: the piercing, shrill wheezes; the staccato rifle reports; the ping echoing from an empty clip after the firing of a final round; the muffled, almost infernal wails. Blood pooling, turning desert dust into mud. She again fought tears.

"I can't," Kamala said.

2

CIRCA 1993
Gorkha District, Nepal, in the
Foothills of the Himalayas

Every year, a boy named Gori came from the neighboring village to help sow the mountain terraces with rice, and every
year, he seemed to make trouble at the celebration held when
the work ended. This time he wrapped a long cloth around his
waist like a skirt and covered his head with a shawl, pretending
to be a girl. He pranced around Kamala as she crouched on the
ground. He poked his nose into her face and sang in a mocking
voice while the other children squealed their approval. As Gori
taunted her, Kamala's gaze tightened. She rolled her hands into
fists. When he flailed at her again, Kamala sprang up to pum-
mel his face with punches, including one across the nose. No
blood spilled, but tears gushed from the boy's eyes as he stag-
gered back and then ran away as fast as he could. The little
girl could fly into such fearsome bouts, so quickly, that few
from the surrounding villages dared taunt her or attempt to
intervene—except for Maya.

"Oh, my *nani*, my baby girl," Maya used to say, gently strok-
ing her baby sister's long brown hair or swirling her hand across
her back, trying to calm Kamala so she could take her by the
hand and lead her home.

Their wood-frame stone farmhouse rose from the side of a
mountain that reached nearly a mile into the sky. The house

stood atop a ledge carved by hand into the mountain's sheer face, near the center of a ridgeline shaped like a horseshoe. Looking out from the farmhouse's porch, one sees the horseshoe ridge open to the north and into a lush valley below. At the valley's end, the earth rises again. A series of jungle-covered ridges climb in succession, each higher than the last, each darker than the last, like layers in the most extraordinary landscape painting. Beyond the last ridge is a sheer white palisade of ice and rock cutting straight across the entirety of the horizon and reaching into the heavens. This is the Mansiri Himal range of the Himalayas. Though located roughly eighty miles north of the farmhouse, it dominates every visible inch of skyline, from the base of the horizon to a peak nearly five miles high. The range's highest visible mountaintop, which is also the eighth-tallest in the world, resembles the silhouette of a fox's head, its twin peaks like ears facing each other across an arched ridge. Its name is Manaslu, which means, "the Spirit Mountain." The farmhouse faces Manaslu almost squarely.

No one is quite sure how long people have been living on and farming the horseshoe ridge, but Kamala's grandfather and his two brothers built the first permanent homes along the narrow path they'd carved into the red earth. Eventually, their trio of farmhouses became a recognized village, called Tin Gharey Toll, which means "the Three-House Street." Eight families lived there in April 1986, when Kamala was born inside her grandfather's house beside the warmth of an open fire.

Seven other villages are scattered along the horseshoe ridge, each holding a cluster of about a dozen homes, many splashed with red bougainvillea, pink hibiscus, or roses carefully cultivated around the edges of their gardens. Terraced farm fields are carved above and below each cluster of homes, winding around the mountain like green staircases climbing into the clouds. The jungle's assault of the valley is beautiful and relentless, fueled by freshwater that streams down gullies in every season; the creeks and rivers may slow in summer, but they never run dry. Relief from the wild comes only from blades driven by human and livestock muscle, sinew, and bone—from the villagers chopping through tangled vines, felling trees with hand axes, and from bulls or water buffalo pulling tethered plows to carve away the jungle by scraping out the mountain earth beneath it.

The red dirt beds of the cleared terraces are sown each season with blankets of seed—corn, millet, rice, and beans, all of which demand constant care. Tiny footpaths trace the terrace edges. When the terraces are thick with life, they look like green banners unfurled throughout the valley, with narrow bands of red trim. Families here eat only what they can grow or rear with their own hands, which requires each household to possess a bit more than an acre to survive, roughly the size of an American football field. Many farmers must extend their terraces all the way to the valley floor in order to assemble enough total cropland from these tiny strips of mountain to get the food they need. The deeper into the valley the farmers go, the wider their fields can get, owing to the more forgiving grade there. Yet the price comes in the climb back up, which grows heavier with each step, especially when the farmers are bowed by the weight of a harvest, which they carry in giant baskets slung over their backs and secured by straps across their foreheads, their necks stiffened atop shrugged shoulders. Often this is the work of girls and women.

As a child, Kamala rose each day hours before the climbing sun had cast its first rays on the peak of Manaslu. Roosters usually roused her, crowing into the coolness of the morning beneath her window. Sometimes she was awakened by familiar shouts of "Ha! Ha-ha!" from her uncle leading a bull through the narrow road. The clearest sign of the new day wafted through the home's windows as the sweetness of wood smoke rose over the village from what seemed to be a hundred kitchen fires lit each morning across the valley. Kamala would scamper backward down the steps of the ladder leading to the ground floor of the farmhouse, step onto the edge of the porch, and turn her back to Manaslu as she slid into her flip-flops. School didn't start until 10:00 a.m. Children across the ridge had four or five hours for chores before the first bell.

Each morning, as the sun rose and lit up Manaslu's peak before the farmhouse, Kamala grabbed an empty plastic urn almost as big as she was, placed it on her hip, and *clip-clapped* down the road, past the peeping chicks that chased one another in and out of open farmhouse doors, past young goats kicking up red dust as they pranced free, beyond the road's last stable, and then along a footpath that ran beside a hedgerow thick with emerald leaves and toward a ravine. Water from the mountain emptied into a shallow stone cistern about the width of a broom closet and built into the hillside at the cut. Behind the well, a thicket of bamboo popped and squeaked like old bones rising against the morning quiet.

Kamala would lean her small frame over the well, skimming its cool water with a pan. She poured pan after pan into the urn until it became almost too heavy to carry, and then muscled it up onto her hip for the trudge back along the footpath. Once home, she would trade the jug for a sack of corn or wheat, which she would hoist off the ground with both arms. She'd then shuffle under its weight to her uncle's house, next door, where a rotary stone grinder had been built into the hardened earth of the porch. Inserting a wooden handle into the face of the heavy grinding stone, she'd spin it continuously with both hands, yielding a rumble that villagers could feel rising from under their feet and up and into their chests. Fetching water and grinding grain into flour were among the few chores Kamala performed alone. She wanted to dispatch them quickly so she could join Maya and her two other sisters, Shusan and Sanu-didi, in the fields.

Maya was the eldest of the four girls, and Kamala rarely left her shadow, even on entering her first year of school. She held Maya's hand, hung from her arm, or, when still little enough, swung up onto her back, wrapping her arms tightly around her big sister's neck. In the fields, she crouched beside or below Maya as they both yanked out the weeds that invaded the family's neatly planted rows. Maya would peer down and see her younger sister mimicking her actions, perhaps by wiping her brow in the heat or waving her hands just as Maya did while speaking, or even echoing the tone of Maya's voice. When Maya rose and moved, Kamala rose and moved with her.

Their mother had had soft skin and thick, long dark hair, and had poured affection on each of her daughters. Not long after Kamala's birth, their mother began suffering intense bouts of abdominal pain. She kept then-eight-year-old Maya by her side to help shoulder some the burden of her daily work. "She couldn't carry heavy loads," Maya recalled of their mother, "so I would carry half." Eating corn or millet, which the family survived on after their rice stocks ran out each year, seemed to sharpen their mother's pain. In 1987, their father took his young wife to a government hospital that was a day away, by foot and then bus, in Kathmandu, bringing along the still breast-feeding Kamala and her toddler sister, Shusan, but leaving Maya on the farm. After several weeks, he sent word to the village that Maya should come to the city to tend to her two youngest sisters, as their mother had grown weaker, while her sister Sanu-didi stayed home to take over their chores. Maya spent a month beside her bedridden mother before escorting her sisters on the intercity bus from Kathmandu back home to Gorkha. The three girls were packed tightly into the hot, tubelike bus for the all-day journey. After the last stop, Maya led the two-hour trek up and over the hills and then onto the horseshoe ridge, carrying Kamala on her back and hip. Before Maya's tenth birthday, their mother died in a small hospital closer to home. Perhaps cancer ate away her stomach, or acute pancreatitis, or something else—no one in the village was quite sure—but the day their mother died, Maya became a full-time mother to her three younger sisters, especially to Kamala, who was then only eighteen months old.

Percussion thumps at the heart of traditional music in Gorkha. The songs have no set lyrics, and singers freestyle to beats a bit like rappers. Tambourines and hand drums, similar to bongos, are the only instruments, though they can be accented or replaced by slapping thighs, clapping hands, and tapping sticks. Kamala and her sisters had mini rap wars daily as they worked the fields. When songs carried the sisters away, Kamala would jump up to dance through the rows, her sisters clapping out the rhythm for her tiny feet as she tried to copy the traditional style of dance in the hills, her hips slowly swirling, her hands and arms rolling out from the elbows as in a slow Polynesian dance.

On the weekends, when Kamala didn't have to go to school, the sisters took their act high above the village, into the uncut jungle and forest toward the horseshoe mountain's peak. The smell of the forest hung thick and wet, held heavy in fallen leaves piled around the footpaths winding up the mountain. The trek gave the girls a chance to gather firewood or cut branches from the kind of spindly trees mostly wiped out lower in the valley, the trees that are covered in broad leaves that their cattle devoured like delicacies. Feeding their livestock these leaves also extended the family's stores of hay and the life of their pastureland.

Kamala could disappear up the trunk of a tree before her sisters noticed she'd left the earth. Any tree deemed impossible to climb by the sisters proved an irresistible temptation for the little girl. They would shout a challenge across the mountainside and then wait and watch and laugh as their baby sister scampered into the treetops. There, Kamala would cut the branches from the top of the trunk, letting them fall and whirl to the forest floor, where the girls would roll them into bales that they would strap onto their backs for the descent back to the village. Aside from the thudding and splintering of tree limbs at the end of the girls' curved blades, these heights held a quiet unlike any other place near the village. You could see and hear the wind rolling up the horseshoe's treetops in waves, like tides filling a cove. Pilgrims came this way each year, crossing over the ridge en route to one of the country's most sacred temples, Manakamana, which translates loosely as "the Heart's Wish."

The four girls were inseparable after their mother's death; they raised one another. Kamala and Maya, especially, were rarely far from each other's sight. Their father, enlisted as a soldier in the Royal Nepalese Army, was gone for all but a couple of weeks a year of home leave. He had remarried only days after the death of their mother, a practice strongly encouraged for widowers in Nepalese society, especially in more conservative Hindu communities.

The reverse was true for widows, no matter how young they were or how long their husbands had been dead. This reality is captured in a sacred Hindu text, estimated to be nearly three thousand years old: "A widow should be long suffering until death, self-restrained and chaste. A virtuous wife who remains chaste when her husband has died goes to heaven. A woman who is unfaithful to her [dead] husband is reborn in the womb of a jackal." Even beyond the question of remarrying, widows traditionally have been considered impure, almost untouchable. In 2015, when Nepal's president, a widow herself, visited a temple in the city of Janakpur, activists performed a "cleansing ritual" because they considered her worship there an unholy act performed upon sacred ground.

Their father's new wife resented the four daughters of his first wife, especially after giving birth to children of her own. Kamala became the main target of harsh words and painful yanks on her small arm. Their stepmother seemed to want to bring the favored *nani* to heel, which only sharpened Kamala's tongue. A harsh word or an open hand directed at one of the sisters strengthened the bond among them all. They needed one another in the fields to survive each season, but perhaps even more to survive without a father and a mother, to give one another the affection, comfort, and love their lives now lacked. Kamala especially spent as much time as she could with their grandparents and aunts on the Three-House Street, but the girls had to come home at the end of every day.

Each night, after the laughter of the sisters fell silent, one of them would snuff out the candle flame twisting in the corner against the red wall in the main room of the farmhouse's second story. All four sisters slept together there, upon a wicker mat covered with a bedsheet spread across the mud-and-plaster floor. In winter months, they would cover the decorative wooden vent built into the wall behind their heads with thickly woven straw pads, to repel the night chill as they huddled ever closer. In the stillness of summer nights, they slept just outside the room, two by two on a narrow balcony facing Manaslu, high above the darkling valley and below a sky drenched in stars.

Kamala would leave her sisters' sides only to attend school. Maya had dropped out at age nine to care for them, but insisted that her *nani* stay enrolled. The primary school rose from a ridgeline along the very tip of the eastern leg of the horseshoe, with valleys opening below both sides of the schoolyard. It took about twenty minutes to walk there from Tin Gharey Toll, and Kamala, wearing the navy-blue skirt and French-blue blouse of the school uniform, would gather her friends from villages all along the way. In summer, they would pick wild *kafal* berries, or bayberries, the irresistible vermilion and purple fruits similar in size and shape to blackberries, stuffing their mouths and laughing at the sight of one another's purple-stained teeth. In the winter mornings, they would marvel as the mist rolled up from the two valleys below the school, to reveal the mountain's contours one terrace at a time, before melting into the sky.

At the start of the school day, Kamala's teachers would carefully sharpen the few pencils they had, shaving away as little as possible, to maximize each one's life as a writing tool. The students shared them. Uday Thapa, a teacher born and raised on the horseshoe ridge, knocked on doors in surrounding villages to scavenge scraps of blank paper, but his stock never lasted long. Usually, he shared the long blackboard at the front of the classroom with his students, an arrangement that at least gave them some way to write out their lessons. A handful of wealthier families from the area sent their children to the boarding schools of Kathmandu or nearby Pokhara, but they were the rare exceptions.

Kamala's teachers kept a concerned eye on her, Thapa remembered years later. They knew she was without parents and that her stepmother had not accepted the four sisters. Yet Kamala didn't need special attention. Whether it was Maya's encouragement or something else, she excelled at school. She even learned to keep her quick fists down at her sides. Her tongue, however, never dulled in the schoolyard or the nearby fields, particularly in the face of what Kamala saw as unfair treatment. This seemed especially true if boys tried to bully her. Girls learn from childhood that men are very much in charge in the predominately Hindu culture of Nepal.* Questioning them or their desires is not typical. Children across the country are taught a folk saying enshrining a norm meant to silence women and keep them from participating in any public conversation: "Only the rooster crows." In Kamala's community, an extra line had been inserted: "The hen that does crow gets its neck snapped and is tossed over the far side of the mountain." Kamala didn't just ignore these mores; she openly challenged them, perhaps owing to an acute sense of fairness that had been sharpened by life in the farmhouse since her mother's death, or perhaps because she and her sisters kept their entire

* Hinduism is Nepal's dominant faith, but Buddhism also has a strong following, as the Buddha was Nepalese. In many families, the two traditions, which share common roots, are blended together, and Hindu and Buddhist priests practice side by side in temples across the country.

world afloat almost completely on their own. Indeed, as soon as she was old enough to speak, Kamala spoke her mind, to boys and girls and men and women alike.

• • •

Kamala watched as the man tethered the boy like a calf and then led him around the courtyard in front of his family and the entire village.

The boy was thirteen, and this was his *bartaman*, the Nepalese equivalent of a bar mitzvah and one of the biggest parties a family can throw. The calf ritual marks the boy's passage into manhood and his acceptance as a full member of his family. This boy's family elders had invited Kamala and another young woman from Tin Gharey Toll to sell home-brewed rice wine spiced with herbs and flowers to the partygoers.

Kamala had been a few times before to this village straddling the ridgeline of the westernmost leg of the horseshoe and like none other in the area. The homes there seemed built atop a narrow peninsula reaching out like a shoreline in the sky. When the musician at the party sang to the beats he tapped on a bongo, his songs carried into the horseshoe valley and two others, the gorge behind the horseshoe to the west and northward, across the peaks toward Manaslu. Kamala found herself lost in the panoramic views. Ever seen since her first childhood visit to the village, she'd fantasized about living amid these extraordinary vistas, and the village's hold on her hadn't loosened now, on the eve of her sixteenth birthday.

A few days after the party, Kamala drove the family's cows down the footpath below her village, clopping carefully on the small stones planted firmly in the mud like steps for hooves. "Ha! Ha-ha!" she shouted, waving a stick in her right hand when the beasts needed a nudge across one of the creeks snaking down the mountainside before joining the wide, clear river below. Kamala and her herd entered a pasture used by farmers from several villages. Another young woman was grazing her own small herd there. "Sister Kamala!" the woman shouted. She seemed unusually exuberant given their passing familiarity. Kamala smiled and waved back.

Sati had attended the *bartaman* party, too, although Kamala hadn't noticed. Born in the village on the ledge, Sati had married and moved to the other side of the horseshoe, closer to Kamala. Small talk between the two young women thinned quickly before Sati made it known that this chance meeting had not been left to chance. She had come to relay a message. The mother from one of the most respected families in the village where Kamala had served wine at the *bartaman* had taken a liking to Kamala during the celebration. After asking around about her and her family, the woman had decided that Kamala might make a good wife for her youngest son, the musician who had filled three valleys with his songs during the party.

Kamala stood heavy under the shock of Sati's words, motionless in the open pasture as beasts grazed around her. She expected to get married at some point, but she hadn't thought the possibility loomed so near.

Matrimony awaits everyone in the mountains. If physical and economic hardship were the primary conditions of existence on the horseshoe ridge, then marriage was the first inoculation against such conditions becoming chronic or critical, something that every young person here is keenly aware of. It takes hands and shoulders and backs to yield enough food to keep hunger at bay, making marriages and the families born into them anchors of security and stability, much as they were in the farm communities of America and Europe in bygone eras.

Extended families also are Nepalese society's sole guarantors of primary care, and having one is the only hedge against the prospect of living alone in old age or infirmity. When Kamala was growing up, it was nigh impossible for almost any woman in the hills to conjure a vision for her future that didn't include joining a family by marriage. Nothing could be more essential to life, except the corn, millet, and rice growing on the terraced land.

Because of marriage's importance for the survival of extended families, coupling decisions are rarely left to young men and women waiting to feel their hearts swell in the mountain moonlight. Marriage normally is not forced in Gorkha, as it can be elsewhere in Nepal, but relatives almost always arrange mates and the ensuing nuptials, allowing the potential betrothed to wield choice solely by veto. A "love marriage" is not only unusual but often scandalous. Love can come after marriage, if at all, though it often does grow between men and women so deeply bound together in the cause of daily survival, especially after they share the intensity and intimacy of having children.

Kamala's stepmother married off Maya and the other sisters as soon as they were old enough, at fifteen and sixteen. "We never planned on marrying so young, but these were the circumstances of our lives at home," Maya would say. Kamala's last sister had just left, and Kamala now lived alone with her stepmother and the three children she'd had with Kamala's father. After the initial shock of Sati's proposal in the pasture, Kamala grew keenly interested in hearing about the possibilities.

Using their herds as cover, the two young women returned each day to the pasture, where Sati pitched the virtues of the musician from the *bartaman* party and his family. Kamala asked

Sati to keep their tête-à-têtes secret. She wanted to make up her own mind and feared interference from her stepmother if word escaped. Destiny might dictate an arranged marriage for her, but she was determined to arrange it on her own, perhaps as a final act of defiance to her stepmother or a first to the culture imposed upon her. What was clear: if there was a marriage, the couple would elope, slipping into matrimony beneath the night sky.

The young man's name was Jeet Bahadur Thapa Magar. Like Kamala, he was the baby of the family. Jeet was twenty years old and had four siblings. His last two names, "Thapa Magar," signified his ethnic group, which was the same as Kamala's. All his brothers shared his second given name, "Bahadur," passed down from their father and meaning "courage." Because a woman formally joined the family of her husband upon marriage, learning about the rest of the family perhaps mattered more than learning about one's groom.

Jeet's late father ascended to the most prestigious station of life achievable by someone from the hills. He had served in the British Army's legendary Brigade of Gurkhas, an elite force whose roots extended to the early nineteenth century during the height of the British Empire, when British forces suffered heavy casualties during an invasion of present-day Nepal, despite far superior numbers. The local warriors rained down the mountains and upon their foreign enemies, wielding their famous eighteen-inch curved knives, called kukris. The warriors were so fearsome that the peace treaty ending the Anglo-Nepalese War included a provision allowing their conscription into the British ranks, where they have remained for two centuries. A famous Indian field marshal serving as a British Army officer once declared, "If a man says he is not afraid of dying, he is either lying or a Gurkha." About forty-three thousand of them died fighting with the British in two world wars. Gurkhas were stationed all over the world courtesy of the reach of the British Empire.

To this day, the entrance exam for finalists for the Brigade of Gurkhas includes a race held not far from Kamala's village. It is known as the Doko, which is the Nepali word for the large basket that farmers sling over their backs and strap across their foreheads. Recruits must run up the side of a steep mountain with a *doko* containing almost eighty pounds of rock. Owing to how difficult it is to gain a spot in the brigade, the family of any Gurkha is revered. Service also comes with something more precious in the hills than status: a pension from the British Army. Although far less generous for fighters in the generation of Jeet's father, it still provided a stable monthly source of cash for his widow and those living under the roof of her stone farmhouse.

Although identical in style, Jeet's house was smaller than the one where Kamala grew up. Rather than building a bigger home, Jeet's family had invested its cash in farmlands on the horseshoe's western ledge and down into the valley. Fields promised security in a way a bigger home never could. The military pension also afforded a rarity in the horseshoe ridge: money for small extras, such as an extra change of clothing, a pair of shoes, maybe a pair of earrings or a necklace, even a transistor radio.

Day after day, Sati filled in more details, interrupted only by the braying of the youngest beasts or questions from Kamala. Kamala's bulls reared their heads and stared squarely into her eyes, dead still and silent, as if waiting for her to answer.

Jeet had lived in India as a young boy with his elder brother, amid the beauty and tragedy of Kashmir, and in the capital, New Delhi. His brother had enlisted in the Indian Army's Gurkha Brigade, another stable income-earning job for men from the Himalayan foothills. (The Indian version evolved from the British brigade following Indian independence in 1947.) But Jeet always yearned for the village on the ledge, and Sati told Kamala that the village loved Jeet like none of its other sons. His music, his talent for playing, singing, and dancing, made him the first guest everyone invited to weddings, *bartamans*, or any other gathering.

Kamala finally agreed to be "taken," the rough-sounding euphemism in Gorkha for eloping. The moment would come during the Holi festival, the most joyous holiday on the calendar in Nepal and India. Known as the "festival of colors," Holi is a national street party marking the end of winter and the coming of spring. Friends, enemies, and strangers douse one another in powdered dyes as they dance in the streets. It is one of the few occasions when all the residents of every village and cluster of homes along the horseshoe ridge gather in the same place, a ledge just below the primary school, on the eastern leg of the horseshoe.

Kamala sat terrified with some of her girlfriends at the festival and waited for her unknown future to arrive. A few hundred farmers, their skin daubed brightly in red and gold and blue, heaved and pulsed and surged all around her. Kamala stayed almost completely silent, straining to imagine the life awaiting her on the other side of the valley with a man she had hardly seen. Until that moment, she believed in the rightness of her choice, as did her friends, but in order to keep her plan hidden from her stepmother, Kamala had not told any elders from her family about it. Now she feared they might ostracize her as a result.

As midnight and the end of the festival approached hand in hand, Jeet sauntered toward Kamala with a small group of friends and family. Sati ushered them over, smiling her enthusiastic smile. "Let's go," someone said. Kamala stepped away from her friends and followed Jeet's party. The group turned and headed together into the bend of the horseshoe and its darkness, staying silent as they cut below the Three-House Street, past the pasture where Kamala had met with Sati, and then around the bottom of the valley. They passed the large, open water well at the base of Jeet's village, where two taps extended from a wall cut into the side of the mountain beneath a canopy of ancient trees and spilled water out onto flat stones set in the basin. They hiked up the steep trail into the village on the ledge, where the breezes never seemed to ebb, to Jeet's farmhouse, which stood near the top of the ridge.

One at a time, members of the wedding party climbed the creaky wooden ladder that was leaning against the far corner of the house and that led to the second-story balcony. Just inside, someone had painted the walls of the main bedroom with bright red mud for the newlyweds. Everything Kamala owned was on her body: the blouse on her back, the flip-flops on her feet. She had borrowed the sarong hugging her hips from her stepmother.

The young couple spent the night in the twisting candlelight, alternately kneeling and crouching on the floor, immersed in the prayers and rituals that bound them together as husband and wife. Before dawn, one of Jeet's female cousins came into the room and placed a single strand of red beads around Kamala's neck, a symbol that she was now a wife. The sun rose across the other side of the ridge, lighting the peak of Manaslu. Kamala had not slept a moment the entire night.

Kamala and Jeet lived together silently at first, almost complete strangers on the precipice of a new life. She could not bring herself to speak, and could barely even look his way. Over time, though, they began to connect through accidental glances. Kamala felt something terrifying and exciting flash between them in these moments, and then something similar but more electric, as when the skin of his bare arm gently brushed against hers while he slipped past her in their tiny bedroom, or when she caught the sweet smell of the jasmine oil he combed into his thick dark hair, as his head rested just below her face on the coolness of their pillow.

Jeet was short, with a thicket of black hair; soft, dark, smiling eyes; rosy cheeks; and a slightly mischievous grin. Despite a small paunch that spilled over the waistband of his trousers, he had the strength of a farm boy. He stood firmly, like a fist; his hands and forearms, heavy with muscle, hung by his sides. Outside the farmhouse, Kamala saw how children ran to greet her new husband. Elders shuffled over to touch or hold his arm. Everyone lit up when they saw Jeet approaching, and slowly Kamala started to as well.

Jeet had been three weeks old in 1982, on the day his father collapsed to the floor of their home from an apparent stroke that left the retired British soldier paralyzed. "I had to take care of the children and my husband while I was still recovering" from childbirth, Jeet's mother remembered. Her husband never improved, dying when Jeet was only eighteen months old, the same age Kamala would be when her mother died in the small hospital not far from their village.

The couple's nearly identical losses, and all that they carried in their lives as a result, created a bond. Sometimes they saw it in each other's faces, as when a visitor summoned a memory of Jeet's father or Kamala's mother. Neither voiced it, but Kamala knew they both understood.

When the couple eloped, Kamala met Jeet's mother only briefly. She was petite and rail thin. Age and sun and cigarettes had loosened and worn the skin hanging from the old woman's arms and face. She occupied the corner bedroom on the ground floor of the farmhouse but filled all three stories with frenetic energy. The old woman's daughter had just given birth in Kathmandu, and the newborn was ill, so Jeet's mother welcomed Kamala with a bony embrace that first morning in the house before excusing herself to rush out toward the footpath that would lead over the far hills to the bus that would carry her to the new, ailing grandchild. She returned a few weeks later, exhibiting for Kamala a kind of warmth that the young woman had not felt since Maya left their home on the Three-House Street. She brought Jeet a small gold chain and a pair of earrings to give to his new wife. Along with the string of red beads, these, for Nepalese women, were akin to a wedding and engagement ring.

The gold necklace's flattened chain links were nearly as thin as paper; a clasp shaped like a twisted snake joined the two ends. Kamala had never seen a piece of jewelry so beautiful. Although it was almost weightless, she took comfort in the feel of it resting over the back of her neck and across her chest. She rarely took it off, not even when she bathed at the community well.

Jeet's mother saw that Kamala had settled easily into the farmhouse and its daily running, along with ably assisting Jeet in tending to their fields and animals. Through her raspy laugh, she told Kamala, "I can die in peace now that I've found a good wife for my son."

Jeet seemed sympathetic to Kamala's struggle with the suddenness of her new life. It took just twenty minutes by foot to reach her own village, yet she was afraid to venture back to face the potential wrath of her family for having eloped. She knew virtually no one else in the village on the ledge, except Heera, an acquaintance from school who had moved back in with her parents after her husband died in an accident in India. Kamala felt anxious the first time she bumped into Heera. What do you say to such a young woman, just a girl in many ways, already a widow? If anything, Heera seemed even more nervous. Hindu widows learn quickly how they are viewed: as carriers of ill fortune, or with suspicion, especially by married women. They are infidelities in waiting, temptresses, even whores. One of the terms in Nepalese for a widow, *randi*, is synonymous with *prostitute*. Kamala didn't feel that way, but the two nonetheless shared only uncomfortable silence. Outside their respective homes, both remained isolated in the village on the ledge, but their lots did not otherwise compare. The villagers would begin greeting Kamala warmly, as a new daughter. The eyes of many turned away from Heera, or worse. They would speak ill of her, and behave rudely toward her in the small everyday exchanges of life. She became something akin to invisible, living among them but treated as if she didn't exist.

Although Jeet gave Kamala space and time to overcome her fears, he rarely missed a chance to woo or gently tease her. He sang to her when they worked in the fields, and all day around the farmhouse. He chipped away at her reticence by making her smile, as he seemed to do with everyone. He even found a way to make her laugh when they argued about how soon to start a family. He wanted to do it right away; Kamala wanted to wait. "If we wait too long, I'll be so old that I'm going to have to lean against the walls of this house to walk while our children do the same as they take their first steps," he told her. He chased her around the three stories of the farmhouse like a schoolboy. As the night air of early spring held on to winter's chill, only a straw mat covered their wooden platform bed, but Kamala could feel Jeet's warmth radiating beside her when he lay down to sleep.

Before two months had passed, she was pregnant.

Kamala's labor began just after sunrise on a cool winter day at the end of 2002. Neighbors started gathering early that same day for a wedding party on a flat pitch cut into the hillside just above Jeet's farmhouse. It was a small public space akin to the village park and hosted some of the most extraordinary views across the three valleys. People from all around the horseshoe who were coming to the party would be in and out of the farmhouse all day to greet Jeet's family, especially because they knew a child soon would be born. This could put the family in a tricky spot vis-à-vis the social etiquette of the hills. It's considered bad luck for a marrying couple if a child is born nearby on their wedding day. And no one wants to jinx or spoil someone's wedding. Kamala's labor started on the farmhouse's first floor, in the main room, near a wood fire burning in the kitchen, but her mother-in-law decided to scoot her up to the couple's second-story bedroom. "Try not to scream too loudly," Jeet's mother instructed. "I know it hurts, but there are a lot of people passing by, so try to keep as quiet as you can." Secrets were nearly impossible in the village, but they would try, at least for one day, to keep quiet the birth of a child.

Kamala's contractions grew more frequent as the party picked up. Her pain deepened and lengthened, and her wails grew louder. Her mother-in-law fetched the family's portable transistor radio—a Chinese-made box about the size of a lunch pail, with a built-in shoulder strap—and placed it in the first-floor window, aimed straight at the wedding party. She rotated the bottom dial, tuning in to the familiar sound of Radio Nepal, and then turned the volume knob as far and as loud as it would go. Kamala's wails were drowned out somewhere between the noise of the wedding party and the Nepali music blaring out the window. About two hours before sunset, a baby girl was born into the spindly arms of her grandmother inside the same bedroom where her parents had been married and where she had been conceived.

Kamala and her baby were moved back downstairs. Kamala lay down on a wicker mat beside the warm kitchen fire cradling her newborn. Someone fetched Jeet from the wedding, where he'd been playing his drum and singing. It seemed impossible Kamala could have given birth so quickly, and he was bursting with shocked joy as he entered the front door and saw the two in the firelight. Because Hindus believe a woman bleeding, whether from menstruation or childbirth, is "impure," Jeet was forbidden from making any physical contact with Kamala for seven days, but he flouted the commandment and sat by and caressed her as she held their daughter. His mother quickly plunged a small piece of gold jewelry into a pan of water, thereby rendering it Hindu holy water, and frantically flicked it at Jeet and all around the house to "purify" it from his peccant behavior. At first Jeet gladly suffered these showers with little more than a grimace, but he soon avoided them by holding his wife only when his mother wasn't looking or when he and Kamala were alone.

In the days ahead, a priest would consult the heavens and give their baby her formal name, based largely upon the position of the stars at the moment she came into the world below, but as was the custom, the family also bestowed an informal name she would go by: Kritika. As Kamala's pain began to subside, she felt her chest swell with a kind of love she had never experienced or dared to imagine.

· · ·

Many Americans view globalization through an understandably local aperture. They watched U.S. companies move factories overseas and export jobs to nations with far lower labor costs, but they benefited, at least superficially, from the importing of inexpensive consumer products, such as cheap blue jeans or flat-screen TVs for every home and budget. Only after the financial crisis of 2007–2008, and the disappearance of easy second mortgages and other readily available credit, did many realize that their American dream had been artificially inflated beyond their livelihood. Now millions feel they learned too late that they were globalization's losers, that they were deceived by their own elites into believing that this particular brand of international capitalism suited their interests. To this day, however, most Americans remain almost completely unaware of the millions of people living on the other side of the world who lost out to the very same system in ways that were more immediate and more sinister.

Globalization looked very different in the rapidly developing countries of Southeast Asia and the Middle East. Rather than exporting jobs, increasingly wealthy nations were importing the cheapest labor they could find to do work that few of their own citizens were willing to do anymore. This meant that by the dawn of the twenty-first century, a growing number of governments in the Eastern Hemisphere were actively importing millions of people from some of the world's poorest countries. Some of these people worked on factory lines. Many more cleaned toilets, dug ditches, did laundry, cooked food, unloaded trucks or railcars, chauffeured women and children, worked on oil rigs, changed diapers, cleaned homes and hotels, and performed virtually any other form of menial labor imaginable— work that could no longer be bought cheaply in these rapidly advancing countries.

The tiny Persian Gulf state of Qatar, the world's richest nation thanks to natural gas reserves, stood at the extreme end of the demand side. Migrant workers made up an estimated 88 percent of the population in a country with the world's wealthiest citizenry. But the global shift under way by 2001 reached well beyond a single petro-monarchy: from the 1990s to the 2000s, twenty-three countries in developing regions of the world went from having net population losses to being net receivers of migrants. Joining Qatar on the list of nations aggressively and cumulatively importing millions of migrant workers were Bahrain, Hong Kong, Kuwait, Malaysia, Saudi Arabia, Singapore, South Korea, Taiwan, and the United Arab Emirates.

Although relatively small, Nepal rose rapidly on the supply side of those charts, quickly entering the world's top ten nations in terms of the number of people leaving—not just on a per capita basis, but also in sheer volume. Because there were no income-earning opportunities in Nepal, then one of the world's least-developed countries, Nepalis were heading abroad in droves to dig the ditches, cook the food, clean the toilets, unload the trucks and railcars, and work on factory lines for a few dollars a day. The vast majority were men. By 1999, the money these men sent home accounted for 12 percent of Nepal's entire economy, and 66 percent of its foreign-exchange earnings. Because of that, the Nepalese government actively promoted this new trade. No one, however, could foresee the exponential growth to come in the years ahead, or just how rapidly the Nepalese people themselves would become their nation's top export.

A domestic industry sprang up in Nepal to feed the boom, and existing businesses retooled to capture some of these benefits. By the early 2000s, the Nepalese government had licensed more than four hundred locally owned agencies to recruit workers and send them overseas. New recruitment agencies sprang up everywhere, in historic courtyards and on high floors of new office towers. Most were small storefront offices. They gave themselves names crafted in English to impress their counterparts in demand-side countries, and to woo the farmers they recruited from the hills, names such as "Bright Star Human Resources," "Divine Insight Overseas," and "Moon Light Consultant." The English- and Nepali-language brochures published by the agencies were packed with superlatives and malapropisms. "We humbly welcome to those clients looking for a reliable, smootheness [sic] and punctuality, recruiting agents in Nepal," read a Moon Light brochure covering forty-two glossy pages. "Our motto is 'Right workers for the right job' so that all of our clients are happy with us." The licensed brokers, in turn, worked through unregistered subagents in towns and villages in almost every district across the country, creating a networked army of thousands of recruiters that reached into some of the world's most remote corners, including the hills of Gorkha. The government left the trade almost completely in the hands of the agencies.

International airlines, such as Qatar Airways and Gulf Air, filled the skies above Kathmandu's tiny Tribhuvan International Airport with jetliners ferrying farm boys to Qatar and Bahrain, or on to nearby Middle Eastern states after connections in the hubs of Doha and Manama. To squeeze more workers onto every flight, Gulf Air used a special fleet of widebody, twin-engine Boeing 767s configured with economy-only seating. All 257 seats often were filled with young men who had barely ever ridden on paved roads much less in a sealed tube hurtling down a runway, and then up and above the mountains and out toward an unimaginable new existence. During takeoff, they heaved their bodies against their seatbelts, twisting and stretching from behind their restraints to try to peer out the windows.

Nepalese travel agents, once reliant on hippies, backpackers, and tourists from wealthy countries coming to Nepal for trekking, started working between the manpower companies and the airlines for commissions on booking the thousands of seats filled with farmers each week. Newspapers that previously had consisted of just a few thin sheets chronicling government pronouncements and the royal family's birthdays were suddenly brimming with advertising, as labor brokers were required by law to publish a public notice of overseas job listings.

If Nepal led the supply side of this new wave of globalization across the Eastern Hemisphere, Gorkha led the way within Nepal. Like Jeet's father, the hardiest of Gorkha's menfolk had, for two centuries, swapped its green valleys and tranquil way of life for a chance to make their names and fortunes overseas with the Gurkha Brigades. Now a much wider swath of Gorkha's men made the same journey, only this time looking for construction or cleaning work rather than war and valor. Soon their numbers would reach into the millions.

Gorkha's warrior past made the idea of crossing seas and borders strangely palatable among a people who were otherwise completely disconnected from the outside world, subsistence farmers living in homes without telephones, electricity, or even toilets. Not only were those who went abroad as Gurkhas respected, but people saw how the money they sent home could benefit the lives of their families in ways no one else could access, allowing them to buy extra farmland or invest in businesses or, in rare cases, even send their children to schools where there were ample supplies of paper and pencils. The two-century history of the Gurkha Brigades made it easier for the region to transition from an exporter of a small band of global warriors to one that exported a much bigger class of global workers.

Ownership of farmland in places such as the horseshoe ridge also aided the flow. Overseas workers had to pay massive fees to labor brokers in order to buy their jobs, fees that often amounted to several multiples of the average annual earnings in Nepal. The country's poorest couldn't afford this, but farmers who owned land were able to borrow money against the acreage they used to feed their families and use the cash loans to pay the brokerage fees. The promise: after two or three years in an overseas job, a worker could earn enough to pay back the loans and all the interest, plus create a small cushion for his family's future.

More than a year before Jeet and Kamala eloped, Jeet had tried to venture onto this path himself. On January 26, 2001, when he was nineteen, he got a passport from the district government office with the assistance of a local manpower agent connected to labor brokers in Kathmandu. Jeet went with a cousin from the village to the nearby agency in Gorkha city, the administrative capital of the district. The agent hung on to Jeet's passport, as the manpower brokers almost always do, to facilitate registration with the government or the issuance of visas from foreign embassies. Yet more than three years passed without Jeet's hearing anything, and it seemed such a remote possibility that he barely mentioned it to Kamala after they married. That changed suddenly in June 2004.

Jeet's cousin informed him that their names had been put forward to a broker in Kathmandu, Moon Light Consultant, for jobs at a luxury hotel in Amman, Jordan. Although the broker had selected only Jeet, his cousin encouraged him to go alone, as such a chance seemed so rare. The brokerage fee would be about a thousand dollars, nearly four times the average annual income in Nepal, and the job would pay in the range of two hundred to five hundred dollars per month. Jeet estimated that he would be gone for only two or three years, and he informed Kamala of his plans. She and Kritika, now about sixteen months old, would be well cared for by his family, and the money he sent home could help them send their daughter to a school beyond the horseshoe ridge, and beyond the hills of Gorkha. He also told Kamala something she didn't know: the family had an outstanding loan on some of its land, and an overseas job would allow them to pay it off quickly.

Kamala didn't want him to go, and she started scratching out some calculations. If they lived frugally and their harvests were strong, the Gurkha pension would allow them to pay back the existing loan in a little more than a year and begin saving thereafter. But Jeet was adamant that he wanted to start earning his own money for his new family, a sentiment he related not just to Kamala, but also to other family members. He convinced Kamala of the soundness of his plan little by little, which was the same way he had softened her heart after their marriage. "Think of our daughter's future," he said to her, repeating this like a mantra in each discussion. It was the refrain Kamala could not answer. After waiting for more than three years, they could not let such an opportunity pass by.

On June 9, 2004, Nepal's Department of Labour and Employment Promotion gave preliminary approval for Jeet and thirty-one other Nepalese men to go to work at Le Royal Hotel, a new thirty-one-story tower clad in white stone and rising above the Jordanian capital, completed in 2003 at a cost of $350 million. Reminiscent of the Tower of Babel, the hotel's main tower rose higher into the Amman sky than virtually any other building. A Jordanian labor broker, Morning Star for Recruitment and Manpower Supply, facilitated the jobs on its end at the five-star hotel. On June 13, the Nepalese recruiting partner, Kathmandu-based Moon Light, published the required notice in Nepal's *Kantipur Daily*, listing twenty-seven different positions. These included slots for a generator mechanic, kitchen helpers, a "salad man," and "room boys."

One day in mid-June, Jeet rose to leave with the sunrise. Kamala had helped pack his rucksack, which contained two extra changes of clothing, including his button-down charcoal-gray shirt, an extra pair of sandals, a bar of soap, and his toothbrush. He embraced Kamala and his daughter inside the second-story bedroom where the couple had married by candlelight and where Kritika had been conceived and born. Crying when someone is embarking on a journey is considered bad luck in Nepal, so Kamala held back her tears, sinking just a little deeper into Jeet's chest as they embraced, inhaling the sweet jasmine. "Take care of our daughter and my mother. Take care of yourself. I'll be back in a couple of years. There's no need to worry," he told her.

It seemed as if every villager had gathered outside the farmhouse to bid farewell to their favorite son. Jeet stood before his eldest brother and bowed as his brother slipped a garland of pink hibiscus flowers over Jeet's neck and offered a simple Nepalese blessing. Like Kamala, no one at the gathering cried. They were stirred with the hope and sadness of a traveler's good-bye.

Kamala watched Jeet walk past the family's store of firewood, then past the single red bird-of-paradise planted at the edge of their property, down to the vegetable patch just below their house, and onto the trail descending into the horseshoe valley. She cried silently that night so as not to frighten Kritika, who slept with her on the platform bed in their room. But Kamala could barely sleep, and when she could, did so fitfully. In a dream, she stood before the bird-of-paradise at the head of the footpath. She looked below and saw Jeet rising back up the mountainside, smiling warmly with his eyes, returning to her.

3

Rumpled and exhausted, Kamala fell onto the platform bed and wrapped herself around her eighteen-month-old daughter. Sowing rice consumed everyone's days. The monsoons were nearing their peak, so the terraces were soaked and boggy, the mud grabbing at Kamala's every step and leaving her limbs heavier than usual by the time nightfall came. Jeet may have been gone, but the burden of his work remained, along with Kamala's own responsibilities—at home, in the fields, and in motherhood.

Word reached the village that Jeet had flown to Jordan on July 3, but no one heard anything else, as the family had expected. Forty-eight days had passed since he landed in Amman to work at the five-star hotel, and months more might pass before a letter made its way from overseas to the village on the ledge, if one came at all. Phone calls were no easier. Just reaching a telephone required a two-hour walk out of the horseshoe and over the near hills to the edge of the village Taksar. There the Kunwar family ran a sort of one-room convenience store on the ground floor of their home by the side of a narrow road choked with buses spinning up dust en route to Kathmandu. The phone sat atop a waist-high display case stocked with Chinese flip-flops and Indian sweets. The Kunwars charged a few rupees per minute to make or receive a call. Phone messages could find their way to the horseshoe if and when someone stopped by the shop on their way to the ridge.

In the two and a half years since her marriage to Jeet, Kamala had come to work seamlessly with her mother-in-law in the daily running of the farmhouse. Kamala rose at about five thirty to light and stoke the kitchen fire. She fetched water from the large community well at the bottom of the hill, and then swept and, by hand, sponged every floor in the house before doing the same on the porch. She worked at her mother-in-law's side to prepare meals and clean up when they were done. The two women grew closer as they split responsibility for managing crops and lives in Jeet's absence.

Warm and affectionate with Kritika, the old woman also gave both her granddaughter and her daughter-in-law things Kamala had never had: a pair of slippers, children's clothes, a sari, and even red bangles for Kamala's wrists, which only Nepalese wives were supposed to wear. The level of security Kamala felt in the farmhouse exceeded anything she had conjured when Sati pitched Jeet's family's virtues under the cover of grazing cattle.

On the morning of August 21, 2004, nearly ten weeks after Jeet had left home, Kamala finished her chores and went down to the large terrace just below the farmhouse, where the red earth stood wet and empty. The time had almost passed to plot the family's last vegetable garden of the year, where spinach, pumpkins, and tomatoes would take root and rise before the mists of winter climbed up around the ledge. Kamala brought the Chinese-made radio with her and set it on the garden's edge. Jeet's songs had long ago replaced those of Kamala's sisters in the fields, but now Radio Nepal offered a comforting surrogate voice in his absence.

A bulletin cut into the afternoon music: a terrorist group in Iraq had claimed credit for kidnapping twelve Nepalese men, the announcer said, before reading the full name of each victim and listing his home village. The third name was "Jeet Bahadur Thapa Magar," from "Bakrang Number Five, Gorkha."

Kamala stood silent—not shocked, not panicked, but curious, questioning her ears and disbelieving. Names in Nepal include each person's ethnic group, so virtually no one's name can be considered unique, especially in an ethnic group as big as theirs. It would be a bit like all Americans having names such as "Peter Joseph Catholic Irish." The name read over the radio could have belonged to anyone.*

"Kidnapped . . . Jeet . . . Magar . . . Bakrang Number Five . . . Gorkha . . ."

Was that his name?

That sounded like my Jeet's name.

That's our village. It can't be. Is it a mistake?

It must be another man with the same name. Is there another man with the same name in the village?

They must be wrong about the village. Did someone steal Jeet's passport?

The terrorists, who called themselves the Army of Ansar al-Sunna, had first posted a statement on an extremist website the day before, saying that their "heroic fighters" had seized a dozen young Nepali men—the statement called them "infidels"—because they had come to Iraq to help "U.S. Crusader forces" who were "fighting Islam." The twelve Nepalis were on their way to the American-occupied Al Asad Air Base in the restive Anbar Province about one hundred miles west of Baghdad. The

* More than 7 percent of the population of Nepal is of Magar ethnicity, and Thapa is among the biggest subsets.

posting included the name and village of each man, taken from his passport as a sort of proof of life. It promised to deliver pictures soon, "so that they will serve as a lesson to others." The statement also included the name of a Jordanian company for which the men worked, something called "Bisharat."

As Kamala stood on the barren terrace, music again poured from the radio, but she didn't hear it. After some time, she gathered herself, picked up the radio, and hastened up the slope toward the farmhouse. Others heard the same news, which spread quickly across the village, albeit in confused and panicked fragments. Neighbors and family converged on the porch of Kamala's home and inside the main room, just beyond the farmhouse's threshold, and as more arrived, the rising sound of worried voices spilled out into the three valleys. Someone made a fire in the kitchen. No one knew anything, but everyone was afraid.

After a while, Radio Nepal news broke in with another bulletin that silenced the room. "Jeet Bahadur Thapa Magar," the announcer said, followed by the government's formal name for the horseshoe ridge that was his home. Someone screamed, and Jeet's mother threw herself onto the hardened earth floor. Kamala froze in place. The assemblage of neighbors and family members melted into panic and grief.

Before the United States launched the Iraq War in 2003, Nepal's government had declined an invitation to join what the administration of President George W. Bush had dubbed the "Coalition of the Willing." Some British Gurkhas were posted in Iraq through their service in the United Kingdom's armed forces, but even in the Nepalese capital, where electricity and television and printing presses had at least some presence among the elite, news of the American war did not play a significant role in daily life. Less than one-half of 1 percent of all Nepalis even used the Internet in 2004. For eighteen-year-old farm wives on the horseshoe ridge, the war was almost completely unknown if not unknowable, but Kamala did understand that Jordan and Iraq were two different countries.

Jeet's eldest brother, Ganga, could not comprehend how Jeet had ended up in an American war zone, let alone in the hands of a terrorist group blaming him for serving the American occupation. Nor could he conceive what benefit anyone might obtain by kidnapping Jeet and eleven others hailing from one of the poorest and most powerless nations on earth. Surely, Jeet and the others would be freed, everyone told Kamala as they tried to comfort her. Kamala herself clung to the hope it was all a case of mistaken identity.

Within a day, a newspaper made its way from the city by bus, then after hours by foot across the hills to the village. The cover displayed a photograph the kidnappers had posted on the Internet of the twelve Nepali men, aged eighteen to twenty-seven, assembled before a large black banner emblazoned with white Arabic characters as if gathered for some kind of macabre class photo. One hostage sat on the floor at the center of the picture, an American flag draped under his chin like a bib. He did not look into the camera, but instead stared down into the field of red-and-white stripes, the others assembled around him. Jeet stood on the far right, wearing the charcoal-gray shirt Kamala had helped him pack, his sleeves rolled up above the elbow, the darkness of the shirt accentuating his wan face and the weight of worry and sleep deprivation in his eyes. Inside their farmhouse, Kamala saw him in the photo and sank into despair.

The day after the radio bulletin, Jeet's brother Ganga trekked down from the ridge before sunrise and caught a microbus for the city of Gorkha, the district's administrative capital, desperate to find someone who could tell him something, anything. Along the way, he entertained fevered fantasies of borrowing money and bribing a Nepalese government official to send a message to the kidnappers on the family's behalf. Many Nepalis understood they could get something done in their country only through the grease of a bribe. Ganga planned to speak with everyone he could find, even local journalists, hoping to discover that plans were afoot to negotiate for the men's release, or that he could rouse someone to action.

Jeet's family had no way of knowing it, but negotiating wasn't a far-fetched idea. Hostage taking in Iraq was much more about capitalism than terrorism, at least in the summer of 2004, when there had been roughly sixty reported kidnappings of internationals in the seventeen months since the start of the war. The vast majority of victims were released, often in exchange for ransom. Americans by and large were the exception. This hit home in startling fashion when, a few months before the Nepalis were seized, a terrorist group kidnapped and beheaded a cell phone tower repairman from Pennsylvania named Nicholas Berg and dumped his corpse on the side of a road regularly patrolled by U.S. forces. The group made a snuff film of Berg's execution—rough, shaky, out of focus, and gruesome—and then uploaded it to the Internet. It was among the first in a shocking new genre of global terror productions that would soon become all too common. It ensured that Berg's murder captured headlines across America, on television and in print, for days. The video's director and executive producer, and the reported executioner, was a man named Abu Musab al-Zarqawi, founder of the terrorist group that would eventually become ISIS.

People in the horseshoe didn't know a thing about Nick Berg. Most had little idea there was even a war anywhere outside Nepal, then consumed by its own escalating civil conflict. Maoist insurgents from rural areas of Nepal, including Gorkha, had launched the fighting in 1996. Inspired by the Shining Path guerrillas in Peru, who wanted to destroy all vestiges of the government and replace it with a peasant-led revolutionary regime, Nepal's insurgents had similar goals in their own mountainous country and saw struggling farmers in the poorest regions as ripe targets for recruitment or intimidation. On October 1, 1999, the war even came to the village on the ledge. Scores of residents had gathered from across the horseshoe for a meeting organized by the Red Cross. Four Maoist fighters pulled from the crowd a man whom they suspected of informing. They confirmed his identity, bound his hands, and then cut his throat before the villagers. They left him to bleed out on the open terrace just above Jeet's farmhouse, the spot that served as a wedding ground and public space.

Maoists also kidnapped hundreds of noncombatants across the country. The vast majority of victims were released following negotiations. In this way, the idea of insurgent kidnappings in the midst of a war seemed oddly familiar in Nepal. Because they often ended in freedom and tearful reunions, those kidnappings formed an almost reassuring backdrop as Jeet's brother Ganga scurried from office to office in Gorkha city. He believed that with the right plan, his brother could come home.

Yet, although each official and politician Ganga met that day personally guaranteed that the family's concerns would be elevated to superiors all the way up to Kathmandu, these were the kind of bureaucratic platitudes that made clear the futility of the mission. There wasn't even anyone to bribe, assuming such a fantasy ever had a chance of being initiated. "I felt so helpless," Ganga would recall. "Nothing made sense to me, and yet I tried to do what I could."

Despite the family's inability to get answers or basic information, hope remained. Government-run Radio Nepal filled the air with encouraging news about efforts to free the twelve. The Ministry of Foreign Affairs had mobilized its missions across the Middle East. The Nepalese embassy in Saudi Arabia held unspecified discussions with unidentified "diplomatic personalities of different countries." Messages went out from the Nepalese embassy in Abu Dhabi to the Iraqi embassy there, and also to the U.S. embassy. The Nepalese ambassador in Doha made a personal visit to the offices of Al Jazeera, the Arabic-language satellite news network bankrolled by the Qatari government, after the broadcaster received communications from the terrorists. That last meeting, at least, appeared to generate something tangible: on August 27, a prominent Iraqi cleric used his Friday sermon, issued beneath the blue dome of the largest Sunni mosque in Baghdad, to call for the release of the twelve Nepalis on the grounds that they were innocents. The plea from Sheik Ahmed Abdul Gafur al-Samarraie went out over Arabic-language radio and television.

Before long, the terrorists released a video, initially broadcast on Al Jazeera, showing the captive who had been draped in the American flag seated in front of a camera. His name was Mangal Limbu, and he was a twenty-two-year-old farmer from a district ravaged by the Maoist war. He held in both hands and in front of his face a statement written out in English by his captors. Desperately, he tried to read it aloud, but beyond an obvious condemnation of the United States, the young man's words were almost completely incomprehensible, as would be the case for anyone barely literate in a foreign alphabet trying to read and speak words he simply could not understand, let alone form with his mouth.

Footage of ten out of the twelve men placed individually before the black banner came next. One at a time, each spoke into the camera, without notes and in his only tongue, Nepali. Several broke down after uttering only a handful of words. Jeet's family didn't see the video, and none of the men's statements was publicly translated, broadcast, or published in the West at the time. Eventually, though, their words would come to haunt two nations, help drive a decade of investigations, and reveal clues that would threaten one of America's most powerful corporations.

On August 31, ten days after news of the kidnapping, Kamala finished the brunt of the day's work by midafternoon, climbed up to the bedroom she shared with Jeet, and stripped off her field clothes. She stepped into the sky-blue petticoat she used for bathing, pulling it up over her chest and cinching it tight, and then backed down the red wooden ladder off the balcony. She walked across the front of the farmhouse, past the wedding terrace above their home, and then down the steep trail leading to the community well.

The well is the biggest on the horseshoe ridge, carved into the green hillside below a thick canopy of ancient shade trees that keep the water cool. Two taps send continuous streams jutting out from a twelve-foot-long stone wall set against the hill. Splotches of emerald moss and black mold creep up and cling to the wall's gray face, giving it the look of an abstract mural, and the water falls and slaps against stone slabs laid in the basin. Kamala leaned forward and dipped her arms into the stream running from the tap, then moved in, drenching herself. Clear mountain water, which runs strongest in the monsoon season, darkened her petticoat as she lingered, trying to wash away her anxiety. Eventually she stepped out of the stream, bowed her head, and twisted and wrung her long dark hair, piling it into a bun on top of her head before heading back up the steep footpath toward the farmhouse, her petticoat and hair dripping. A drizzle had started falling from the sky and onto the mountain.

She kicked her feet out of her flip-flops, stepped up onto the porch, and crossed the threshold and went into the main room of the ground floor. She heard a whimper, turned, and, once her eyes had adjusted to the darkness, saw one of Jeet's nieces sitting on the floor in the corner, crying. Her two sisters-in-law then entered, filling the house with wails. They told Kamala that people had been hearing on the radio that the terrorists had murdered Jeet and the other men. Their executions were on a video like the one of Nick Berg. Kamala began hyperventilating.

Jeet's mother had already left. She'd gotten the news earlier, from the same woman weeping in the corner, and had asked her grandson, who was also in the house, if it was true. He said it was. For a moment, Jeet's mother stood still, and then, not knowing what to say or do, and noticing the drizzle outside, she asked her grandson to bring in the clothes that were hanging on the balcony. Her grandson refused. "What's the point of anything now?" he said. With her grandson's refusal, the truth washed over the old woman, and she felt numb. She shuffled out of the farmhouse, off the porch, down the footpath, and toward the gloomy shade cast by thick jungle that had never been carved away, wanting only to wander until she was lost and starving—perhaps the cleanest and oldest way in the hills to end one's own life.

After a time, the old woman reached a cluster of homes along the path. A distant nephew saw her there. He had heard the news. Everyone had. "Auntie, where are you going?" he called out. She did not answer, and kept walking. The young man then drew even with her, took her hand into his own, and led her to his house. He kept her there for a time while he finished some chore. "You should go back home," he told her. When she refused, he kept her longer. "Do you think you can hold me here like this forever? I'll go wherever I want," she said. Again, he took her by the hand, leading her all the way back to the village on the ledge, where her family and the other villagers placed the old woman on a makeshift suicide watch, making sure no one left her alone or able to wander free.

The killings made news internationally, albeit briefly, that same night. "The twelve Nepali men were kidnapped ten days ago by an extremist Islamist group, Ansar al-Sunna," a BBC News anchor said. "And today, all twelve were brutally murdered, shot in the back of the head, or beheaded." *ABC World News Tonight* used still frames taken from the execution video, as anchor Peter Jennings introduced a correspondent in Baghdad. "The video showing the slaughter of twelve Nepalese construction workers was posted on an Islamist website this morning. Most of the four-minute tape is too gruesome to broadcast. These are edited stills. One of the hostages is beheaded; the others are lined up, facedown, and shot at point-blank range," said ABC's Mike von Fremd. The piece lasted a little more than a minute.

By then, attacks on foreign contractors in Iraq were old hat, and had dominated headlines for months. They were the softest targets, the outer ring of the American occupation, and they were deliberately targeted in an effort to cripple it. The violence had started in full force five months earlier on March 31, 2004, a year after the U.S. invasion, when Iraqi insurgents ambushed a convoy of security contractors near the center of Fallujah, hitting their SUVs with a fusillade from automatic weapons and rocket-propelled grenade launchers. The four American men killed that day worked for a company called Blackwater USA, and were guarding a delivery for a catering firm. Insurgents dragged the four from their smoldering vehicles and paraded their charred corpses through streets filled with cheering mobs, before hanging them from a bridge spanning the Euphrates River. Video of their deaths aired worldwide. It was a signal moment in the war, when the rage against the U.S. occupation, at least from within Iraq's once dominant Sunni population, stood naked for the world to see and made undeniable the reality, size, and force of the insurgency.

In the days, weeks, and months that followed Fallujah, a wave of attacks crashed down on truck drivers, interpreters, engineers, oil workers, and more security contractors. There were roadside bombs, ambushes, and kidnappings. There was Nick Berg. By the end of the summer of 2004, these murders no longer shocked. Nearly one hundred contractors were killed in the months following Fallujah. News outlets ran the story of the Nepalis' murders as a contractor death story like any other—but it was not.

For starters, this was far and away the deadliest such massacre to date, although this fact generally did not make the news. Comment from coalition authorities in Iraq also seemed strangely absent, unlike in the aftermath of other such killings. And while death in Iraq was routine, everything else von Fremd said to Peter Jennings made little sense. *Nepali men?* Nepal was one of the remotest lands in the world, and it wasn't a member of the Coalition of the Willing. Yet these men—these "construction workers," who had probably barely ever seen a paved road let alone ridden in a car before they left Nepal for the Middle East, men who quite likely had never plugged anything into a wall socket or pulled open a refrigerator door or turned the handles on a faucet—were the victims of the deadliest such massacre in Iraq? How on earth had they gotten there, from mud-floored homes and villages without roads—and then four thousand miles away, across heavily guarded borders, and into a fortified American war zone? Who had brought them? What were they doing there? What possible vital skill set could a dozen farm boys from the foothills of the Himalayas have held for the American government? And for whom were they working?

In addition to raising more questions than they answered, the news reports that followed understated the horror of what had happened to the men.

The film opens at eye level of the man behind the handheld camera, looking down on the ground at Mangal Limbu, the farmer who had been draped in the American flag. His torso cuts horizontally into the center of the frame from the left side. He is lying on his back in the desert dirt beneath the open sky. His hands are bound behind him, and the knot they create beneath his back causes him to twist slightly onto his side. A bright chartreuse shirt is in tatters beside his head. The shirt has been sliced away from his body, exposing his bare chest, his shoulders, and his arms. His head and eyes are wrapped with a wide white blindfold, which looks like a strip torn from a bedsheet. The same white cloth is wrapped around his bare abdomen, and is apparently what's binding his hands.

A man in a desert camouflage uniform moves into the picture from the top of the frame, wearing a matching baseball cap with the bill pulled low to hide his face. He crouches above his captive and, with his left hand, cups the young man's chin to steady the head. Roughly, quickly, the camera zooms in, filling the frame with the farmer's head and the white blindfold. With his free hand, the killer draws a large hunting knife across the farmer's throat and begins to saw, slicing through the cartilage of the windpipe and into the carotid artery running up beside it, but stopping short of severing the spine. Bright red blood spills into the dirt and begins rapidly spreading across the absorbent white blindfold.

The man with the knife quickly backs out of the frame. The camera lens widens, pulling back with him. The farmer writhes. Another man stands above the farmer, stepping down on the young man's right hip to force him flat onto his back before the world. His vocal cords are severed, making it impossible for him to speak, but ghastly squeals of air, almost porcine, scream up from his lungs and through the gash in his windpipe, each squeal lasting the length of his breath, each growing longer and higher-pitched the more desperate his body becomes for air.

Finally, he falls silent. Thirty-five seconds have elapsed. His corpse is decapitated. In the remaining three and a half minutes, the eleven other men, lying prone in a ditch, are shot in the back and the back of the head, one by one. They are not bound. They submit to their deaths, and to their last moments beneath the sky becoming political theater, although it is difficult to imagine how they could have done otherwise.

In 2004, there were no online social networks in Nepal, or smartphones to carry them, and there was virtually no Internet penetration, yet the video spread rapidly across the country's cities through makeshift public screenings, the media, and then word of mouth. Within just one day, tens of thousands, perhaps hundreds of thousands, of angry rioters choked the streets of Kathmandu and other cities.

They spontaneously and simultaneously attacked scores of manpower agencies throughout the Kathmandu Valley and across the nation, beginning with Moon Light Consultant, the broker in Kathmandu that had sent Jeet and the others to Jordan. They ransacked offices and burned the passports of would-be workers, shattered windows, burned signboards, and smashed or burned virtually every piece of office equipment they could find inside agencies around the nation. Often, they later returned to the same brokerages to make sure they had damaged everything possible. They attacked virtually every business affiliated with the manpower agencies in the entire foreign employment network, from clinics providing preemployment health checks to photo studios where workers were sent for passport pictures. They went after the offices of travel agencies and the airlines. They attacked the biggest national newspaper that made money publishing the public notices for foreign jobs. Almost no one in the system, or even on its fringes, went unharmed. In response, the government instituted a nationwide curfew that lasted four days.

The sprinkling of stories on the riots that appeared in the international media highlighted attacks on Muslim institutions. The mob's real target, the system sending Nepalese farm boys off to foreign employment, had been overlooked in the coverage. The true meaning of the nation's rage would become clear outside Nepal only once the footage of each man speaking in Nepali, as he stood before the black banner, had been translated and disseminated beyond the Himalayan kingdom.

Calm returned after a few days, and a sort of national mourning settled over Nepal.

Mourners filled the farmhouse. Everyone tried to comfort Kamala, but it sounded as if they were all speaking from a distant room. She heard words but could not discern meaning in them. Only Kritika seemed clear, fixed in her sight. The child was not yet two years old, the same age Jeet had been when his father died and Kamala had been when she lost her mother.

Jeet's eldest brother, Ganga, initiated the rituals of death. After the murders were announced, people across the country prayed for the return of the men's bodies. Hindus and Buddhists believe the soul cannot be free until the body of the dead person is cremated. "We said, 'Give us his breath, bring him home alive,' but now we asked for his body—give us his breath or his body," Ganga said. Soon they knew neither would be theirs.

Ganga met with elders on the horseshoe ridge to discuss something he had heard of but never seen, something that he believed could free Jeet's soul: an ancient ritual for creating and burning an effigy of a dead man whose body has been lost, perhaps at sea or in a faraway battle. Priests crafted such an effigy from dried holy grass, called *khus*. The grass is rare in the foothills of the Himalayas, but it does grow in monsoon season. Ganga began scouring the jungles each day.

The meaning of loss, not just the loss of life but also the loss of a loved one's remains, is acknowledged through the reconstruction of his body from the stalks of the sacred grass. Three hundred sixty stalks are to be used, a figure believed by the ancients to be the number of bones in the human body as well as the number of days in one of their calendar years. Specific prayers are recited at each stage, beginning with the same prayer that is uttered when a child is born. There is even a mantra for placing the heart of the man who is lost into the effigy. There were no priests on the horseshoe ridge, so Ganga did his best to adhere to the rituals as he had learned them from the old men. He prayed aloud and spoke to the effigy as he crafted it, as if speaking to his brother. The effigy was about the size of a newborn. As a child, Ganga had held his baby brother the same way after his birth. "Even though you suffered a terrible death, I hope you will find a place in heaven, and that the afterlife is more beautiful," he said as he bound the head and arms to the body with twine.

About two hours before sunset on the ninth day after Jeet's death, Ganga and almost every man in the village gathered at the farmhouse. Kamala, bearing a set of Jeet's clothes and a pair of his shoes, backed down the ladder from the room she had shared with her husband. She handed the clothes to the men and then hid herself away, unable to bear the thought of what was to come. The men placed the effigy on a small bier fashioned from bamboo poles. Ganga held the bier from the front, like a pallbearer, and a cousin took up the rear. They led the other men in a procession over the footpath and down the western side of the ledge behind the horseshoe, trekking for about an hour, until they reached the Sauney River in the valley below. There they gathered wood and made a pyre on the river's edge. Dousing the wood with kerosene, Ganga placed Jeet's clothes and effigy on top.

Stalks of dried *khus* blacken and bend above a fire, but they do not wisp up into the wind as embers or ashes, especially when densely twisted together. Some varieties of the grass are even made into perfume, and the sweetness of the white smoke's smell is soft but discernible in the air. The men watched the fire. As the flames twisted in his eyes, Ganga prayed again for his lost brother, wondering if there could be freedom or justice for Jeet's soul. The fire dimmed as darkness settled into the valley.

Ganga removed his shirt and sat on the riverbank. Hindus believe hair is an adornment and a symbol of vanity and that one must be free of vanity to grieve for a departed soul, so one of the men took a razor and shaved Ganga's head clean by the water's edge. Ganga rose and wrapped a white cloth around his waist, like a pauper Hindu priest. He left his chest bare and placed a white scarf on his head in the style of a bandanna. Such are the Nepalese symbols of mourning. The men began their trek back up the mountain and into the jungle darkness.

In the bed she had shared with Jeet, Kamala tried not to think of the fire, but she couldn't keep the image of its hungry flames out of her mind. She felt her love burning on the mountain river.

PART II

The Body Shops

4

Eyad Mansour eyed me warily from behind a large desk with a dark lacquer finish. Thick curtains drawn across the window behind him kept the fierce Middle Eastern sun from glancing off its polished surface. Mansour's pendulous cheeks bristled with stubble, and the forearms exposed by his short-sleeved dress shirt suggested he had once earned a living somewhere other than behind a desk, perhaps swinging a pickax into something unyielding, or holding sway over a crowd. With nervous distraction, he hovered over two cell phones and two landlines, the handsets all lined up below his nose.

I knew Mansour to be a small but critical player in two worlds I was reporting on, or, more accurately, two multibillion-dollar global industries. The two industries were opaque, in part because they had been constructed without any kind of architect overseeing a logical, easy-to-understand structure, so no single source of information held a key, and also because men with significant stakes intentionally obscured their true nature. One of these industries encompassed the side of globalization unfolding beyond the sight of the West, in the other half of the world: the "export" and "import" of cheap labor in the form of human beings. The other was the unprecedented profiteering from the privatization of warfare unfolding in Iraq. Eyad Mansour seemed to be at the intersection of these two worlds.

On the other side of Mansour's office curtains, Amman, long the plain sister in a region dazzled by Beirut, Damascus, Cairo, and Baghdad, basked in the daylight and danced into the night. In the two years since the U.S. invasion of neighboring Iraq, Amman had become an Arab capital on the make, a sort of Casablanca for the Iraq War, teeming with the wealthiest Iraqi refugees and awash in wartime cash from Washington. Its hotels, private housing, and commercial office stock overflowed with workers for aid organizations, contractors, and hustlers previously based in Baghdad. Many had relocated to avoid the carnage inflicted by the growing insurgency and a looming civil war. Amman also teemed with the displaced and dethroned ruling class of Saddam's Iraq, members of the Baath Party, who had been frozen out of the new nation the Bush administration wanted to create.*

Five-star hotels clad in white stone sprang up across Amman's modest skyline as businessmen surged into luxury shops and new restaurants below. In nightclubs attached to the cheaper hotels, Russian women danced under lights shimmering through clouds of smoke from hookahs and Cuban cigars. New construction suddenly rose across the sleepy city at a rate of more than 10 percent a year. The boom also rippled a short drive away into the Jordan Valley, whose lush though rocky landscape had not changed much since followers of the Old Testament God ordained it a land of miracles. Now people there were getting rich growing tomatoes and milking cows. Farmers sold fruits, vegetables, and dairy products at soaring prices to help feed three squares a day to each of the more than 130,000 American soldiers stationed next door in Iraq, along

---

* Malcontents among the most committed former Baathists would form a significant part of the insurgency, up to and including the so-called Islamic State.

with an almost equal number of civilian contractors. Foreign direct investment in Jordan jumped sixfold in the first year of the war and would increase fortyfold in only four years, becoming one of the largest sources of the country's GDP. It wasn't entirely clear where all the money was coming from, but Jordan obviously benefited from some of the estimated ninety cents in corruption skimmed out of each U.S. dollar being spent on rebuilding Iraq, even as the country continued to burn.

I had flown to Amman to write about these changes as a reporter for the *Chicago Tribune* and was planning to attend something called the Rebuild Iraq Expo. Owing to the spiraling violence, however, the exposition ended up having little to do with reconstruction and, instead, became more of a trade show for armored vehicle salesmen and companies peddling bulletproof and batter-resistant doors for homes. My remit was to write a feature story and try to use the expo to develop some contacts, but I took the opportunity to buy passage to Jordan, so I could find and speak with Eyad Mansour.

The massacre of the twelve Nepalis seven months earlier had captured my attention as an investigative journalist. Maybe it was just a dark and obscure moment in this bigger global tragedy unfolding in Iraq, but aspects of the story suggested it might represent and mean much more. For months I had made little progress trying to dig into it from my desk in Washington, but then one day I had happened upon Mansour, who appeared as a disembodied quotation in the archives of the Associated Press International wire.

An AP reporter in Jordan interviewed Eyad Mansour in the immediate aftermath of the executions and identified him as the head of a firm called Morning Star for Recruitment and Manpower Supply. Mansour had told the wire service that he had hired the twelve men "through the Nepal-based Moon Light Co. *to work in factories in Jordan.*" Factories? The story didn't mention which ones or explain how the men had wound up in Iraq, or whom they were meant to be working for there. Nor was there any mention of Iraq in the paperwork filed with the government in Nepal, which showed that Mansour's firm had supposedly arranged jobs for them at one of Amman's newest five-star hotels, Le Royal.

Mansour made a brief appearance in another, earlier AP story, after the men were first kidnapped but before they were killed. He admitted that his firm had arranged to bring the twelve Nepalis to Amman, and he identified another company that was to be the men's "immediate supervisor" in Iraq. It was called Bisharat, an Arabic word that means "good news" or "good tidings." In fact, the kidnappers themselves, when they first announced the abductions on an extremist website, had said the men were working for Bisharat.

The AP story revealed nothing more about Bisharat except that a reporter could not reach anyone there for comment. Public record searches of Bisharat and Mansour's firm revealed virtually nothing. Reporting out of Nepal was even thinner, especially given the almost total lack of Internet usage there. I couldn't even find a comprehensive listing of the identities of the twelve men, including each of their names and home villages, something that would be critical to even asking the right questions.

Seven months after the massacre, my desk reporting had left me with only two clues about anyone who might possibly have direct knowledge of how and why these twelve men had died for the United States of America: the names of two Jordanian companies and the name of one man, Eyad Mansour.

Eyad (pronounced, EE-odd) was the son of a Filipino maid and a Jordanian father. He had built a successful business bringing foreign workers into Jordan from the Philippines, India, and beyond to work in factories, in hotel laundry rooms, and at construction sites, or to do housework for wealthy Jordanians. Mansour and his firm made up a tiny slice of the newly booming global trade that had lured Jeet and subsequent millions from the farm fields of Nepal and other poor countries to the Middle East and Southeast Asia for their labor. The business had just blossomed in Jordan thanks to some perverse consequences of the Arab-Israeli peace process and to the U.S. Congress.

After Israel and Jordan officially ended their status as enemies in 1996, Congress provided an incentive to keep the peace: goods jointly produced by Israeli and Jordanian businesses could be imported into the United States duty free. Garment factory production bloomed across the Jordanian desert, churning out clothing for top-selling American brands such as Nike, Puma, and Hanes, with the program creating some forty thousand jobs by 2003. That's where Eyad Mansour came in.

Factory owners set the hours so long and the pay so low that they had to import migrant workers from India, Sri Lanka, and other poor countries. Those workers accounted for almost half of all the jobs created, meaning that the U.S. program benefited factory owners far more than the multitudes of Jordanians who otherwise might have had a personal investment in peace. Dark realities for workers inside some of the garment factories were not yet widely known in 2005. That wasn't the case for other, wealthier Middle Eastern nations, where endemic human rights abuses against the millions of foreign workers they were importing had been documented in a growing body of academic studies, investigations by human rights groups, special volumes published by bodies of the United Nations, and even official publications of the U.S. government. All agreed that this looked like human trafficking. Workers routinely were lured abroad after paying for jobs based on fraudulent contracts, discovering only upon arrival that their journeys had been launched on lies. "Recruitment agencies [in Nepal] are also known to cheat people by using fake demand letters from overseas employment agencies and duping the prospective workers," wrote Ganesh Gurung, a Nepalese sociologist, Fulbright scholar, and head of a small migration-focused think tank in Kathmandu who wrote a chapter on Nepal in a report by the United Nations' International Labour Organization.

Many endured conditions akin to slavery in a region where the most influential countries, Saudi Arabia and the United Arab Emirates, had not even outlawed the practice until the 1960s. Employers or labor brokers in the destination countries seized and held workers' passports almost as a matter of course, eliminating their ability to leave or move about freely. Employers and brokers routinely refused to pay workers, or withheld wages for extended periods as a form of coercion. Some even refused to house or feed their migrants. Physical and sexual abuse was common, especially for women, who reported enduring rape as a routine matter of employment. Employers and brokers also used their nation's corrupt criminal justice systems to jail migrant workers who refused to work under such conditions, who attempted to organize or flee, or who defended themselves against abuses. There were regular reports of foreign workers being executed following secret trials in which they had no legal representation.

The ILO expert in Bangladesh, a political science professor from Dhaka named Tasneem Siddiqui, pointed to another important change in the system that had further corrupted the transnational process, just as the new surge of migrant workers spread farther and wider. In the earliest days of migration to the Middle East, following the oil boom of the 1970s and stretching into the 1990s, employers and brokers in the "receiving" nations typically paid recruiting agencies in places such as Nepal to find them reliable workers. These agencies paid the workers' airfares, arranged their visas, and covered all their costs. Now workers were expected to "buy" these jobs themselves in their home countries by paying massive brokerage fees, which were used to enrich brokers and cover all the business's expenses for importing workers.

It's not clear who first figured out that aspirational farmers would mortgage the lands they used to feed their families and hand over the cash based solely on the promise of a job paying a few dollars a day in a faraway land, but the shift came easily, and with extraordinary effects. It transferred the costs of importing millions of workers away from businessmen and onto some of the world's poorest people. It also shifted all the risks to the workers. If things didn't work out, only the workers and their families would suffer, not the businessmen in the already prosperous nation.

Perhaps most significantly, the change also created deeply insidious conditions that made it even easier to exploit and abuse workers once they arrived. After having borrowed vast sums of money to pay labor brokers, often several times the annual per capita income in places such as Nepal, the farmers had no choice but to do what they were told upon arrival in the destination countries, to accept whatever bait-and-switch terms were foisted upon them. Brokers and other business owners knew that migrants would accept almost anything just so their families could pay back the loans they had secured in order to buy the jobs in the first place. In this way, it became possible for millions of people to sacrifice years of their lives away from their families in exchange for no net benefit.

With this shift, a once mutually beneficial arrangement between wealthier nations that needed workers and poorer nations that needed cash evolved into an often inherently exploitative relationship, almost as if by design. Someone other than the employer may have been holding the debt, but this was, in effect, indentured servitude.

Those in the international marketplace in cheap human labor also seemed to quickly realize that globalization in the developing world yielded a buyer's market. Better communications and new airline routes to places such as Kathmandu created a nearly unlimited pool of desperate people from which one could draw "supply," and oversupply in any market always means falling prices. Between the early 1990s and the early 2000s, wage rates plummeted by more than half in Saudi Arabia. In Kuwait, employers slashed them even deeper.

Scholars, legal professionals, and diplomats began using a new lexicon to describe what all the pieces of this trade added up to. Phrases they employed that once might have sounded over-the-top, such as "debt bondage," or "human trafficking for forced and coerced labor," or even "the modern-day equivalent of slavery," gained acceptance, and then even gravitas. This booming new trade and its dark side hardly came up in chats at most American dinner tables, yet it also wasn't the exclusive preserve of experts and human rights lawyers.

Officials across the U.S. government knew of these abuses, and not just superficially. Diplomats working in U.S. embassies throughout the Middle East had been documenting and condemning them in human rights reports approved and published by their bosses back in Washington. By 2004, American diplomats had gathered so much damning evidence about these practices that the Bush administration was forced to publicly shame four of the United States' closest allies in the Iraq War, Kuwait, Qatar, Saudi Arabia, and the United Arab Emirates, by adding their names to the top tier of the U.S. government's human trafficking watch list.* By 2004, inherent abuses in the system had grown so ghastly, and were taking place on such a large scale, that they could no longer be ignored.

The practices outlined in these investigations and reports resembled the kind of sophisticated practices and transnational criminal complexities I had seen covering organized crime and drug cartels as an investigative reporter years earlier, in Chicago. Still, I was struggling to understand how all this connected to the U.S. military in Iraq, which, for all its many and gaping faults in the war, was largely a law-bound bureaucracy. How might the Pentagon have ended up doing business with Eyad Mansour and other men like him across the Middle East to fight the war in Iraq?

• • •

* The official designations came in June 2005 but were based on conduct by these governments that occurred in 2004.

"Get it?" Mansour said, using one of his favorite phrases. "The factory is in Nepal. I receive the goods and I pass them on." The "goods" were the Jeet Bahadur Thapa Magars of the world. As Mansour explained it, his small firm acted as a middleman in a global supply chain. The lexicon of commerce he used, which was common to the industry—referring to people as "imported goods," like commodities or even cattle—reached beyond the metaphorical, as I would soon learn.

After I showed up and introduced myself as an American journalist, Mansour had welcomed me, albeit with some suspicion, into his office to discuss his business. Hospitality to visiting strangers has for millennia been in the cultural DNA of the Middle East, where survival in the desert depends upon the kindnesses of people you come across on a journey, whether for just a moment of shade inside a Bedouin shelter, a drink of water, some food, or anything else. This makes it easy for you to knock on doors as a journalist and then to get past the threshold, but it doesn't necessarily make it any easier once you're inside, because a cultural obligation to welcome traveling strangers doesn't include an obligation to tell them the truth. Such was the case with Mansour.

During that initial meeting, Mansour told three different stories about the twelve men. First, he said he had absolutely nothing to do with them, and that Jeet and the others simply must have made their way to Amman on their own and then found jobs in Iraq. Later, he said the Kathmandu broker, Moon Light, *had sent* the twelve to Jordan, along with dozens of others, but that Moon Light dealt with a different firm in Jordan, not his. Finally, Mansour claimed that Moon Light had coordinated with him and sent the twelve workers to Jordan through his firm, but he said he had then sent the men to another Jordanian labor broker, who sent them into Iraq. This final account at least partially matched what Mansour had told the Associated Press in the immediate aftermath of the kidnapping and massacre.

After our meeting, I decided that politely and relentlessly pestering Mansour offered the best chance at getting more out of him. I hoped that, sooner or later, short of having me arrested for trespassing in his office, he would realize I wasn't going away. My Jordanian interpreter and assistant, Nader Rabadi, and I even brainstormed about slightly mad plots as cover for repeatedly showing up at Mansour's house. Not long after my first meeting with him, we walked into his office again—again unannounced—and Nader launched into a speech in Arabic, so I was mostly clueless about what he was saying, but his body language revealed some sort of entreaty. Mansour listened intently. At one point while Nader was speaking, Mansour pressed and rubbed the palm of his hand across his forehead and then drew it down over his eyes, the universal symbol for a man under stress. When Nader finished, Mansour asked him a question, also in Arabic. Nader answered and then turned to me and said we should begin.

We returned immediately to the specifics of the twelve men from Nepal, explaining, gently, that Mansour had previously offered different versions of what had happened to them. Which one was true? Suddenly, Mansour was more forthcoming. He said the twelve had not been alone, but were part of a much larger group of nearly eighty men. And beyond even those eighty men there were far, far more coming through Jordan, from Nepal and other impoverished Asian countries. Mansour said he had been doing a vigorous business since the start of the Iraq War, with the owner of the Moon Light agency in Kathmandu, a man he had met in Saudi Arabia. Nepalese workers were especially popular right now, Mansour said, "because they are good, they are honest, and they accept low salaries."

According to Mansour, Moon Light charged each Nepalese man somewhere between seven hundred and a thousand dollars, a fee multiples beyond the average annual earnings in Nepal. The agents had only had one cost: a one-way ticket to Jordan, which could be had for about four hundred dollars apiece or even less. The rest belonged to the broker, and the profit off a single man equaled more than the national per capita income for an entire year. Multiply that by twelve, or several dozen, or hundreds, then thousands, tens of thousands, and the business of selling overseas jobs to farmers looks incredibly lucrative, on the supply side alone.

As the middleman, Mansour said he received e-mails or faxes from the agency in Nepal containing the names, passport details, and flight arrival information for men landing at Queen Alia International Airport. Sometimes there would be just a few Nepalis, and sometimes they would come in batches of twenty or more. Mansour would send some men to meet each group as it arrived at the airport. Farmers from the hills of Nepal were never too hard to spot amid the crowds arriving on flights from Doha, Manama, or Dubai.

Each Nepalese man carried with him a sealed envelope, which he was told never to open, and that he must hand over directly to the local broker upon arrival at the airport. Brokers in Nepal sternly warned each man of this sacred rule, and threatened that opening the envelope or losing it ended with one certainty: *You will be sent home immediately. All will be lost.*

After his men collected the imported Nepalese "goods" from the airport, Mansour said that he would send them straight to another man in Amman, named Ali al-Nadi. More than anything else, this was what I really needed from Mansour: more names, more links in the human supply chain.

Al-Nadi ran what Iraq War contractors called "body shops." If you needed the "bodies" of menial laborers, you went to Ali al-Nadi. His shop's name, Bisharat, was the same name that Mansour had given to the Associated Press in the wake of the kidnappings, and the same name the kidnappers themselves had posted on the extremist website. Al-Nadi had been a dry cleaner prior to the war, Mansour said, but the U.S. invasion of Iraq had made him wealthy: "He is very rich from America. One American contract is all you need." Al-Nadi provided Mansour with locations in and around Amman to drop off the men after the airport pickups. These small apartments sometimes housed up to thirty men, who would wait days, weeks, or perhaps even months for paperwork clearing their way into Iraq, including documents issued by the Pentagon.

By the time Mansour finished his account, it was clear his involvement consisted of little more than typing "demand letters" on his stationery for nonexistent jobs in Jordan, sending them to Nepal, receiving e-mails containing the names of workers and their arrival information, and arranging airport pickups. His middleman role filled the smallest possible window, incurring virtually no costs, which made it a perfect enterprise— money for almost nothing. For this, Mansour received a total of three hundred to five hundred dollars for each Nepalese "import" he sent through the system. Some of that cash, we would eventually learn, came via the envelopes the men would hand-deliver when they got off their flights, meaning it came literally from their own pockets, and their families were indebted to pay it back. The rest came via a commission paid by al-Nadi, according to Mansour. Al-Nadi's body shop exclusively supplied men to a single Jordanian company, Daoud (pronounced DOW-ude) and Partners, which had contracts to serve American forces in Iraq. Mansour claimed it was one of the biggest contractors in Iraq.

Mansour claimed that Daoud operated as a sort of cutout. In the same way that Mansour was a middleman, Daoud's work was being done solely for, and at the behest of, another company, KBR Halliburton. Halliburton had been much in the news; it had not only the largest contract in Iraq, but also the largest wartime contract in history. Before 2000, when he left to campaign as the running mate of George W. Bush, U.S. vice president Dick Cheney, a prime backer of the war, had served as Halliburton's CEO.

It wasn't clear yet if Mansour had told the whole truth in this latest round, but he had been dramatically more forthcoming that day. As we walked out of Mansour's office and into the Amman heat, I asked my interpreter, Nader, "What happened in there? What did you tell him when we first arrived?"

Nader replied that he had warned Mansour that I was something akin to a manic police detective who would keep showing up at his office, and maybe at his home, too, until a full and honest version of events emerged. Nader confided to Mansour that the best way to make me go away was to be as cooperative as possible.

"And then what did he ask you?" I said.

"He asked me if you were really a journalist," Nader said, "or if you were secretly some kind of government agent."

"What did you tell him?"

"I told him you were a journalist," Nader said, "but I couldn't be sure about anything else."

I burst into laughter. Nader just smiled uncomfortably. He had worked with dozens of reporters who had flooded into the Middle East during the war, including some real characters, but this was certainly a far stranger adventure than any he had ever undertaken before. I suspect he was slightly worried about what I was up to, and what I might be getting him into.

• • •

Daoud and Partners' presence, at least on paper, left room for doubt about Mansour's veracity. A report from a financial research company said that Daoud's total staff numbered just twenty-five people. The company "principally engaged in hotel cleaning and catering," but also "freight forwarding and clearance services," and had only an average credit rating. The research firm assessed Daoud's "operating trend" as "steady," not booming beyond belief. Most important, at least in terms of gauging the veracity of Mansour's story, the research firm said Daoud's reported annual revenues were less than a million dollars in 2003, the first year of the Iraq War, and a smidge higher in 2004. That seemed beneath a pittance, given that the United States spent an average of almost fourteen billion dollars per year on contractors in Iraq.

The company's physical presence in Amman also did not seem to befit a major wartime contractor. None of that booming construction across the Jordanian capital appeared to include a single building for Daoud, let alone a tower, or even a significant set of suites. In short, Daoud did not appear to be the glistening Arab incarnation of Halliburton.

Mansour had feigned losing the contact details for everyone

he had done business with, but had let loose some vague details about one Daoud office. Knocking on a few doors led to its location, in a converted apartment on the top floor of a four-story residential building. It was located in the Abdali neighborhood of downtown Amman, where government bureaucrats are stashed inside gray concrete office blocks. Daoud's converted apartment resided in a building behind the Jordanian Ministry of Industry and Trade.

At the top of the stairs and beyond the threshold, a balding, slightly sunburned, middle-aged Daoud employee named Haitham Shwarham sat behind a reception desk in what had been the apartment's living room. The room was spare and colorless, beyond Shwarham's slightly reddened dome.

We asked for Ali al-Nadi, and were informed that al-Nadi did not work directly for Daoud. But, Shwarham said, "he brings the workers here."

If the flat functioned as a transit point for Mansour's "goods" from Nepal and beyond, then it made sense that Mansour knew this to be the company's office. Maybe Mansour had been telling the truth, or some version en route to it, after all.

Could Shwarham please provide contact information for al-Nadi? we asked. He refused.

Would he consider dialing al-Nadi's mobile number himself from the office phone and then handing over the receiver? Reluctantly, he agreed.

Al-Nadi answered immediately, and when the phone was handed over, he sounded flustered, saying he was attending a funeral on the outskirts of Amman, so he couldn't meet with us. He also said that while sometimes he uses foreign workers in his cleaning business, he didn't know anything about the twelve Nepalese workers who were murdered in Iraq, and that he had

had nothing to do with them. He said he would be happy to meet once he returned to Amman, but he declined to offer his phone number or even the location of his firm. He promised he would be in touch if we left contact details at the desk where we were standing.

We did that, but Shwarham had warmed to us just enough to offer the location of al-Nadi's office, a couple of miles away, and we headed straight there. The receptionist said he wasn't in, but offered us his business card. It carried an amateurish-looking logo crafted from the word *Bisharat*, which means "good news" or "good tidings," the same firm named by the terrorists following the kidnapping.

Ali Kamel al-Nadi spread his legs wide, leaned back into the sofa, and drew hard on a filtered American cigarette, the tip crackling and glowing in front of his face. From behind the bursts of smoke, he repeated claims he had made over the telephone in the previous two days: it was completely possible that the twelve Nepalese men in question had somehow found their way to Amman from villages across the Himalayan kingdom and perhaps even to his laundry business before slipping away into a convoy bound for Iraq that he had no involvement with. These things happen. Workers come and go every day, he said.

Al-Nadi had agreed to meet us for drinks in the lobby of Amman's Grand Hyatt Hotel, a space so filled with gold and garish fixtures and highly polished marble that it resembled the palace of a nouveau riche king. Al-Nadi's sunglasses were atop his head, nestled in his tight, thick dark hair, and his gangling, long limbs loosely filled an olive-colored business suit. He carried a protruding belly above the waistline of his trousers, evidencing a fondness for lager.

He was accompanied by two men whom he introduced as his partners. One dressed younger than his years, in designer jeans and a fashionable long-sleeved T-shirt. Al-Nadi called him "Ghaleb." He was the only one in the trio without a wedding ring. The other had longer hair and a thick mustache that veered toward handlebars at the ends. He wore an ill-fitting suit cut from inexpensive cloth. A bright gold watch hung languidly around his left wrist in the fashion that requires the occasional jiggle of the hand to make it drop below the cuff. Al-Nadi introduced this man as "Abdullah" and sometimes looked his way before answering questions.

Service at the Grand Hyatt tended toward the obsessively attentive in that colonial-era style often displayed in five-star establishments of the Middle East. Waiters streamed over, bearing fresh glasses of beer, clearing the empties the second they were dry, and constantly swapping dirty ashtrays for unsoiled ones. It wasn't just for show, as al-Nadi could empty a glass of beer in just a few tilts, and each man seemed to light another cigarette the moment he'd tamped out his last.

The men answered questions about their livelihood with hedged statements or hypotheticals, frequently retracting comments and contradicting one another only moments after each had spoken. "Abdullah" seemed most often to lead these retreats.

Were they in the business of delivering workers from poor Asian countries into Iraq to work for the U.S. occupation? *Maybe* that was a profitable line of business in Jordan right now, they said, and *maybe* they were involved. Maybe they were, and maybe they weren't.

As the beer and smoke flowed more freely, al-Nadi increasingly seemed to enjoy being the center of attention for an American journalist, which perhaps explained part of his motivation for agreeing to the meeting. How many other businessmen in Jordan were holding court at the Grand Hyatt for the pages of an American newspaper? The more he drank, the bigger he seemed to feel, and that was a feeling worthy of cultivation.

Did al-Nadi's cleaning business ever broker foreign workers to firms doing business in Iraq? Yes, al-Nadi said, but usually these were just human loans and did not last very long, maybe only a month or two.

Did they specifically send workers to the company called Daoud and Partners, the firm Mansour had identified as the major Iraq contractor?

Ghaleb jumped in. He said they indeed delivered workers to Daoud.

Immediately, Abdullah became unnerved. "There are some things about our business that we keep even from our wives," he said.

Yes, the ringless Ghaleb chimed in. "We don't even tell our mothers."

Assuming hypothetically that such contracts even existed, they would surely contain clauses demanding confidentiality, Abdullah said, a statement that seemed crafted to remind his partners that they should be more cautious.

I returned frequently to the twelve dead Nepalis by asking slightly different questions about them, but the answers never went far beyond the initial hedged denial from al-Nadi. After one such question, al-Nadi reached into the inside breast pocket of his suit jacket and removed a slender calendar book, the kind banks used to give away for opening a new account. He said that if I wrote down the names of the twelve dead men, he might be persuaded to try to check whatever employment records he could find to see if they had possibly worked for him before wandering off on their own and getting themselves killed in Iraq.

Al-Nadi never expressed or feigned remorse over the executions of the twelve men in the video, but he did say that checking whether they had been in his employ could be useful. After all, he said, "If they were my workers, maybe I should be compensated for losing them."

A cigarette hung loosely from al-Nadi's mouth as he strutted out of the lobby bar and to the front of the hotel, where we waited for the valet to bring his car around. Abdullah remained by his side. As the parking attendant pulled up, al-Nadi said he needed to show me something in his car, something I absolutely had to see. He popped the trunk and placed a DVD into a player mounted inside it, and we spun around into the rear passenger seats where there were two small screens on the backs of the headrests in front of us. He said he had installed them to quiet his children with cartoons.

A newscast popped up on the screens, and suddenly al-Nadi and "Ghaleb" were in the frame, appearing at some sort of formal meeting. In the car, "Abdullah" leaned in from the open door and, acting as a sort of sycophantic member of his boss's posse, pointed insistently to the screen at a well-suited man. "You see," he said, "the ambassador!" Al-Nadi smiled.

The man in the frame was the Philippine ambassador to Jordan. I pretended to be duly impressed to be in the presence of a man who had been in the presence of an ambassador on the television news. The broadcast was in Tagalog, the dominant tongue in the Philippines, and I had no idea what anyone was saying.

I urged al-Nadi to give me a copy of the DVD, which he seemed to think was an excellent idea. "Abdullah" immediately objected. Al-Nadi ignored him, and we spun out of the car and back around to the trunk. Al-Nadi fumbled as he tried to keep a cigarette dangling from his mouth and simultaneously eject the DVD. "Abdullah" grabbed at his arm to physically try to stop him from handing over the disc, but al-Nadi grew angry and firmly shoved his partner's hand away. "Abdullah" then fell silent.

Al-Nadi passed the disc to me, and I thanked him profusely. No problem, he said, adding that he'd had many copies made. It seemed like a sort of business card, evidence of his bona fides. We shook hands and said our good-byes and promised to be in touch.

The video the half-drunk al-Nadi had proudly handed over contained a newscast that had aired a few months earlier, on ABS-CBN, one of the largest broadcasters in the Philippines. After all the rhetorical dancing in the lobby of the Grand Hyatt, the newscast identified al-Nadi as the official representative of Daoud and Partners as he shook hands with the Philippine ambassador. The two were holding a formal meeting about Daoud's use of Filipino citizens as menial laborers on U.S. military bases in Iraq.

A story appearing in the *Manila Standard* a few days after al-Nadi's meeting with the ambassador provided more details. It reported that the Philippine government had formally barred its citizens from working in the increasingly dangerous war zone and that Daoud had been taken to task for violating the ban. The story added that foreign ministry officials finally had "secured an agreement with the Jordan-based firm Dawood [*sic*] & Partners to stop deploying Filipino workers to Iraq," which it had been doing on a large scale and in defiance of the Philippine government.

Within a week of my meeting with al-Nadi at the Grand Hyatt, a new story appeared in Philippine newspapers, reporting that government officials were blacklisting Daoud after finding that Filipinos in Manila had signed two-year contracts specifying they'd be working in Amman, "but upon their arrival, they were brought to the U.S. military bases" in Iraq. One of the bases was Al Asad, where the twelve Nepalis had been headed when they were kidnapped. In addition to the alleged bait-and-switch, the news story mentioned force: some workers said they had been forced to go to Iraq. Indian newspapers had been reporting similar allegations about Daoud, even before the twelve Nepalis were taken into Iraq and kidnapped.

Not long after, officials in one Amman embassy for a major "feeder" country showed me a shelf of three-ring binders filled with correspondence between its government officials and Daoud executives about the alleged mistreatment and deaths of foreign workers under its employ on U.S. military bases.

The weight of all this evidence made clear that Mansour had been telling the truth. Al-Nadi in fact ran a body shop, and he did so for Daoud. The paper trail at the embassy of the feeder country and interviews with others in Amman also confirmed that Daoud itself operated as a body shop for KBR Halliburton. This appeared to be much bigger than the tiny, fly-by-night operation portrayed on paper. Still, I lacked hard, specific evidence connecting Jeet and the other murdered men into a global supply chain stretching from Nepal to KBR and the U.S. military.

5

LATE 2004 TO EARLY 2005
Gorkha and Kathmandu

Kamala put on her petticoat and gathered a plain white sari prepared for the day, the ninth day since Jeet's death. She walked alone down the steep trail beside the farmhouse and toward the well below the village, where she would take a ritual bath to mark her permanent passage into widowhood. As a wife in Nepal, she had been considered half her husband's body. As a widow, she would be considered half a corpse. She was expected never to remarry or be with another man, staying faithful to her husband even after his death. An old woman was already at the well when Kamala arrived, standing at the far tap. She saw Kamala's white sari and stared in silence.

Kamala finished bathing and wrapped herself in the cloth. Only a widow dresses in a white sari, a garment meant to serve not the wearer but the world. Widows are considered impure and the bearers of bad fortune, and must be marked clearly to make it easier for others to steer clear of them in the streets or to exclude them from ceremonies, for fear that their presence will curse the gathering and the gathered. They also must be marked easily for shaming if they are in the company of men who are not their sons or fathers. A woman, especially a young woman, who once was but no longer is married is no longer under the control of a man. Because she possesses sexual experience, she is considered dangerous. No matter one's ethnic group, the widow's duty to wear the white sari is shared across virtually every divide in Nepal: high caste or low, rich or poor, educated or illiterate.

Once Kamala had shrouded herself in white, the old woman who had been watching from the other tap broke her silence. "What has the world come to, to see a day such as this?" she said. The words were sympathetic, but pounded into Kamala's chest, and she struggled to maintain her composure in what was meant to mark the first moment of her new life. How on earth could she ever escape her grief if everyone forever saw her as this old woman did in this moment?

Four days later, Kamala's father, long absented from her life and the lives of his other daughters, came to the village on the ledge. He stood before her in Jeet's farmhouse bearing fresh clothes. He handed them over to Kamala and implored her to remove the white sari and never wear it again. "Do not stop dressing as you want," he said. Then he asked her, "Where are your bangles?" The red bangles that Jeet had given Kamala are symbols of matrimony in Nepal, and unmarried women or widows are socially prohibited from wearing them, along with anything else that is the color red, as red symbolizes desire and is reserved solely for wives of the living. Kamala had removed them before donning her white sari. "Put them back on your wrists," Kamala's father told her. She changed her clothes as her father had commanded, and then silently cupped and extended her fingers and slipped the bangles over them and onto her arms. Kamala was stunned that her father would insist she break some of the most powerful taboos of their culture, but she did not question him. Perhaps, unbeknownst to her, he had witnessed the suffering of widows of fellow soldiers with whom he had served during the nation's brutal civil war, or maybe one of his other daughters had implored him to take Kamala's side. Regardless, from that day forward, Kamala would find the strength to ignore the disapproving stares she felt shoot down at her wrists. The weight of the red bangles reminded her of her father's concern, and perhaps his love.

Jeet's family had been so supportive of Kamala since her first day in the farmhouse, and then also of Kritika, that Kamala felt little fear for their security in the immediate aftermath of her husband's death. Some extreme thoughts, some irrational fears, however, are inevitable when one is in a state of shock and grief. On one such day, a relative of Jeet's offered Kamala a cigarette, telling the young widow that drawing the smoke and nicotine into her lungs would ease her anxieties. A single fear seized Kamala's mind, one she immediately expressed: *If smoking that one cigarette puts me in the grip of addiction, how will I afford the habit and still feed my daughter without a husband?*

Your worries are irrational, the woman said. "You have a brother-in-law and a mother-in-law who love you. They will take care of you and your daughter." Still, Kamala chose not to smoke even one cigarette that day.

She felt alone inside the walls of the home and among the family members who had once made her feel so welcome. Jeet's mother was encased in her own pain, and the entire village watched her with concern. On occasion, the old woman still spoke of slipping into the gloomy shade of the mountain never to return. She no longer engaged with Kamala as she had before Jeet's death, and turned away from her when the young widow cried out Jeet's name and sought comfort. Likewise, when her own tears came, the old woman would not turn to Kamala for an embrace.

Kamala's mother-in-law had asked the family's eldest son,

Ganga, to move back into the farmhouse immediately upon Jeet's death, even though Kamala and the old woman had been managing the home seamlessly since before Jeet went to Jordan. Upon moving back, Jeet's brother's wife took to the old woman's side and assumed the kitchen and household duties that had been Kamala's exclusive preserve for nearly three years.

At first the daughters-in-law shadowed each other in the tiny space. Kamala found herself grasping at air when she reached for pots and pans that were now hanging elsewhere. Before long, Kamala's daily duties shifted out of the farmhouse and into the fields. Crops and cattle then became her responsibilities, though for many households, this often was the work left to children or to farmhands from outside the family. As she moved back onto the land, she carried Kritika on her hip, and would leave her crawling at her feet through the fields or in the forests as she assumed her new role in Jeet's family.

The centuries-old stigma of widowhood in Nepal can be difficult to shed even in the most progressive and educated families, even for a woman who refuses to wear a white sari. In more conservative communities, the isolation and rejection of widows can be instant and complete, with women and their children literally cast out from their dead husband's homes. It was more subtle and insidious for Kamala. She felt her value as a member of Jeet's family slip away without mention or negotiation, as regard for her as a bearer of ill fortune hung around her like a cloud inside the farmhouse. Villagers who had once embraced her as the wife of their favorite son now averted their eyes. When she approached small groups, their conversation would abruptly stop. Inevitably, Kamala believed they were speaking ill of her. What she knew for certain was that people neither accepted her as before nor treated her with disdain. She had to endure not only a lack of compassion for her predicament but also a feeling of invisibility, which she found impossible to shed.

Jeet gently untangled the pumpkin vines with his strong hands, or carefully sculptured the red earth beneath the spinach stalks as he dipped between the rows of the vegetable patch on the terrace just below the farmhouse. He wore the long-sleeved white shirt and soft gray khakis he had worn on the day he left for Jordan. Usually this was how Kamala saw him in her dreams, standing in the middle distance on the terrace below the farmhouse and tending their vegetables. He never sang or spoke to her, as he had done in life, but she watched as he worked in silence, a vision she had seen hundreds of times before. At other moments in these dreams, she would see him closer to her, but still beyond her touch, smiling and contented beneath the mountain sky as he sipped her homemade rice wine. It wasn't every night that Jeet came home in her dreams, but he appeared often enough that it brought Kamala a measure of comfort before she rose to face the isolation of her days.

Kamala's mornings now began with her trudging up the switchback paths and into the forest high above the horseshoe so she could gather branches and leaves for the family's cattle, as she had done with her sisters in childhood. Kamala thought of them as she climbed into the heights where the wind rolled up the treetops in waves. Her eldest sister, Maya, heard the news of Jeet's death and she feared that Kamala might try to end her own life. But when Maya visited Jeet's farmhouse in the first days following his murder, she instead found her *nani* hardened to the world. Kamala refused to show her suffering to anyone. "I cried even more after seeing her this way," Maya said.

Kamala ascended the gorge to resume the chores of her childhood with the one person from the village with whom she now shared a bond, the young widow Heera, her acquaintance from their school days. Heera had moved back to the village and into her parents' home after her husband died in an accident in India when she was just seventeen years old. Kamala always had felt ashamed at how the village regarded Heera, but she had never mustered the courage to break through the social constraints that kept her distant from her former friend. Heera had been the youngest widow in the village until Jeet's death bestowed this shared status on Kamala, who was now eighteen. The two women immediately took comfort in each other's company, but conversations about their dead husbands were rare, and when they did occur, they usually centered on prosaic matters, such as the differences between the men's funeral rituals. The women did not speak of the inner and outer discord that ruled their lives on the ledge. Still, they became inseparable, each plainly visible to the other in a way she could not be with anyone else, and this was enough.

When she wasn't chopping branches with Heera, Kamala sometimes accompanied her mother-in-law and Jeet's eldest brother, Ganga, on long treks across the valley to the nearest town, where they had countless tasks related to Jeet's death. Outcry over the murders had prompted the government to provide small charity payments to the families, but the paperwork appeared endless. For hours on end, Jeet's eldest brother and his mother would not speak to Kamala on these long walks, marching far ahead on their own as Kamala fell behind, slowed by the weight of Kritika on her hip and surrounded by the end-less silence of the footpath.

Kamala's prized possessions remained the wedding gifts from Jeet's family, the gold necklace crafted from paper-thin links and the small gold earrings he had given her not long after they eloped. These were the first pieces of jewelry she had ever owned, and she thought of her husband when she touched them or felt the gentle tug of the necklace's weight. One night, Kamala lent them to her sister-in-law, who was attending a festival, but afterward, the woman didn't return the jewelry, and Kamala discovered that her mother-in-law had taken the pieces.

Kamala delicately approached the old woman in the farm-house kitchen. "My neck feels strange without that chain," she said.

"Who cares?" the old woman replied. "No one's going to look at you now." The old woman told Kamala that she had given her son the jewelry in the first place. "Your husband didn't earn the money for this; my husband did," she said. "I bought it for you, so it's mine, not yours."

The pain of isolation and rejection became physical for Ka-mala. She hid alone in an upstairs corner of the house, praying for strength. She prayed she wouldn't have to rely on the family she had become so dependent upon. She clung to Kritika, who was just two years old, and spent as much time as she could outside the farmhouse, and in Heera's company.

• • •

The final approach to Kathmandu can be unnerving, even for those unaware of the city's history of airline disasters. Jungle-covered mountain peaks ringing the Nepalese capital appear frighteningly close as soon as the belly of a plane dips beneath the clouds. Turbulence above the Kathmandu Valley often makes it feel like one's plane is bouncing across these peaks in a descent that can unfold in flashes of blindness induced by thick fog or rain shrouding the city. When patches of sky do open, the city nestled beneath the mountains appears like none other, its thousands of low-slung buildings, most made from bricks fired in kilns across the valley and rising no higher than the treetops, are packed into chaotic clusters dotted by ancient pagoda temples and golden stupas, shrines built to honor Nepal's most famous son, Buddha.

I flew into Kathmandu in May 2005 fresh from my trip to Amman. At this point, even basic information about the twelve men from Nepal remained beyond reach, as did specific evidence linking them into the KBR and U.S. military chain.

The only way to try to discover what had happened to these men was to retrace their journeys, from their villages up to the moments recorded in the four-minute video of their deaths, to find and speak with their families and others who had known them, to find the brokers in Nepal who first sent them, and any others whom they had encountered along the way.

Yubaraj Ghimire was the editor of *Samay* ("Time") magazine, in Nepal, and one of the country's most respected journalists. He had once been forced into exile after someone tried to assassinate him because of his work, and in 2001 he was arrested on treason charges by order of the nation's king after he dared to publish something written by a Maoist. It cost him his job as editor of Nepal's largest newspaper. Warm and soft-spoken, Ghimire believed in the importance of trying to piece together what had happened to the twelve. He agreed to help gather whatever official documents existed on the case.

After the killings, the Nepalese government had ordered a special inquiry, but the charge of the investigative commission was focused not on the twelve murdered men but, instead, on the riots that broke out across Nepal after the execution video aired. Of central focus to the panel, headed by a former justice of Nepal's supreme court, was that the riots had targeted an industry that had become the biggest pillar of Nepal's economy: the foreign labor recruitment business. The estimated one billion dollars wired home each year by overseas Nepalis had quickly outpaced all exports, tourism, and foreign aid combined. Ghimire provided a connection to a source who provided a copy of the commission's secret report.

Even with such a narrow focus, the report included a substantial background section about the events preceding the riots, which could help me retrace the men's journeys. It listed each man's permanent home address, along with brokers involved in Nepal. It also had gathered up everything about the twelve held in the files of every Nepalese government agency, including contracts filed with the overseas employment office. The agency's records showed that the twelve men "had been recruited on the condition of being employed at Le Royal Hotel through the Morning Star company" of Jordan. That was Eyad Mansour's firm. It also gave identifying information about the main labor broker involved in Kathmandu, registered as Moon Light. Mansour himself had given me the same name.

Nine of the twelve had won "final approval" from the government to work at the Amman hotel. Such approval amounted to a rubber stamp, literally pressed into each man's passport to get him past an airport check. Paperwork for the three remaining men had been lost within the Labour and Employment Promotion department, an unimaginably overburdened, understaffed, and noncomputerized labyrinth, with file rooms that on most days resembled paper mountains. The trio hailed from the same hometown in Eastern Nepal's lowlands. The report also said that the twelve dead men were among a larger group of at least thirty-two Nepalis whom Moon Light had won permission to send to Jordan in applications filed simultaneously in June 2004. Eyad Mansour had put the overall group's number at about eighty men.

Amid the rusted-out cars, motorcycle rickshaws (called *tuk tuks*), and trucks belching black fumes across Kathmandu, a tiny two-seater no bigger than a clown car in an American parade rolled silently across a dirt road not far from the diplomatic quarter in Kathmandu and into its parking spot behind an iron gate in front of a three-story redbrick house. The car, imported from India, might have been Nepal's first all-electric vehicle, if for no other reason than that electricity service in Kathmandu sometimes functioned only a few hours a day. The driver, Ganesh Gurung, a U.S.-educated sociologist raised in the mountain air near Gorkha, put up with the disruptions to make a small and silent stand against the increasingly dangerous pollution choking his city. The three-story brick house on the dirt road served as the headquarters of the Nepal Institute of Development Studies, a small Nepalese think tank he had established in 1998 to conduct research into the economic development policies and needs of his country.

Gurung had devoted himself to the study of foreign labor migration since long before Nepal's government saw how critical it had become to the nation's economy and how easily Nepalis were trapped and abused inside the unregulated global trade. He knew more about the system than anyone else, and had written a paper on it ahead of a 2003 conference of the United Nations' International Labour Organization focused on human rights abuses against migrants from Asia. We had spoken extensively by phone previously, and he had agreed to help me figure out what had happened to the twelve should I ever come to Nepal. Over a cup of tea and a handshake across his desk, he allowed me to hire a fixer and a young sociologist from his staff, and helped me find a driver. He also warned me how difficult it would be to retrace the journeys of the twelve men, given the obvious hurdles.

For starters, the government report showed that except for the three men whose paperwork had been lost, and who were from the same village in Nepal's low-lying plains, the victims of the massacre had come from towns and villages scattered across the country, all separately drawn into the same nation-wide recruitment pool through different channels. It was natural to assume that they were somehow all connected by more than their fates, yet all but three had been strangers to one another before they went to Jordan, and perhaps right up until they were kidnapped and killed together in the ditch across the border in Iraq.

Logistically speaking, this meant that even with "home addresses" for their families, it would likely take weeks to reach them all. They were scattered across a nation with few phones and fewer roads, a nation spanning more than fifty-six thousand square miles and rising across some of the most inhospitable, albeit breathtaking, terrain in the world, a nation in the throes of civil war. It could take hours or even days of walking before reaching villages in places such as Gorkha. And after the murders of their sons, husbands, and brothers, some of the families had moved, which meant that even the most basic information about them in the report could be useless.

Gurung knew of a charity that had raised a small amount of money for the families, and its leaders might know how to reach the survivors. And one of the nation's richest businessmen, who ran a conglomerate that owned the famous Gorkha Brewery, had offered surviving family members jobs in his offices and factories. His company also might help us reach the families. After a few phone calls, we had a rough idea about how to locate some who were now living in and around Kathmandu, which was the best place to start.

Thousands of Nepalis packed the narrow alleyways and streets in the ancient city of Patan, dancing in a procession both leading and trailing a towering effigy of the Buddhist god of rain. Men pulled long ropes to raise the effigy on a pole hewn from the trunk of an old-growth tree felled in the surrounding mountain forests. It tottered as the men wheeled it on a chariot through the streets. Thousands of tiny flames, held in brass candles burning clarified butter, danced in the breeze at outdoor temples and altars around every corner, with Patan's red chariot festival in full swing. Amid the chaos of the festival, we found the single-room ground-floor apartment that Bishnu Maya Thapa shared with her last living son.

Her firstborn son, Bishnu Hari, had left for Jordan less than a year earlier, age eighteen. He stood barely five feet tall, and his face sported fuzz that wouldn't trouble the dullest razor. He always wore blue jeans and sandals, and if we judge by the blurred images of a young man in long sleeves and jeans captured in the four-minute video, the terrorists executed him fifth.

His mother had soft light-brown eyes and waist-length hair that she wrapped in a bun when she went out in public. As she spoke, she held her face between her two hands, which were thick, like those of a retired boxer. She looked well beyond her four and a half decades, especially around her eyes. She'd earned much of her living smashing stones with a hammer at a roadside quarry in their hometown northwest of Kathmandu. Stone breaking was an old and steady way to survive in Nepal, if not a lucrative one.

In the early years of her marriage, a common saying throughout Nepal and India formed the basis for a kind of mantra in her prayers: "May you be the mother of a hundred sons." Sons are equated with prosperity. Daughters marry and move in with the families of their husbands, so it is believed that only a son can bring security by bringing a wife and children home to help raise food and shoulder some of life's burdens, or even to earn a salary should he leave home.

Before Bishnu Hari, his mother had given birth to three daughters. So grateful was she that her prayers for a son had been answered that she lavished love and attention on him. By the time he had graduated from the equivalent of high school, he wanted to do whatever he could to keep her from spending more of her days breaking stones into gravel.

Many from their small town, in a district ravaged by Nepal's civil war and about a five-hour bus ride northwest of Kathmandu, had moved to the capital city to find work overseas. Bishnu Hari followed their path, aided by a former neighbor who had started earning commissions by connecting young men from his town with brokers in the capital. He worked as a *dalal*, a Hindi-derived word that had once been used to identify a pimp and that had, in the new age of global labor, become synonymous with "middleman" or "agent." *Dalals* are vital to the overseas labor system in Nepal. They're paid in cash, sometimes by labor brokers (who slice off a piece of the *dalals'* commissions from the workers) and sometimes by the prospective overseas workers themselves. They're not licensed by the government the way the main brokerages are.

Bishnu Hari's *dalal* was named Kumar Thapa. He sported a faux-leather baseball cap and a pencil-thin mustache, and claimed that he had helped Bishnu Hari get a job working at a restaurant called the New Bamboo Cottage, a tiki hut tourist restaurant in Kathmandu where the smell of clarified butter, scorched cumin, and sweat hung heavy in the brown thatch used for the walls. In exchange for his labors, Bishnu Hari got to eat for free and sleep at night on linoleum tables that he shoved together side by side and end to end to form a sort of platform bed. When he wasn't working, he combed newspaper ads and visited some of the city's hundreds of labor brokers.

In June 2004, Nepal's leading daily newspaper published a public notice–style advertisement for jobs at Le Royal Hotel in Amman. It promised more than one hundred open positions for Nepalese men, each fetching two hundred to five hundred dollars per month. A logo appeared near the bottom of the ad, a crescent moon and six stars slung low over two mountain peaks. Arching over the stars and the mountains like a rainbow were the words "Moon Light Consultant Pvt. Ltd.," the Kathmandu broker. Its government registration number was there, too, lending an air of credibility. The Moon Light ad mentioned that a "demand letter" for the hotel jobs in Amman from its Jordanian counterpart (called Morning Star for Recruitment and Manpower Supply) was on file with the government, as required by Nepalese law. No one reading the advertisement could have known that Eyad Mansour had done nothing more than simply type some words on his letterhead and fax the paper to Nepal. The ad said that job interviews would take place at Moon Light's office the next day. The *dalal* said he had arranged for Bishnu Hari to get in, although he accompanied the nervous young man only to the Moon Light office and through the process of what passed for an interview.

Bishnu Hari would have been a standout that day. He had more schooling than most young Nepalese men, and rudimentary training in welding and wiring had given him an extra edge. Perhaps his strongest qualification: he could afford to pay for the job.

The agency called the New Bamboo Cottage about two weeks later and said that Bishnu Hari should come back with some two thousand dollars, or about eight times the average annual income in Nepal. He got word to his mother. The family borrowed all but four hundred dollars of the cash from local lenders, who charged an interest rate of 36 percent a month. He took the bus back to collect the money from his mother, and bade her goodbye the next day, telling her not to worry. "I will earn and send money home. We'll buy land and build a small house to live in."

Bishnu Hari flew to Amman on July 3, and his younger brother moved to Kathmandu and took Bishnu Hari's place at the New Bamboo Cottage, encouraged by his brother's success and eager to find his own overseas job. He was at the restaurant several weeks later when his brother called long-distance, the first time anyone had heard from him since he left.

"How are you?" Bishnu Hari asked his younger brother, but the line cut immediately, and he didn't phone back.

In August, Bishnu Hari called again. The restaurant's owner, a woman named Gana Magar, answered and recognized Bishnu Hari's voice right away. "Where are you?" she asked him.

"In Jordan," Bishnu Hari said. Then he added, "I am done for."

Before he could explain, before his brother could come to the phone, the line went dead, Gana Magar told me. It is the last known time anyone in Nepal heard from Bishnu Hari until his anguished visage, taken from captivity in Iraq, flashed on television screens days later.

Interviews—with Bishnu Hari's mother, with his younger brother, with the *dalal* with the pencil-thin mustache who had accompanied him to the labor broker, and with the restaurant owner who had employed him and who received his ominous call from Jordan—plus the advertisement in the newspaper and the paperwork gathered by the government commission all showed that the eighteen-year-old had been the victim of the kind of bait-and-switch common to the "supply side" of this newly booming slice of globalization, but far more sinister than usual in both its specifics and its consequences. More than the terms of the work had been changed—the advertisement and the paperwork filed with the government were as clear as they were fraudulent. Everyone who had dealt with Bishnu Hari throughout the entire process said the brokers spoke only of Jordan, not Iraq, and that included the *dalal* accompanying him throughout the interview. Bait-and-switch techniques common to the new global trade could cost people two or three years of their lives under conditions akin to peonage and coerced labor, and then years of crippling debt for their families who purchased the jobs, but these techniques were on another scale entirely. It appeared they had cost eighteen-year-old Bishnu Hari his life.

"My child is dead, my son who I brought up in the midst of hardship and difficulties, crushing rocks, carrying gravel," his mother recounted. "I want to die myself." She pulled out one of the only clear pictures of him she still had, a passport-size head shot barely bigger than a postage stamp. She held it gently in both her hands and raised it to her lips, then closed her eyes and kissed it. If she had known what awaited her son, she said, "I would have kept him by my side, even if I had to do back-breaking work."

She had remained in Kathmandu to make sure that her last living son stayed in school and did not try to pursue his own dream of working overseas. "I've tried to persuade her," the young man told me, "but she says no." At this his mother, squatting on the floor beside him, reached for her son's leg and wrapped her arms around it, trying to hold him in place as much as embrace him, and began to cry.

Across the Kathmandu Valley and beyond, the stories and paperwork were turning out to be as similar as the heartbreak. Each man appeared to have succumbed to the bait-and-switch. Without exception, each family had to borrow money to pay small fortunes in order to buy the jobs on offer in Jordan. Even so, the sums they had paid varied, sometimes widely. *Dalals* were involved in every case, but some, such as the young man from Bishnu Hari's village, acted like ushers for the Moon Light agency in Kathmandu and collected only small fees. Others inserted themselves much more aggressively into the middle, and this allowed them to control the process. These *dalals* set the price for the jobs exorbitantly higher, keeping bigger cuts for themselves. The farther from Kathmandu, the easier it was for *dalals* to be more controlling and to charge higher fees, as "locals" far from the city had no idea how the business worked, and little chance of discovering this on their own.

In the lowland plains of southeastern Nepal, the families of the three young men from the same town paid more to their local *dalal* than any of the other families: roughly $3,500 apiece. The jobs in Jordan, the *dalal* told them, would pay $700 per month. The three young men, ages twenty-one to twenty-four, were the closest of friends. The oldest worked in the local cinema as a ticket taker, and he marveled that just one month's salary in Jordan would be more than four times what he earned all year at the movie house. His two friends, a farmer and a student, were equally dazzled.

Even though the paperwork filed by Moon Light with the Nepalese government had said the men were bound for hotel jobs in Jordan, the local *dalal* had told the young men and their families that they would be serving food to American soldiers at a U.S. military camp in Jordan. The families had no idea what brokers had typed onto permit applications filed with the government to get their sons and brothers out of the country. They did express concern to the *dalal* about the safety of the trio, given that the job involved the U.S. military. The *dalal*'s response was: "Don't worry—you are working for American soldiers. The plane will take you to the camp, and in the camp, there is no danger."

Together, the three families agreed to borrow money to pay the broker, believing that $3,500 apiece was, in the end, a good investment for the future, given the salaries. The young men boarded a night bus together in late June 2004. It rolled down a road where oxen pulled carts filled with dung and straw before passing under a canopy of mango trees and reaching Nepal's only east–west highway en route to Kathmandu for their flight to Jordan.

Not long before they were taken from Amman and into Iraq, the three called the only phone in their village, a local pay phone maintained by a shopkeeper, and their families were summoned. The young men on the other end of the international line were panicked. The Jordanian brokers had dramatically changed the terms of the jobs the families had already paid for, and now they would have to surrender two months' pay to Jordanian brokers as an additional fee for their jobs. They also would have to accept less than half the monthly salaries promised in Nepal. The bait-and-switch terms meant it would take at least a year for their families to pay back just the principal on each man's loan, assuming they could put 100 percent of their salaries toward their loans and nothing else, and that didn't include the interest. Effectively, they would have to work two years for free just to break even with the debts they had incurred to buy their jobs. In addition, the young men said, they were being taken to "an American camp" across the border in Iraq. They wanted to come home, they said.

The families responded that they needed to weigh their options. They asked the young men to phone back the next day. That night, the families decided collectively that the debts they had incurred to buy the jobs were so great that they had no choice but to ask the young men to proceed, lest they all face certain ruin. Even if they couldn't pay back all the money borrowed to buy the jobs, they needed to pay back as much as they possibly could. Even if they had decided to reject the new terms, it wasn't clear how they would get the men home without incurring more debt. They had no choice.

They spoke again the next day at the preordained time,

relayed their decision, and said their good-byes. The families never heard from their sons and brothers again.

I asked the families if they knew from where in Amman the young men had telephoned them, and whether the young men had provided any way to get in touch. The brother of one of the three pulled a billfold from his back pocket and carefully plucked out a small folded piece of paper that had been stashed there for nine months. It contained three handwritten phone numbers, which he had taken down the day the young men phoned home. He had asked his brother for the numbers, in case the line went dead, as frequently happened during calls to Nepal, but he had never had cause to use them. Each number began with a Jordanian country code and an Amman exchange. Two were clearly for the same business, as they were just one digit off from each other. We made a copy of the piece of paper and then handed it back.

Five days after burning an effigy of Prakash Adhikari, his family received a letter. A computerized stamp on the envelope's face read August 1, 2004. The letter had taken forty-four days to reach their village along the eastern edge of Nepal, not far from the border with Darjeeling, India. The same stamp indicated that it passed through a postal facility called "Amman City Center." And the envelope's handwritten characters were all from the English alphabet, drawn in block letters. Many had been written over or crossed out and written again by the sender's unsure hand. Across the left side were the words FROM PRAKASH ADHIKARI, JORDAN.

In the letter, Prakash asked after everyone in the family and sent them his best wishes. His father suffered from diabetes, and he urged the family not to work too hard during the sowing season. In his absence, they should hire a farmhand to help make sure their father didn't suffer, he suggested. Prakash then assured them that he was well. But, in hindsight, something clearly had been amiss. He mentioned that he had attempted to call the local *dalal* in the village from whom the family had bought the job, but said that the agent had not responded. Prakash did not explain his need to reach the *dalal*, but he did write, in a matter-of-fact way, that soon he would head into Iraq after being "in Jordan for a month without work." He also wrote, "I have realized that life is like a flowing stream. Until yesterday, I was in Nepal. Now I am in a foreign land. Why? Who knows? Maybe it's the times, or the situation, or maybe I had no choice."

When rioters tore Nepal apart following the executions, the first building they ransacked held the offices of Moon Light Consultant. The businessman behind the agency was named Prahlad Giri. Had Giri still been around, it is likely the mob would have dragged him into the street and killed him, but by the time his office and his nation were ablaze, he had disappeared. Government paperwork listed Giri as the agency's general manager and part owner, although the true ownership of the brokerage houses in Nepal often was obscured. It seemed imperative to find and speak to Giri. What did he know? What had he told the men, and the *dalals* he did business with, about the jobs, and about where the men were ultimately headed? Many Nepalis assumed Giri remained in hiding abroad, most likely in India, and the government had yanked the operating license for Moon Light.

Through contacts we'd developed among other brokers in the capital, we discovered Giri hiding in plain sight, operating another overseas recruitment agency on the edge of town, under someone else's name. He worked from a single-room office built as an addition atop the flat roof of a three-story building in a strip mall just off the main road ringing the city. The agency was called Sea Link Overseas. We found Nepalese men lingering outside Sea Link's main lobby area, hoping for one of the jobs in Qatar, Saudi Arabia, or the United Arab Emirates trumpeted in "Urgent Demand" notices hanging from a bulletin board on the veranda.

Giri was born into Nepal's Brahmin, or upper, caste, which gave him a whiff of social and ethnic superiority that he could easily use to exploit people from lower classes. In a country where the men in many major ethnic groups stand little more than five and a half feet tall, Giri towered at six feet. He spoke near-perfect English, excepting his use of malapropisms of the ilk so often found in the brochures of overseas labor agents. Like Eyad Mansour, when I entered he was sitting in his office behind a high desk with the curtains drawn, the hot air swirling through the blades of an oscillating fan on a pedestal in the corner.

Giri insisted he had no idea the twelve men had been bound for Iraq, even though Eyad Mansour had said that he and Giri were working together to send Nepalese men into Iraq via Jordan—and via false paperwork that Giri had knowingly filed with the Nepalese government. Giri instead blamed Mansour, who he claimed had deceived him. "I am just the one guy who was unlucky, who faced the problem," Giri said. In conversation, Giri often poked the air with his slender fingers, or touched the tips of all ten fingers together and propped his hands below his sharp chin, like a man who believed deeply in the profundity of his own words.

Giri said that he didn't mention anything about Iraq to the *dalals* who brought him applicants or to the applicants themselves, but, he said, he did warn prospective workers that Eyad Mansour's Morning Star "is a multinational company, and it might send you somewhere else." In reality, Mansour operated from an office smaller than Giri's, and earned his commissions by doing little more than arranging for foreign workers to be picked up at the airport in Amman. He scarcely had the makings of a multinational tycoon. Yet, as hard as it was to believe that Giri did not know he was sending men into Iraq via Jordan, he would clearly never admit to it, at least not to me.

It also became increasingly clear that the murders of the men he had sent into the Middle East exposed far deeper problems with workers being tricked into buying jobs in neighboring countries, only to be forced into Iraq to work for the U.S. government. After finding Giri in Kathmandu, I met Indra Tamang, a twenty-four-year-old Nepalese farmer. He had been in a compound in Kuwait with about fifty other Nepalese men when the execution of their twelve countrymen appeared on Al Jazeera. The company that operated the compound was called First Kuwaiti, and like the Jordanian company Daoud and Partners, it worked as a major subcontractor in Iraq to KBR, the Halliburton subsidiary.

Tamang said that many of the men in the compound did not know that their ultimate destination would be Iraq until after they had paid for their jobs in Nepal and arrived in Kuwait. When news of the executions spread, panic swept the compound, and many of the men demanded they be returned home. Initially, Kuwaiti supervisors watching over them, and holding all their passports, were not sympathetic. "They told us that we could not return to Nepal; we had to go to Iraq," Tamang said. "We could not go back because we did not have a plane ticket and passport, or any money."

Still, some of the men who were there were able to phone home, providing details about their plight to their families and urging them to contact the Nepalese government, said Lok Bahadur Thapa, the then-acting Nepalese ambassador to Saudi Arabia. He got urgent orders to fly to Kuwait, where he said he discovered a crisis situation inside the compound.

Following the broadcast of the executions, First Kuwaiti supervisors had gathered the workers together and issued an ultimatum: Agree to go to Iraq, and you will get more food and water. Refuse, and you will get nothing and be cut loose onto the streets of Kuwait City to fend for yourself and find your own way home, and perhaps face arrest. "The company was forcing them to go to Iraq," the diplomat said. A First Kuwaiti executive, Wadih al-Absi, later acknowledged that Thapa had helped Nepalis at the firm's compound return to their homeland in the wake of the executions, but denied that anyone from his company had tried to force or coerce workers into Iraq.

Thapa said he discovered men similarly deceived and coerced at Kuwaiti compounds run by other contractors working for the United States.

The international market in cheap human labor, already rife with human rights abuses, had taken a far more sinister turn when the United States tapped it to prosecute the war in Iraq. Deception, fraud, and coercion were widespread with regard to sending men to work in a war zone through U.S. subcontractors based in the very same countries on the top tier of Washington's human trafficking list. The nature of the system meant that responsibility was diffuse. There was no single villain pulling every string from the top; instead, there were several individual actors making up an overall chain of conduct. It was an inherently transnational enterprise, making use of both a supply chain extending across multiple countries and an extensive transnational network to succeed. And it was run through a thick web of recruiters, contractors, subcontractors, parent corporations, and subsidiaries crossing jurisdictions, countries, and continents. Each participant undertook individual actions (such as recruitment, collecting exorbitant fees from the workers' families, transportation, detention, and employment), all of which had to come together for the system to work. While some of these actions in isolation may not constitute human rights abuse, when taken together they amounted to something abhorrent.

The full translation of the Nepalese commission report contained a transcript of statements made by ten of the twelve men and recorded by the terrorists just days before their deaths, and this helped flesh out details of the critical forty-five to fifty days between when they left Kathmandu and when they were kidnapped in Iraq.

Each man stood before the terrorists' black banner, one by one. Each faced the camera head-on. Each looked terrified as he gave a clearly unprepared statement in Nepalese, which the captors could not have understood. Each said he had been forcibly held in Jordan and then forcibly sent into Iraq. Each man knew these were likely to be his final words, and several indicated so.

Budhan Kumar Shah, one of the three best friends from the town in Nepal's lowlands, the men who desperately called home after realizing they had been deceived, lashed out at the agents behind the trio's journey. He also said, "I was held in Jordan for one and a half months. While being held in Jordan, I was repeatedly asked to go to Iraq, and ultimately, I was forcibly sent here, and now I have been handed over to [the terrorists]." He closed with the following: "I do not know when I will die, today or tomorrow."

One of his companions from the same town, Manoj Kumar Thakur, also lashed out at the brokers, and identified one of the Jordanian middlemen involved. He said the man's first name was "Amin," but his effort to render an Arabic surname was incomprehensible.

The farmer who would have his throat slit in the gruesome execution video said that he, too, had been kept in Amman against his will and suggested that he had been in contact with Giri, the manager of Moon Light in Nepal. "After keeping me there for one and a half months, he did not let me return to Nepal when I tried to do so. Instead, he evaded the issue and sent me to Iraq. While being sent to Iraq, we have been captured along the way and are being killed this very day."

Jeet Bahadur Thapa Magar, who came from the hills of Gorkha, spoke sixth. "We arrived in Jordan through Moon Light, and stayed there for one and a half months," he said. "Thereafter, we were sent to Iraq. From the day before yesterday until today, the terrorists have captured us—and now . . . now we . . ." Jeet stammered and stopped speaking, then lowered his head, unable to continue.

The final captive's statement on the tape came from Ramesh Khadka, just nineteen. He uttered a single, broken sentence, as

sorrow and fear overtook him, yet his incomplete words somehow made perfect sense many months later, as the truth about
what had happened began to emerge. "Through the agency . . .
trapped by Moon Light . . . in Jordan, Jordan . . ."

• • •

After journeying across Nepal for weeks, we had located and
met with nearly all twelve families, but there was another person I wanted to find: the widow of Jeet Bahadur Thapa Magar.
She was just eighteen when her husband had been executed,
and she had a young child. We had learned from relatives that
she had recently moved from Gorkha and into a home for
destitute widows and their children on the outskirts of Kathmandu, but no one from the family we dealt with seemed to
know where, which seemed odd. Soon I learned enough about
the treatment of widows in Nepalese and Hindu cultures to
understand perhaps why they didn't know where to find her—
because they didn't care. Historically in Nepal and India, some
ashrams for widows were little more than warehouses or dump-
ing grounds, where women could be abused, including being
forced into prostitution.

With a bit of effort, we identified and found the place, which
consisted of a small assemblage of redbrick buildings, some
dating to the property's original development in 1926, off a
dirt-and-gravel road on the backside of Kathmandu's Tribhuvan International Airport. It stood behind a high wall, the
drive blocked by an iron gate. The ashram's director said that
Jeet's widow had been there only a short time. Her name was
Kamala Thapa Magar.

Dressed in the blue sari that served as a uniform for the ashram's women, she met us at a stone-and-wooden gazebo on the

grounds. Giant black crows, which Nepalis believe carry the souls of the dead, cawed in the thick trees above. Kamala had just turned nineteen years old but looked so much younger, and she carried her daughter, not yet three, in her arms and on her hip, clinging to the child as the gazebo shielded us from the summer sun. The young widow could barely utter her own name. She responded to questions with a grief-stricken silence, which seemed to last an eternity, staring down at the ground or folding and unfolding the end of her blue sari with her small hands, occasionally lifting its edge to wipe a tear or to cover her mouth as she cried. In other moments, she held her daughter tightly to her chest, almost hiding behind the child. We had no idea how the young woman, in many ways still just a girl herself, had arrived in this place or at this moment, because she could not tell us; nor could anyone else in the ashram. She seemed to be alone there.

Not long before I arrived in Nepal, Kamala had sat by herself in a sea of folding chairs, staring up at an empty stage in a silent Kathmandu auditorium. A charity was holding a benefit for family members of the twelve dead men, and Kamala had arrived hours too early. Trips to the capital gave her respite from her increasingly dolorous existence on the horseshoe ridge, but deep anxiety and worry remained her constant companions, no matter how far from home she traveled.

Her late husband's family had received a small amount of charity from the Nepalese government in the wake of the riots, to be divided between Jeet's mother and Kamala. Kamala had hoped her share might provide a chance to move away from the farmhouse and start afresh, but the government wired the entire sum to Jeet's mother, effectively giving her control because widows in Nepal had no inheritance rights. The old woman locked the funds in a bank account that Kamala could not access without her mother-in-law's signature, and claimed she did this to protect the future of Jeet's only child, Kritika.

Seated alone in the auditorium, Kamala knew she could never return to anything resembling her status in the village on the ledge before Jeet's death. She now realized she also could not move out on her own and provide for herself and her daughter. She would remain dependent upon whatever Jeet's family chose for her, and whatever it chose to give her. Thoughts of being caught in an existence she could no longer bear and yet being powerless to escape it filled Kamala's mind as she stared at the stage, waiting for the charity benefit to start.

A keynote speaker for the event, the chief executive of Nepal's oldest social service group, arrived not long after Kamala. The woman's name was Bhadra Ghale. Though nearly five decades older than Kamala, Ghale was as sturdy as a fist, with soft brown eyes and a broad, welcoming smile. Ghale noticed Kamala sitting alone, and she must have seen a look on Kamala's face that she had seen cross those of hundreds, if not thousands, of other widows in Nepal, a look that told her Kamala must have been the wife of one of the men killed in Iraq. Ghale sat down beside Kamala and introduced herself, and seemingly from nowhere, she told Kamala, "I can help you find a future. I know a place. I can help." A woman Kamala had never met had identified her needs in an instant: a future, a place, help. For the first time in so long, Kamala's anxious mind relaxed, at least for a moment. No one she knew growing up in the horseshoe had possessed such an incongruous combination of strength and gentleness. Ghale wrote down her phone number,

handed it to Kamala, and told her to come over to her house
for dinner before leaving town.

Ghale ran a small society established by Tulsi Meher, a Nepalese
lifetime disciple of Mohandas K. Gandhi who had studied at
Gandhi's side during an exile in India. Both men had been
unpopular in their homelands for promoting human rights and
equality, and for speaking out against the shameful treatment
of women. In the 1970s, the disciple won a small fortune from
a humanitarian prize and used it to open a campus behind
Kathmandu's Tribhuvan International Airport. Ghale turned it
into an ashram that served as a home for destitute women and
their children. She knew the hopelessness and discrimination
single mothers in Nepal faced, and she believed that teaching
them skills that would help them secure a living could break
the cycle. She guaranteed a good education for their children,
who lived in dormitories with their mothers.

At dinner a couple of days after the benefit, Ghale tried to
convince Kamala to move into the ashram, to move away from
her pain, and build a new life for herself and her daughter with
women who shared her experiences. The first commandment
of the ashram, Ghale said, was this: although the caste system might rule the larger society, it had no quarter within the
ashram, where every woman was equal to every other woman.
Excepting a head cook, the women divided all the chores of
daily living among themselves, and then rotated with the turn
of each month. The lowest-caste and highest-caste women
could sweep floors together, or chop vegetables, or tend to animals and crops side by side, a proposition that would be unimaginable, subversive, or even heretical to many in the world

beyond the ashram's walls, where those from families at the bottom of the ethnic ladder are born to serve those at the top.

Women stayed in the ashram for two years. They practiced yoga when they rose before dawn each day, and then devoted themselves to the ashram's workshops. By the time she graduated, each woman knew how to spin yarn, weave cloth on a loom, and tailor clothing on a treadle sewing machine. Also, illiterate women learned to read and write. A widow paid for nothing, and all her material needs were met. Ghale knew that the women she recruited needed little persuading. "The women are taught to love themselves and each other," she said. Sharing a bond was the most powerful draw. The youngest widows feel this pull more than the older women, Ghale said, because of how painful their lives are inside the homes of their dead husbands' families.

After her dinner in Ghale's home, Kamala returned to the horseshoe and to her daily duties in the fields with Heera, the other young widow from her village. She told Heera with excitement about the possibilities offered by Ghale's ashram. Day after day, she tried to convince Heera to apply for one of its spots—before realizing that she had actually been trying to convince herself.

Once Kamala told Jeet's family that she wanted to move to Kathmandu and join the ashram, word began to spread in the village. Jeet's family encouraged her to go but said she should leave her daughter with them. "Everyone in the village told me I should keep Kritika, as she was all that I had left now of Jeet, and that I should send Kamala alone," Jeet's mother recalled. Kamala was pained by her in-laws' response. She had expected at least a show of resistance from Jeet's family, even a feigned plea for her to stay, but she never expected they would want her gone and her daughter left behind. *They want to take everything from me, everything I have left*, she thought.* Of course, there was no way she would abandon Kritika.

Kamala moved forward with the application process, convincing Heera to apply with her. Both women were accepted, and early one morning, Kamala hoisted a bag of clothes over her shoulder, bundled her daughter in her arms, and headed down the same path Jeet had taken the day he left for Jordan, beside and below the vegetable path and through the sweet smoke of kitchen fires rising from the valley. She felt the sadness of a good-bye, but none of the hopelessness she had felt inside the family home, her isolation deepening by the day in the wake of Jeet's murder. There was trepidation in not knowing what lay ahead, but Kamala felt lifted by a sense of relief as she and Heera, who had joined her along the path, descended the trail into the horseshoe valley.

After their bus arrived in Kathmandu and they made their way to the ashram, Kamala and Kritika were assigned to a room with other mothers and children on the ground floor of a redbrick dormitory off the main courtyard, where a murder of crows bowed the branches of the tall trees. The room had high ceilings and long windows, and their bare feet were cold on the plaster floor. Eight beds were arranged against the room's outer walls. For most of her first nights in the ashram, Kamala held Kritika and lay awake. With each step or shift in weight of a woman above, the ancient boards in the ceiling creaked like the towering bamboo of the horseshoe ridge. Women in

---

* Jeet's mother told me she was desperate to keep Kritika by her side and was heartbroken at the idea of her absence, but said she never asked Kamala to leave the child behind. "The pain of separation from your child always kills you, and I didn't have the strength to do the same to Kamala," she said.

Kamala's room seemed to take turns weeping throughout the night, perhaps after waking suddenly from a dream of their lost life or from a nightmare about wicked in-laws, or perhaps overwhelmed by thoughts they could not outrun. Kamala was grateful she had found a refuge for herself and her daughter, but the desolation she heard in the nightly cries made her realize how far away from family and home she was for the first time in her life. She was as alone in the world as everyone surrounding her.

6

JULY 2005

Amman

Critical details about the time the twelve Nepalese men spent in Jordan, and definitive proof about for whom they were working, remained out of reach but seemed so much closer than they had only weeks before, and Jordan was the only place those details, that proof, could possibly be found. If anyone could help provide clues that led to filling in the missing forty-five days, it would be the man who was my investigation's erstwhile ally and obstructionist, Eyad Mansour. I flew back to Jordan.

Aside from figuring out where the twelve Nepalis were kept and who was involved, I also needed Mansour to flesh out the details of how they were delivered to their deaths, which could reveal as much about the nature of the human supply chain as any other link. I returned to his office and Mansour told me that the twelve were seized by the terrorists from two cars as they were being taken into Iraq in a larger convoy ferrying almost eighty men to the Al Asad Air Base for Daoud and KBR Halliburton's operations there. The convoy required at least ten vehicles, but as Bisharat's al-Nadi tried to organize it in August 2004, driver after driver across Amman refused the job.

It required a four-hundred-fifty-mile drive down the Amman-to-Baghdad highway, which, despite being as wide and smooth and well paved as any American interstate, had become perhaps the deadliest stretch of tarmac on earth. The vast majority of the journey cut straight through the heart of the desert badlands of Iraq's Anbar Province, the center of the growing insurgency against the U.S. occupation. At a cloverleaf interchange just west of the Euphrates River, the convoy would have to turn north and head up a road running parallel with the river for the last fifty miles, until reaching the American-occupied base near Haditha.

Bandits plagued the Amman-to-Baghdad highway almost from the first day the border crossing opened between Jordan and Iraq following the invasion. Scouts on motorcycles buzzed up beside vehicles, seemingly from nowhere, craned their necks, and peered through windshields and windows. They'd then signal to AK-47-wielding accomplices following close behind in pickup trucks or even taxicabs. These would brandish or fire their weapons to force drivers or terrified aid workers, journalists, and others to veer off the road and hand over cash, satellite phones, computers, cameras—and whatever other treasures were stowed on board to facilitate long stints on duty inside a nation cut off from ordinary supply lines, a nation at war. Some Westerners had taken to calling the road the "Mad Max Highway" or the "Highway Through Hell." Before long, it was mostly supplies being ferried on the road, not people.

Even though human cargo from Amman became more limited, as personnel flew on up to sixty commercial flights per day at the newly opened Baghdad International Airport, the passage for goods being delivered by road from Jordan grew far more dangerous as the insurgency blossomed in 2004. By the end of that summer, three hundred trucks were hijacked, robbed, or destroyed, and about forty Jordanian drivers were killed, according to the estimates of a Jordanian transportation group. Mohammad Tayla was among those spared after armed men pulled him out of the cab of his truck. "They tied me up, and I saw them putting gasoline on my truck, and they burned it. They said, 'If you open your mouth, we'll kill you,'" he said. The four Blackwater men who were murdered in March 2004 had been guarding a delivery of kitchen equipment rolling down the Highway Through Hell.

By June 2004, the danger had so intensified that the Iraqi government publicly announced plans to provide armed escorts accompanying deliveries from the Jordanian border all the way to Baghdad. In the end, the promise appeared to be little more than public relations. The government had been forced by all of the bad publicity to speak, but it didn't seem able or willing to act. U.S. Armed Forces accompanied some vehicles "working in support of the coalition," with a military spokesman telling the Associated Press that summer, "We take the protection of our contracted civilians very seriously. They are essential partners." Clearly, though, the lives of some contracted civilians were more essential than others'.

The month before Bisharat's al-Nadi tried to organize his convoy for the Nepalis to Al Asad, two Bulgarian drivers were kidnapped. One was beheaded; the other was never heard from nor seen again. Insurgents released a kidnapped driver from the Philippines only after his government agreed to withdraw the few dozen troops it had stationed in Iraq, a decision deeply embarrassing for the United States.

By the summer of 2004, because the dangers were so abundant and clear, American civilian personnel were flown, not driven, into the country, and the American government warned that travel by road should be undertaken only if absolutely necessary, and only then with proper security.

On July 26, 2004, a little more than three weeks ahead of al-Nadi's attempt to assemble a convoy, the threat came directly to the door of KBR Halliburton contractor Daoud and Partners. Insurgents kidnapped two of its drivers and demanded that the company cease working in Iraq. Otherwise, the men would be murdered. Daoud issued a statement declaring it would withdraw all its personnel from Iraq and no longer work for the U.S. military. Daoud's statement achieved its goal, but it was a lie. Insurgents released the drivers; Daoud did not pull out of Iraq. It was a dangerous game, one that significantly raised the stakes for any and all future Daoud personnel delivered into Iraq on the Highway Through Hell, by choice or by coercion.

Little wonder al-Nadi had such a hard time finding the phalanx of drivers necessary to bring the Nepalis to the American air base. Not only was it one of the most dangerous drives in the world, but it was a particularly risky undertaking for anyone associated with Daoud. Still, flying the men to Baghdad was out of the question for KBR because it was considered too expensive. It's also clear that security for the convoy was never provided, according to both Eyad Mansour and Prakash Mahat, who was then Nepal's foreign minister.

What happened next marked perhaps the signal moment in which the lexicon used by the men who ran the industry—referring to people as "imports" or "goods" or basic commodities—translated in a very literal way into how they treated the human beings they traded in. Essentially, the twelve men and the others with them were to be transported down the Amman-to-Baghdad highway in gypsy taxicabs screaming out of Amman, driven by whatever drivers remained who were willing to make the run without armed escorts, without a single professional consultant or security guard of any kind, and without even armor plating. According to Mansour, the drivers who were on the job also violated the most basic rule for convoys in dangerous places: stick together. The two lead cars carrying the twelve Nepalis ended up separated from the rest.

About forty miles south of the air base, just after the turnoff from the Highway Through Hell, men wielding weapons and wearing the uniforms of Iraqi security forces stopped the two cars at some sort of flying checkpoint. Leave the workers at the checkpoint, the armed men told the drivers, and the Americans will come from the base to collect them. Foolishly, the drivers complied, apparently communicating with no one, either at the base or back in Amman.

Word went out to Daoud and KBR executives hours later from the base: the convoy of workers had arrived, but it was twelve men light. Security men operating the checkpoint were, it appeared, working with the insurgents, or were even in their ranks. Within ten days, the bill of a security forces ball cap pulled low would hide the face of the man who sliced the Nepalese farmer's throat before the camera.

Not only were the jobs in Jordan fraudulent, but the sons and husbands of the families I had met were sent across another international border and into a third country, a nation that was host to the world's deadliest war zone. Bundled into an unprotected convoy, without any security precautions, they were driven into Iraq against all public warnings issued by the U.S. government and against all common sense—even though they were apparently headed there to serve the U.S. government. It is difficult to imagine a greater disregard for their lives.

After having made it clear that he had "possessed" the twelve "goods" from Nepal before passing them on to Daoud and its body shop supplier, Eyad Mansour changed his story one last time, or rather, he added a new twist. He claimed he actually never had full custody of the twelve, because a disloyal former employee had intercepted these specific men at the airport in Amman. The former employee's name was Amin Mansour, Eyad Mansour told me. (Amin and Eyad are not related but shared the same, common surname.) He said Amin had gone into business with al-Nadi, becoming one of al-Nadi's partners. "I don't blame Amin," Eyad said. "He's ambitious and wanted to build something for himself."

I gave Eyad Mansour physical descriptions of the two men al-Nadi had introduced to me as his partners, in the lobby of the Grand Hyatt. Without hesitation, he identified Amin as "Abdullah," the short one with the thick handlebar mustache who had tried to keep al-Nadi from handing over the DVD. As his true name emerged, a previously inexplicable tidbit seemed to make sense: One of the twelve Nepalis had used his final statement before the black banner to name the Jordanian broker involved in their ordeal. Although the surname came out jumbled, he clearly uttered the forename into the terrorists' camera: "Amin."

As I concluded our interview, Eyad Mansour noted that I had asked, the first time we met, whether he possessed documents related to the twelve murdered men. "I just found this," he said, handing a folder across his desk. It held photocopies of the men's passports, including copies of Jordanian entry stamps. How had he come by these after having just denied even possessing the men who bore the passports? It didn't matter. I was happy to have the copies just the same.

Each of the twelve dead men stared back from his own passport page against a background as black as the terrorist banner each had posed before when speaking his final words. In the photo, each looked straight ahead, trying assiduously to suppress a smile, although a couple of the youngest, the ones who were just boys, let one through, including Bishnu Hari Thapa, who was seventeen the day someone set him on a stool to take this picture. He wore a traditional Nepalese cap, called a topi, which is not too dissimilar in style from a garrison cap like the one a Boy Scout would wear.

Prakash Adhikari wore a tie for his portrait, taken less than a month before he left home. How many other times in his life had he put on a tie? His face unsmiling, Jeet Bahadur Thapa Magar, whose widow now lived in the home for destitute women, wore a dark T-shirt emblazoned with 100% PURE WHOOP-ASS, a phrase popularized by the American professional wrestler "Stone Cold" Steve Austin. Jeet was cheeky enough that he might have had some knowledge of what this meant, but millions of T-shirts like this, along with other clothing items that Americans leave in charity bins in cities across the United States, routinely make their way through the global aftermarket to Nepal and other poor countries, where they are worn without irony.

The lack of opportunity in Nepal that had sent each man to his labor broker had been etched onto a blank line in his passport below "Profession": farmer, helper, laborer. Each was inscribed by his hand or perhaps that of the broker who had helped him get the passport after promising that life in an exotic land would yield a reward so great there wasn't even a familiar word in his language for the sum of cash he would earn over two or three years. Each passport also had been stamped in Jordan with the same urgent command, eight words in block letters: CONTACT THE NEAREST POLICE STATION WITHIN TWO WEEKS. A similar warning appeared on signs near the airport's immigration queues: FOREIGNERS REMAINING IN JORDAN FOR MORE THAN TWO WEEKS MUST REGISTER AT THE NEAREST PO-LICE STATION.

Nader Rabadi, my Jordanian interpreter and assistant, led me through a maze of cold, spare corridors inside the gray office blocks of downtown Amman's Abdali neighborhood. We trawled government offices in search of the right department and the right official within the right department with whom to plead our case. We were after three different sets of records for each man: the record of his passport being scanned by border guards at Queen Alia International Airport upon entry into the country; a similar record when he exited the country at the road crossing into Iraq; and finally, and most important, a police registration shedding light on where he stayed during the nearly fifty days between those two points.

The soft resistance of Middle East bureaucracy is not dissimilar to the resistance of bureaucracies everywhere. It most often revealed itself in blank expressions across the faces of those who professed to have no idea how such a record could have been generated, no idea about who would be able to do it, and no idea about who could even authorize the granting of such a request from a foreign journalist. No one seemed inclined to pick up the phone to try to find out. Each exchange ended courteously enough. Everyone we saw simply sent us to someone else. In this way, everyone appeared to be helpful without actually helping or conveying any information that could come back to haunt him. When we weren't bouncing down government hallways, Nader worked the phones in search of an answer. It seemed hopeless.

As the second straight day of bouncing began drawing to a close, Nader believed we had finally found the right office within a division of Jordan's Ministry of Interior. Clocks in every government building marched in unison toward quitting time, and each corridor would empty as quickly as a sink after the drain plug is pulled. Despite the hour, we managed to get an audience with a senior-looking official. He wore the light-blue shirt and thick mustache of a security agency employee, with flat epaulets carrying officer's markings on his shoulders, and a beret. As I pleaded my case for the records, and Nader interpreted, the officer stared straight at me with the poker face of a skeptical cop, revealing absolutely nothing while also reading every line in my face and each movement of my eyes. Finally, I pulled out my passport and flipped to the page with my visa from Nepal. I told him that each of the twelve Nepalese men had left his home to come to Jordan, and yet all twelve were brutally executed in Iraq before the eyes of the world, including those of their families. I told him that I had traveled across Nepal to find those families, and then I handed him my passport, open to the Nepal visa page, as proof. "They just want to know what happened to their husbands, sons, and brothers," I pleaded, Nader echoing my words in Arabic.

The officer took the passport and examined the page. He then stared again squarely and silently into my face for what seemed an eternity. Suddenly, he jumped to his feet, a wide smile breaking below his thick mustache. "I think you speak more Arabic than you're letting on!" he said, laughing and wagging his index finger at me, which I took to mean that he liked me. He handed back my passport and agreed to help. We typed a formal request on *Chicago Tribune* stationery, handcrafted from a photocopy of my business card in the top corner of a blank sheet of paper, and attached a list of all twelve names and their passport numbers and copies of my press credentials from Washington. We faxed it to the number the official provided, and then waited.

One potentially significant lead remained: the photocopy of the scrap of paper that had been produced by the brother of one of the three victims who had come from the same town in Eastern Nepal's lowlands. It contained three handwritten phone numbers, all landlines that rang in Amman. The first two numbers differed by just one digit and clearly rang at the same business, a small storefront shop at the edge of a gritty working-class Amman neighborhood. The shop, called Horizons East for Computers and Communications, offered international calls and Internet service. The shop had a couple of plywood phone booths, and each one, tall and narrow, covered in a thin oak veneer, held barely enough space for a flaccid plastic garden chair and a corner shelf for the telephone. One could imagine the three young men from Eastern Nepal packed against one another in a single booth like rush-hour commuters on a New York subway car, calling home to say they feared going into Iraq.

The store's owner did not recognize pictures of the three men, but said that hundreds of foreign workers came into his shop. His business relied on them. Someone kept foreign workers housed in the residential neighborhood just up the street, he said, but he was unsure exactly where.

We followed the street around a bend and into the nearby neighborhood, landing on Malfuf Street, which was carved into the side of a winding hill. The low side of the street had dirty concrete privacy walls cutting parallel to the edge of the sidewalk for each property. There were small gates in the walls. Behind each, a staircase descended to a concrete block home built into the hillside below.

The street was quiet—it was residential, and these were working hours—but we showed pictures of the three best friends to almost everyone we saw. No one recognized them, but like the phone shop owner, all were aware of droves of foreign workers living somewhere on the street. Two independently directed us to the same house, at No. 58 Malfuf Street. It was on the low side of the hill, behind one of the dirty concrete walls, meaning the house could not be seen from the road. We left without trying to get past the gate and down the stairs, deciding we would knock on the door once we knew more, or if we ran out of other leads.

One unchecked Amman phone number remained on the photocopy of the slip of paper from Nepal. Nader soon discovered it belonged to none other than Amin Mansour, the chain-smoking business partner of Ali al-Nadi who had been introduced as "Abdullah" during our meeting at the Grand Hyatt—the same man who Eyad Mansour had claimed took the Nepalese workers from the airport after they landed.

The phone's registered address, and Amin Mansour's home, was at No. 58 Malfuf Street.

After a few days we received a three-page report from the Jordanian government detailing official records on the twelve men inside the country. It showed the twelve had arrived in three different groups. The three best friends who had phoned home from the Horizons East booth landed together on June 30, 2004, and five more arrived on July 4, including Jeet; Bishnu Hari, the young man who had phoned the restaurant in Kathmandu to say, "I am done for"; and Prakash Adhikari, whose parents received a letter from him after they had burned an effigy of his lost body. The last four men came two days later, on July 6.

There was no way to know how many other Nepali workers had arrived within each group, but Eyad Mansour's estimation that these twelve had been among scores arriving from Nepal at the time made it likely there were many more traveling with them on the same planes.

The next column in the report documented each man's exit from the country, specifying which border crossing. It confirmed that a border guard scanned all twelve passports on August 19, 2004, at the Karameh Border checkpoint when the convoy crossed into Iraq on the Amman-to-Baghdad highway.

The final column detailed each man's police registration for his residence inside the country during the weeks between the border passport scans.

The four who had arrived in the last group, on July 6, were registered at different locations. Perhaps that was because, as Eyad Mansour had claimed, so many workers had been coming into the country that the body shop operators were running out of space for them.

The remainder—all eight of the men who had landed in the first two groups, including Jeet, Prakash Adhikari, and the three best friends who had phoned home—were kept together in the same residence. The police records registered all the men as residents of No. 58 Malfuf Street.

The phone number registered for them, also required by the

authorities, was identical to the one on the scrap of paper: the landline of Amin Mansour.

Le Royal, the hotel where the men were supposed to have guaranteed jobs, towers above the neighborhood in central Amman that is home to the Zahran Police Station, where the men were taken for their registrations. In fact, it is on the same street.

We phoned Ali al-Nadi to arrange one last meeting. Trying to get past his dissembling felt like a useless exercise. The only thing we needed now, from him and his partners with the fabricated names, was their picture. We felt strongly that photos of them should be published, and accordingly, we scheduled our afternoon meeting in an outdoor bar, so José Moré, a veteran *Chicago Tribune* photographer, could shoot them from a public place and at a discreet distance. We scoped out the bar in advance, to plan where everyone should sit.

Al-Nadi and Amin Mansour arrived on time and arranged themselves around the table as planned. They ordered lager; they smoked. Al-Nadi volunteered almost immediately that he had, in fact, checked his records to see if the twelve men had ever worked for him, as he had promised to do the first time we met, because, as he had mused then, "If they were my workers, maybe I should be compensated for losing them."

This time, al-Nadi said yes, the men had at some unknown point been on his books, but he didn't really have any idea what had become of them. More dissembling.

For tactical reasons, we played dumb, because much more was at stake than just a vain quest for answers to fill holes in an article. U.S. law required contractors and subcontractors to pay lifetime compensation to survivors of anyone killed working for them, or on their way to work for them, in a war zone.

Compensation came from a government-regulated fund, and not only were the families entitled to the compensation, but contractors and subcontractors could be prosecuted for a federal crime if they failed to follow this law. None of the victims' families in Nepal knew the law existed, because no one had ever contacted them about filing claims.

So, the dissembling and denials from al-Nadi and his partners, not to mention those from people farther up the chain, created a potentially consequential roadblock for the families of the men they had sent into Iraq in gypsy taxicabs at the end of a trail of fraud and deceit and coercion. It could conceivably frustrate attempts to win even a small measure of justice.

José Moré secured his cameras out of sight. He came to our table, signaling to me that he had what he needed. I introduced him as my colleague, and we said our good-byes.

Past the gate at No. 58 Malfuf Street, we walked down the steps leading to the two-story house built on a concrete slab in the side of the hill above the ravine. Its primary resident, Amin Mansour, aka "Abdullah," did not expect us. He didn't know that we knew his real name, let alone where he lived.

The bottom of the steps opened onto a small courtyard on the concrete slab. Amin's front door was at the back. No one was about. Empty clotheslines strung across the courtyard overhead dipped gently beneath the weight of plastic pins of pink, purple, and blue, and someone had shoved a dull, faded sofa without feet into a corner, exposing it to the elements. We moved silently as we scanned the large porch, gesturing at things we saw of potential importance.

To the left, an odd extension (a one-story, box-shaped addition) had been tacked on to the side of the home, with its own, separate exterior door, secured from the outside by a chain. A tower of ratty foam sleeping mats, piled higher than our heads, rose and teetered to the right of Amin's front door. We counted twenty-one in the pile, and José snapped a picture.

I rapped on Amin's door, and he answered. He gasped. Then he smiled uncomfortably and invited us into a small reception room just beyond the threshold. It was eerie to be there, in the last place Jeet and the others had found themselves before being driven to their deaths. I sat next to Amin on the sofa. No one said a word; the room was tense. In the corner sat a giant sack of rice, like the kind used to feed an army. José Moré fired his camera, and the pop of the shutter, rapidly opening and closing to let in a burst of light, broke the silence. "No pictures!" Amin shouted. "You are forbidden from taking pictures in my house!" Quiet immediately fell over the room once again.

I turned to Amin and handed him the three-page report we had received from the Jordanian government detailing official records on the twelve men. Their residence from the time they entered the country until they left, the very home where we were sitting, had been highlighted for Amin's convenience, along with his phone number.

He placed the three-page report across his lap. He flipped the pages, one by one, silent and transfixed, his eyes at first wide and then appearing to narrow and fill with fear. Nader discreetly phoned Amin's landline from a cell phone and handed the cell phone to me.

Suddenly the landline rang loudly in the silent room, startling Amin, whose head popped up from the records in his lap. I turned to him on the couch, holding the cell phone in front of his face with one hand and pointing to his number on the screen with the other. Then I pointed back down to the records before him. "You see, Amin, that's your phone number," I said. I let his phone ring another time or two before pressing the hang-up button on the cell phone in an exaggerated way, making certain he saw me do it. The ringing inside the home died as suddenly as it had begun.

Nader echoed my words in Arabic as I told Amin that we now knew that he and his partner had been lying to us all along. Either they had lied to us, I said, or they had lied to the Jordanian police.

Amin rapidly fired back in Arabic with more dissembling. I cut him off and told him he had a big problem reconciling the truth and the lies. "Why don't we go to the Zahran Police Station now and speak to them together," I said, "and we can sort out with the police whether you lied to them or to me?"

My hope was that once he was cornered, Amin could be convinced to come clean with at least some additional details. This clearly had been naive. Good cop, bad cop works only if someone else is in the room to play the good cop, and probably only if the person being questioned is a prisoner. Instead, Amin exploded, jumping to his feet and screaming a river of curses in Arabic. Nader tried to calm him, but it didn't work. It seemed foolish to bark back, and I told Nader and José that we should leave.

Quietly we walked out the door, up the stairs, and away from No. 58 Malfuf Street, with Amin probably still cursing behind us. Nader never told me all of what Amin had said, but when we reached the street, he cautioned, "I should have warned you. In Jordan, a man has a right to kill you if you are on his property without his permission."

It would take almost a decade until something emerged resembling the full truth about what Jeet and his compatriots experienced over their nearly fifty days in an overcrowded, locked, windowless room. But we walked away that day from No. 58 Malfuf Street with everything from Jordan that could be had, and much of what we needed to proceed.

7

1996–2005
Texas to Baghdad

Richard B. Cheney wanted to run for president in 1996, but garnered so little Republican support that he formally bowed out of the race more than a year before the first GOP primary. He needed twenty million dollars just to get into the conversation and had managed to raise only a million. Texas businessman Thomas H. Cruikshank was among the disappointed. "I was ready to support him to lead our country, but since he has chosen not to do that, we want him to come do the next best thing," Cruikshank said. Apparently the next best thing to being president of the United States was the job of Cruikshank, who served as chairman and chief executive of the Halliburton Company in Dallas, Texas. It was August 10, 1995, and Cruikshank was at a podium with the fifty-four-year-old Cheney by his side, about to retire after twenty-six years and hand over the reins of his company to the Republican politician.

Cheney had no experience running a business, having spent his entire career in politics and government. It was a leap for Halliburton, too. Playing politics, especially in the revolving-door fashion of Washington, was not part of its modus operandi. The outcome of this gamble would prove fateful for all sides.

By 2004, Halliburton had become a global household name, one synonymous with outrage over the Iraq War. Dick Cheney was now vice president, and the war's strongest advocate inside the Bush White House, and his former company was the war's largest private partner, owing to the fact that Halliburton earned more than any other contractor.

Damage to Halliburton endured beyond the war. Thirteen years after the invasion, and five years after the full withdrawal of U.S. forces, the company ranked second to last in a Harris Poll of American attitudes about the nation's one hundred most visible companies. Only Volkswagen ranked lower in 2016, after admitting it had rigged tailpipe emissions tests.

The outrage, however, has been somewhat misdirected. Behind Halliburton's Iraq controversies was not the company with the household name but, instead, a subsidiary called Kellogg Brown and Root, or KBR. Allegations of undue political influence, wartime profiteering, massive cost overruns, fraud, abuse, and waste rarely had been linked to Halliburton, but that wasn't true for KBR. Such allegations clung to the firm almost from its founding in the early twentieth century.

Herman Brown, the son of a grocer, got his start in the public works business in 1914, at the age of twenty-one. He ran a crew of roughnecks and broken-down cowboys who lived in tents erected in the Texas dirt. When his men weren't in county jails for their weekend high jinks, they were building public roads for Brown after he had arranged bail with local sheriffs. These weren't painted highways but, instead, primitive trails carved from tangles of brush, sometimes following paths already worn into the earth by cattle herds. Brown started with four mules and a single Fresno scraper, a plow pulled behind beasts. His old boss had given him the lot in lieu of back pay after going belly up. Road building was a tough business, and not just physically. It was notoriously corrupt, and Texas was largely broke. That meant funding for Brown's work relied on a shallow public trough. To stay afloat, he needed to invest his meager funds wisely, in the right Texas politicians.

Herman Brown wasn't terribly affable, but his younger brother, George, seemed well suited for political work. Someone inscribed George's high school yearbook with the words "gains his power through his ability to make friends." Dan Root, who was married to the Brown brothers' sister, loaned Herman twenty thousand dollars, and Herman named the business Brown and Root as a thank-you.* He made George a full partner.

Although contemporaries considered George more genial than Herman, the two were alike in their extremism. Robert Caro, who interviewed George Brown extensively for his multivolume biography of Lyndon B. Johnson, described the brothers as ultrareactionaries. They were racists, virulent antiunionists, and stridently antitax and antigovernment, even though their firm would rely on taxpayer-funded contracts. (Herman Brown also made a tidy sum squeezing impoverished African American residents of tenements he owned in the slums of Austin, Texas.)

The Brown brothers used their money and influence to build Lyndon Johnson's political career, despite the New Deal supporter's seeming to be their ideological antithesis. They had always seen Johnson as a practical investment, and considered him more of an opportunist than a true believer. As George Brown told Caro, "Basically, Lyndon was more conservative,

* It wasn't renamed Kellogg Brown and Root until 1998.

more practical than people understand. You get right down to the nut-cutting, he was practical. He was for the niggers, he was for labor, he was for the little boys, but by God . . . he was as practical as anyone."[*]

Brown and Root's lawyer and chief fixer orchestrated Johnson's first nomination to Congress, in 1937, and he did it so Johnson could orchestrate something vital for the company in return. The company needed someone to get authorization and funding through Washington for its first federal contract, construction of the Mansfield Dam,[†] on the lower Colorado River in Texas. The Browns had put their own money into equipment, but the project had stalled in a legal and bureaucratic morass. Strictly speaking, it also was a boondoggle. Johnson went to work as soon as he landed in Washington in March 1937, and his frenetic efforts on behalf of the dam culminated weeks later with a now legendary go-ahead for the ten-million-dollar project from President Franklin D. Roosevelt. "Give the kid the dam," Roosevelt reportedly told one of his aides. Given the fortune Brown and Root made from its construction, he more accurately could have said, "Give the Brown brothers the dam." Johnson immediately obliged the Brown brothers a second time, untangling a political and legal snarl to secure the extra seventeen million dollars they sought for an expansion of the same project. Their thanks were so great, and so widely known in Washington, that Roosevelt's aide and master fundraiser Tommy Corcoran later told Caro, "Lyndon Johnson's whole world was built on that dam."

---

[*] Apart from George Brown's deplorable sentiments, Caro himself would come to hold a view of Johnson not too terribly dissimilar to Brown's, telling an interviewer in 2012 that Johnson "really had compassion, he really wanted to help. But whenever ambition collided with compassion, it was the ambition that won."
[†] It was originally called the Marshall Ford Dam.

Johnson and the Brown brothers entwined their fortunes together for the next three decades. Their relationship grew into one
of the purest examples of the symbiosis between corporate money
and political power that Washington had ever seen, and certainly
one of its most intimate. Brown and Root reaped billions from
government contracts with Johnson's help while financing his rise
to national power, which culminated in the presidency.

Brown and Root gave and generated millions of dollars for
Johnson throughout his career—Johnson even flew in the company airplane to campaign stops—raising campaign cash from
the oil elite of Texas and squeezing contributions from its own
army of employees and subcontractors. And the cash wasn't
just for Johnson's own races. He channeled the Browns' largesse through the Democratic Congressional Campaign Committee to build power and influence across Congress and the
nation. Caro would conclude that the Brown brothers, through
their support for Johnson, had pushed the corporate corruption
of American politics to an unprecedented level.

If Johnson's mammoth ambition drove his desire to attain the
most powerful office in the world, Herman Brown's ambition
did the same for him in the world of business. "We were always
reaching," said George Brown. "We never had any walking-around
money, because we were always reaching above our heads. We never
felt we had it made. We were always reaching for the next plateau."

Roads and dams funded by taxpayers could build a fine
and profitable Texas company, but only one thing could take
Brown and Root to the next plateau: a war.

As the 1930s drew to a close, Congress gave Roosevelt permission to spend $1 billion to expand the U.S. Navy and extend

its reach into the waters of an increasingly troubled world. In April 1939, the president authorized a first round of about $67 million for building new naval bases. Johnson served on the House Committee on Naval Affairs, so Brown and Root bid on a contract to build a naval base in Puerto Rico, which navy brass unceremoniously rejected. Johnson, still a novice, used the little clout he possessed to press for an explanation, and received a terse reply from a low-ranking navy staffer, amounting simply to this: Brown and Root wasn't qualified. The Browns quickly found another way to break through. In 1940, Roosevelt faced a contentious challenge from within his own party, and via Texas. The Brown brothers quietly orchestrated key support for the president through their chief fixer, who assumed fund-raising duties for Roosevelt's campaign in Texas. The administration gave the fixer a senior post over public works contracts, a ripe and rich source of campaign cash.

The Navy Department suddenly learned that it had to consult with none other than Lyndon Johnson before awarding any contracts in Texas, and almost overnight, a long-stalled plan for a naval air station to train pilots in Corpus Christi went from bureaucratic limbo to top priority. Just months after deeming it unqualified to build the naval base in Puerto Rico, the navy gave the nearly $24 million Corpus Christi job to Brown and Root. The contract had an unusual feature, guaranteeing Brown and Root would recoup all its costs, *plus* earn a 5 percent profit—what is known as a "cost-plus" contract. Guaranteed profits are a contractor's best friend, but they are not always so great for the taxpayer, as they give the contractor a massive incentive to run up the bills—the bigger the tab, the bigger the profit. As expected, almost as soon as the first shovel turned Texas earth, costs at Corpus Christi soared, with the price tag ultimately inflating more than five times. Still, Brown and Root finished a big piece of the job early, allowing operations to start ahead of schedule. In a pattern that would become familiar for decades to come, the significant price inflation got approved with nary a blink of an eye, and the navy gave Brown and Root a coveted commendation, the Army-Navy Production Award. Cost-plus contracts would become the norm for Brown and Root going forward.

The company's first experience with defense contracting held clear and valuable lessons. America's vast wealth endowed its military leaders with the freedom to care much more about deadlines than dollars, especially in wartime, so boosting the price is easy once a contract is awarded. Costs can skyrocket so long as the work is done reasonably well and on time. The Browns could apply such lessons also to a separate shipbuilding company they had launched for the war, which would land them more than five hundred million dollars in contracts.

Over the next two decades, Brown and Root's taxpayer-funded growth surged, but so did controversy about the company. Critics sent skeptical glares its way, including from Congress, because of the firm's flagrant use of its political clout. After the 1960 presidential election, *Life* magazine spoofed a conversation between President John F. Kennedy and his vice president, Lyndon Johnson, linking Kennedy's Catholic faith to Johnson's own personal savior.

"Now Lyndon," Kennedy says in the cartoon, "I guess we can dig that tunnel to the Vatican."

"Okay," Johnson replied, "so long as Brown & Root get the contract."

After Johnson became president, government business came Brown and Root's way as never before. Johnson's decision to sink America deeper into the Vietnam War created the windfall. Nine hundred American soldiers were in Vietnam in 1960. By 1966, the number had reached 385,000, and by 1968, it had hit 536,000. Brown and Root became part of a private joint venture that built infrastructure in Southeast Asia to facilitate Johnson's massive troop buildup. The firm carved landing strips and roads from jungle, and built bases, ports, and virtually anything else the military required across the length of South Vietnam. Between 1965 and 1972, the firm's share of the work reached $380 million, the equivalent of more than $2 billion in 2016 dollars. Vietnam was a cost-plus contract.

Auditors from the then-named General Accounting Office, the independent congressional watchdog agency, found that, in less than five years, the joint venture's tab had risen from an original estimate of $25 million to $1.3 billion. Controls and oversight were virtually nonexistent in the face of the rapid troop buildup, the auditors said. By 1967, about $120 million in equipment was unaccounted for.

As more American conscripts came home in flag-draped boxes, George Brown became the poster boy for profiteering in an increasingly unpopular war. Newspaper stories about the Vietnam contracts prominently mentioned his role as "one of President Johnson's principal financial backers." Antiwar protesters began to target Brown personally, including during a public ceremony in Texas. None of this hindered Brown and Root's fortunes, and by 1969, it had become the world's biggest construction company, with $1.6 billion in sales that year.

Herman Brown died before the firm reached that milestone, and Halliburton, an oil services company that rose side by side with Brown and Root in the American South, purchased Brown and Root in the wake of his death. Yet Halliburton allowed Brown and Root to keep its name and operate independently, leaving George Brown at the helm until his retirement in 1975. Before he retired, *Texas Monthly* declared that some had regarded George Brown as perhaps "the most powerful man in the entire nation, and, by extension, the entire world."

Ghosts of Vietnam hovered over American policymakers for nearly two decades. With the Gulf War in 1991, Brown and Root went back to war, too, earning a contract to assess damage inflicted by Saddam Hussein's occupying army in Kuwait. Halliburton independently had its own war contract, with its workers capping oil fires lit by Hussein's fleeing forces.

After the rapid success of the Gulf War, the U.S. military in 1992 gave Brown and Root a four-million-dollar contract to produce an unprecedented, classified report. The aim: to show in detail how a contractor could serve all the military's logistical needs for potential deployments in more than a dozen specific global hot spots. It likely was the first time the Pentagon entrusted such critical planning functions to anyone outside the government, let alone a private company.

Brown and Root's study formed a kind of blueprint. Contractors could use it to be at the ready for rapid deployment alongside U.S. forces in each hot spot. They would no longer just build foreign bases and their mess halls, as Brown and Root had done in Vietnam. They would also peel all the potatoes and serve all the food inside those mess halls—and fulfill virtually every logistical need in between, including buying and delivering fuel for vehicles and generators, pumping the gas, storing ammunition, piping in clean water, rooting sewer pipes, cleaning latrines, and washing and folding laundry. It didn't matter if the hot spot came without roads or other critical infrastructure. Contractors would do it all.

The idea benefited substantially from the times. The promise of a "peace dividend" after the Cold War had created pressure to downsize the military, and the perceived necessity to privatize public services had become something akin to gospel across all levels of American government.

In 1992, as Brown and Root drew up the Pentagon's secret plans to privatize logistics for the most powerful military in the world, Dick Cheney was serving as the U.S. secretary of defense. His then boss was George H. W. Bush, the father of Cheney's future White House boss. The Dick Cheney of 1992 believed in privatization in general and in Brown and Root's ideas in particular. Cheney's Pentagon therefore converted Brown and Root's classified blueprint into contract requirements, creating the Logistics Civil Augmentation Program, or LOGCAP, in militaryspeak. LOGCAP's size and scope were open ended; its term lasted five years. It also was, of course, a cost-plus contract. A national contractors' lobbying group would call it "the mother of all service contracts." Unlike Saddam Hussein's hollow threat to give America "the mother of all battles" in the Gulf War, the lobbying group's quip would prove a dramatic understatement. LOGCAP would become the fattest prize in the history of wartime contracting.

In 1992, Cheney's Pentagon awarded the deal to the same company that had drawn up the secret plans: Brown and Root.

Beginning in 1992, with the growing international mission in Somalia, and continuing as interventions multiplied around the world, Brown and Root's workers increasingly deployed beside U.S. forces. In 1995, after Cheney ditched his presidential ambitions and assumed command of Halliburton, the workload escalated dramatically as a sixty-thousand-man peacekeeping force gathered in the Balkans. When the LOGCAP contract expired two years later, the United States gave it to a competitor, but carved out an exception for the Balkans work, which stayed in Brown and Root's hands. That's how valuable the firm had become. "The first person to greet our soldiers as they arrive in the Balkans, and the last one to wave goodbye, is one of our employees," Cheney said as Halliburton's CEO. The Balkans also were, far and away, the most valuable piece of the LOGCAP business.

Before long, though, government auditors raised concerns about overruns in the Balkans, just as they had thirty years earlier, in Vietnam. The former General Accounting Office, now called the Government Accountability Office, found that the company had overstaffed the vast majority of its projects in Bosnia, paying large swaths of the workforce to sit idle for extended periods. It had also billed taxpayers for other massive redundancies, including unnecessary backup electricity, estimated to cost an extra eighty-five million dollars over five years. Still, servicemen and women gave Brown and Root's work high marks. Comforts from home were available, often in abundance. The firm delivered hot showers, ice cream, folded laundry, and steaks. By 2000, its employees and contractors had served beside U.S forces not just in Bosnia, but also in Albania, Croatia, Greece, Haiti, Hungary, Italy, Kosovo, Macedonia, Rwanda, Somalia, and Zaire. Revenues for the company, now called Kellogg Brown and Root, or KBR, reached two billion dollars that same year, under the original LOGCAP contract and its Balkans extension.

The LOGCAP contract neared its expiration on September 11, 2001, the day of the worst-ever terrorist attack on U.S. soil. America did not seem likely to shrink from the world, especially with Cheney and George W. Bush in the White House. In December, the government gave a new LOGCAP deal to KBR. In hindsight, the agreement looks like a planner's road map for a very long war. The contract would last ten years, instead of five, and required rapid action on a massive scale. The company promised to deploy an army of private workers capable of meeting the needs of twenty-five thousand combat troops with only seventy-two hours' notice. KBR would have to build and run seven camps and a rear-support base with housing for four thousand troops. Total troop numbers could reach fifty thousand per deployment. "Halliburton KBR must be ready to furnish these warfighter services 24 hours a day, 7 days a week, 365 days a year under any condition and at any location around the globe," the company said in a December 17, 2001, press release. Beyond that, virtually all mention of the contract award escaped public notice. The world had fixed its attention elsewhere.

The morning Halliburton issued that press release, Secretary of Defense Donald Rumsfeld beamed confidently from a picture atop the front page of the *New York Times*, shaking the hand of an American soldier in Afghanistan. Celebration seemed justified. A small team comprising U.S. Special Forces and allied troops had overrun Al Qaeda positions in a cave complex in the country's White Mountains, at a place called Tora Bora. They had routed Al Qaeda, and its Taliban allies had been deposed. A new government ruled Afghanistan. This looked like victory. The first paragraph of the story, next to Rumsfeld's picture, datelined Washington, noted the apparent triumphs but said that the Bush administration was "putting out two messages: It's not over till it's over, and even when this first phase of the war does end, Mr. Bush plans to move quickly to other terrorist havens."

The piece anonymously quoted one of Bush's "exuberant senior aides" saying that the president was "on a roll," a phrase captured in the headline. The story openly questioned "where [the president] should next take the war on terrorism," and then listed a few other purported terrorist havens. President Bush faced "some difficult choices in the next few weeks. Is it taking the war to Iraq, where Saddam Hussein is clearly seeking nuclear and biological weapons? Or does it make more sense to focus on easier Al Qaeda targets—Somalia, or perhaps Indonesia and the Philippines?"

The piece also said, "Pentagon officials have openly agitated to finish off Mr. Hussein. Today, speaking on the NBC News program 'Meet the Press,' Secretary [of State Colin] Powell disclosed that efforts to find new ways to destabilize the Iraqi leader were under way."

Adjacent to Baghdad International Airport rose Victory Base Complex, a massive, sprawling base of numerous military camps, all enclosed in razor wire, dividing its U.S. and allied soldiers, contractors, and detainees from the rest of Iraq. Under LOGCAP, KBR provided services to the base. Many of Victory's camps were like distinct neighborhoods, the majority comprising relocatable "containerized housing units" provided by KBR. The Americans called their headquarters within the complex Camp Liberty.

KBR acted as a boardinghouse, construction company, public

works agency, repairman, utility company, backup utility company, launderette, gas station operator, car mechanic, barber, plumber, air-conditioner repairman, and maid. The base PX, or "post exchange," a retail store, resembled a Walmart in the desert. As big as an airplane hangar, it sold Beyoncé CDs, video game consoles, big-screen TVs, Red Bull, and barbecued pork rinds. Camp Liberty may have been America's biggest camp, but similar, albeit smaller wartime cities and hamlets had sprung up throughout the region under LOGCAP. There, too, the comforts of home could exceed even those that KBR had flown into the Balkans, as did the price tag.

Contractors at war were nothing new. In World War II, there was one civilian contractor for every seven American soldiers. When the United States invaded Iraq in 2003, it brought one contractor for every two and a half soldiers, and by 2006, civilian contractors in Iraq would outnumber U.S. forces. The growth of private security firms such as Blackwater drew global attention. Yet security contractors made up only 16 percent of the private workforce. The vast majority of contractors, about 60 percent, were not hired guns but hired hands, as *The New Yorker* magazine would put it years later.

Aamer Madhani, a Chicago native born to Pakistani immigrants, was a young, smart, hungry reporter who had risen fast at the *Chicago Tribune*. He was one of about two dozen reporters the *Tribune* sent to Iraq when the war started. There, Madhani distinguished himself. Many journalists stayed inside the protective bubble of the Green Zone, or civilian headquarters, in central Baghdad. Madhani climbed into a ratty car and made his way, sans security, to Karbala, about sixty miles southwest of Baghdad, to investigate the murders of two Americans working for the Coalition Provisional Authority and their Iraqi interpreter. These were the first such killings of the war, marking a major turning point. Madhani's reporting drew praise and international attention. Editors made him a regular in the paper's Baghdad rotation.

"You're immediately struck by how many civilians it takes to keep this war going," Madhani said of his earliest impressions inside Camp Liberty. Also, gone was the army mess hall of old. In its place, KBR, through LOGCAP, had built something called a DFAC (pronunced DEE-fack), militaryspeak for "dining facility." At the DFAC, Madhani noticed something else that many had overlooked: the faces of those who served him his meals. "There are all sorts of different skin colors," he said. "You see Filipinos, you see Indians, you see Pakistanis, you see Nepalis. There are people from throughout the world." KBR's army as a whole may have been hard to miss, but individually, they seemed invisible.

Knowing how good Madhani's reporting from Iraq had been, I asked him if he'd be interested in helping me investigate the wider system that had delivered the twelve Nepalis to their deaths. I needed the help. Basic questions had gone unanswered under the veil of "security" that had lowered as the insurgency rolled across Iraq. We had learned that KBR relied on forty-eight thousand people working for roughly two hundred subcontracting companies to operate at Camp Liberty and direct the rest of the war's noncombat logistics. Many assumed that these subcontracting firms were fly-by-night Middle Eastern companies cashing in on what P. W. Singer, an expert on the privatization of warfare, called the unprecedented gold rush atmosphere of Iraq. Daoud and Partners was among them.

KBR called a large segment of the forty-eight-thousand-man workforce TCNs, short for "third-country nationals."

They were not Americans, Brits, Australians, or Iraqis. Instead, they came from "third" countries, or what used to be known as Third World countries. Essentially, TCNs was shorthand for the brown faces Madhani had seen behind the counter when he ate burritos inside the DFAC. Like the twelve, they had come to Iraq from some of the poorest corners of the world through labor brokers who had routed them via other Middle Eastern nations, often nations that were themselves chided by the United States for human trafficking. A few women were there, too. In all, the TCNs executing KBR's LOGCAP contract numbered thirty-five thousand during 2004, and their population was growing fast. Unlike Westerners, they could not move freely about Camp Liberty or the other camps inside Victory Base. KBR's subcontractors typically kept the men in internal camps, behind armed guards. If Camp Liberty was a sprawling city, then the TCNs were living in its ghetto.

I had developed a KBR source who worked as a foreman for a crew of TCNs at Camp Liberty. After Madhani agreed to help, he went to Camp Liberty on an "embed" in 2005. The source had agreed to smuggle him in his pickup truck past the guards at Liberty's "Indian Camp," which he did with little effort. No one gave Madhani a second look in the company of the white KBR supervisor. Once inside the camp, Madhani found the men living twelve to a single "hooch," as the containerized housing units were called. With them packed in so tightly, Madhani could barely stand and hold his notebook in front of him as he tried to conduct interviews.

He confirmed much of what we had heard about the TCNs. Many of the men worked under conditions akin to indentured servitude, bound to their jobs in Iraq by crushing debts accumulated by their families to pay excessive brokerage fees back home. Brokers employed myriad bait-and-switch tactics. Many of the men there earned far less than had been promised when they bought the jobs, a fact that gave them little choice but to stay in the war zone to pay back their families' debts. Typical earnings per man amounted to $65 to $112 per week, depending on which country he came from. Workdays lasted twelve hours, and men could go weeks without a day off. Sometimes companies withheld wages, especially if workers refused to give up their passports. Subcontracting bosses routinely took and held these documents, a practice which the U.S. State Department and others viewed as a key indicator of human trafficking, and which the top U.S. commander in Iraq, General George Casey, would later make clear that he viewed as illegal in Iraq under U.S. law. Also, TCNs often got none of the safety equipment Westerners received, even as mortar and rocket fire fell from the sky. In short, we found that the war ran on a pipeline of cheap foreign labor, mainly impoverished Asians, who were often deceived, exploited, and put in harm's way in Iraq with little protection or regard for their lives.

The day after he first entered the base, Madhani returned with the whistleblower for a second round of interviews. Electricity died campwide, which was not unusual, and the TCN workers kept the hatch of their hooch flung wide open, to try to circulate the stale desert air in the steel box they called home. They crowded onto bunks to speak to Madhani. He wanted to focus most on the seizure of their passports but quickly lost track of the time, riveted by tales of how the men had landed in an American war zone. After a couple of hours, the shadows of two men crossed the threshold of the open steel door. They were private security guards, and they ordered Madhani out of the container.

He turned off his tape recorder and complied, identifying himself as a journalist. "I'll be glad to leave," he recalled telling the guards. "I have a ride out that I can go meet." He started to walk away at a brisk pace—not quite a sprint, but not a stroll, either—but the guards grabbed him, each one taking an arm, and marched him to their guard shack at the front of "Indian Camp." They, too, were Nepalis, former Gurkhas; even the security contractors used TCNs. One made a phone call to his boss. Shortly afterward, a British private-security man pulled up in a pickup truck.

The security chief asked Madhani for his identification but refused to identify himself. Madhani handed over his military-issued press ID. "Can I have your passport? I want to see your passport," the security guard said. Madhani reached into his back pocket, pulled out his passport, and handed it over. Inside his vehicle, the security man sat down and placed the passport under his rump. Madhani asked for it back. "We'll eventually give it back to you," the security boss told him. They drove to the headquarters of the KBR subcontractor Prime Projects International, a Dubai-based company. Two other security men with British accents greeted them. The pair were a bit less polished than their boss. "They were furious that I had gone to interview their workers, and they started screaming at me," Madhani said. "They said they were going to get the military police involved—but they first thought it might be a good idea to take me out back and kick my ass."

The men also told Madhani that he had trespassed and they wanted him to be charged with a crime. Fine, he said. Call the military police. Let's bring them here now. No indication emerged that any military officials were coming, but the security men refused to release Madhani. He continued to worry that they would carry through on their threats to harm him as they interrogated him about precisely what the workers had told him. The security contractors then told Madhani that because he had trespassed, he could not print anything he had learned from any of the men he'd interviewed. Madhani scoffed. Then they said he would be endangering the men's lives, and those of their families back home, by printing their stories. Madhani scoffed at that, too.

Eventually, the security contractors released him, without carrying out their threatened beating. They gave back his passport, too. Military police never came.

We had more than enough evidence to put the twelve Nepalese men into the supply chain of Daoud and Partners, KBR Halliburton, and the U.S. military's operations in Iraq. Thanks to Madhani's efforts before his detention, we also had enough to show that the wider system went far beyond the twelve men and a single, rogue subcontractor. Not surprisingly, KBR Halliburton and the U.S. military did not reveal how much they knew about the twelve or about how Daoud and Partners and the two hundred other firms on KBR's contract had acquired the tens of thousands of foreign workers making up the invisible U.S. Army, the one keeping the Iraq War fueled, fed, and running.

We gave Halliburton sixty detailed, specific written questions resulting from an investigation that spanned several countries and involved interviews with scores of people and thousands of pages of documents. Lawyers crafted Halliburton's replies, or at least provided substantial input. The company directly answered few questions, and avoided acknowledging any connection to the twelve dead men. Halliburton would not say whether anyone had been reprimanded—not just in the case of the Nepalis, but also for any conduct involving so-called TCNs anywhere during the war. It said that it hired subcontracting firms through a "government-approved procurement system," and explained that the TCNs employed under its contract in Iraq, and how they got there, were the responsibility of the subcontractors, and that "questions regarding the recruitment practices of the subcontractors should be directed to the subcontractors." It said it would "fully investigate" any allegations of wrongdoing by those firms, but would not say whether it ever had investigated any of them. It refused to provide copies of contracts or even contract clauses, because that might "impact future contractual relationships and represent a breech [sic] in operational security."

Also, someone had cut-and-pasted one line multiple times into the response. Each occurrence included the same typo. "KBR operates under a rigorous Code of Business Conduct that outlines and [sic] legal and ethical behaviors that all employees and subcontractors are expected to follow in every aspect of their work."

The U.S. Army, which had oversight for the contract, went a step further in washing its own hands of responsibility. "Questions involving alleged misconduct towards employees by subcontractor firms should be addressed to those firms, as these are not Army issues." Not army issues. Given all that, figuring out specifically what KBR and the U.S. government knew before, during, and after the ordeal of the twelve men, about their case and the broader system, looked impossible. Determining what they reasonably should have known, and what they had failed to do, was easier.

Beyond the obvious litany of failures within the step-by-step journey of each man to his death, neither KBR Halliburton nor Daoud did anything after the murders to seek out the twelve men's families. Clearly, those families were entitled to legally mandated compensation. Payments are made out of an insurance pool, so they would not have cost either company a dime. The reason behind their failure to do anything on this front dovetailed with Halliburton's refusal to answer questions about Jeet and the other men. Lawyers for both companies likely feared that the slightest admission of involvement regarding the twelve might subject Halliburton and Daoud to litigation, potential liability, or even a criminal investigation. Implicating Daoud even through a compensation case also would involve KBR Halliburton, by necessity.

More broadly, KBR Halliburton executives at multiple levels knew, or clearly should have known, that there was a massive human trafficking problem in the very same countries they relied on to source foreign workers for their Iraq contract. Numerous warnings and reports about the routine nature of human trafficking across the region were readily available, both publicly and inside government files.

For starters, U.S. diplomats the world over had gathered enough evidence by 2004 to put the White House's four leading Middle Eastern allies in the Iraq War on the U.S. watch list for human trafficking, even as the Pentagon relied on scores of firms from those nations to bring tens of thousands of foreign workers into Iraq under KBR's contract.

And prominent figures had publicly raised specific concerns with government officials and company executives. Hillary Clinton, then a senator from New York, and her fellow members of the U.S. Helsinki Commission had in 2003 flagged fears to the Bush administration about human trafficking into Iraq. The commission is an independent government agency run by appointed U.S. senators and House members. Clinton also specifically asked Department of Defense officials in a hearing on September 21, 2004, to investigate labor trafficking and debt bondage in Iraq, which they had promised to do. Still, in its correspondence with me a year later, the military had absolved itself of any related responsibility.

In meetings with senior U.S. military officials, representatives from the government of India, and other "feeder" countries also had complained about the treatment of their nationals by contractors and subcontractors working for the United States. There even had been a handful of news stories in 2004 and 2005 raising questions about the same issues, including questions addressed directly to Halliburton, in the *Washington Post*, the *New York Times*, and a couple of other publications. There were stories in the foreign press, too.

Defense Secretary Donald Rumsfeld personally had an idea about what was happening, although his actions at the time would not emerge for a decade. Just two weeks after the twelve Nepalis were murdered, Rumsfeld penned an internal memorandum addressed to the secretaries of all the military departments, to the chairman of the Joint Chiefs of Staff, to all undersecretaries of defense, to his own lawyers, and to the Pentagon's inspector general. The subject line read, "Combatting Trafficking in Persons."

The reason for the timing of the memo is unclear, but in his very first sentence, Rumsfeld pointed out that he had, in fact, originally sent around a memo on this very subject way back on January 30, 2004. Next, he wrote, "Trafficking in persons is the third largest criminal activity in the world, after illegal arms and drugs sales. It enslaves thousands of people. I am especially concerned with commercial sex exploitation and labor trafficking practices in areas near our overseas locations . . . Trafficking includes involuntary servitude and debt bondage. These trafficking practices will not be tolerated in DoD contractor organizations or their subcontractors supporting DoD operations." He also wrote, "No leader in this department should turn a blind eye to this issue." The memo went into files at the upper reaches of the Pentagon. Whether Rumsfeld's memo was written out of genuine concern or was simply a classic work of that Washington literary genre known as CYA (Cover Your Ass), defined by William Safire as the bureaucratic art of avoiding future accusations of wrongdoing through advance deflection of responsibility, remains unknown.

While Halliburton's answers to our questions did little to shed light on what had happened, the company had offered some valuable insights in a completely different context. They came via Alfred V. Neffgen, the CEO of KBR's government operations division, as he defended KBR Halliburton from allegations of profiteering.

By mid-2004, controversy within the Beltway and beyond engulfed Neffgen's company over its cost-plus, no-bid contract awards for Iraq. The furor reached levels the company had not experienced since Vietnam. Fanning the flames: Cheney, the former Halliburton CEO, and his White House boss were up for reelection in November. The situation was similar to what had happened to President Johnson with Brown and Root during Vietnam: critics blasted Cheney, charging that his continuing financial relationship with his former company gave him a personal stake in the war. In fact, the ties between Cheney and the company were even clearer and more personal than they had been with Johnson. Throughout his first term in the Bush White House, Cheney got a deferred salary and bonuses from Halliburton totaling almost two million dollars by the end of the summer in 2004. He also held unexercised stock options.

GAO auditors issued a report in July 2004 citing poor management practices at both KBR Halliburton and the Pentagon. Auditors said the company lacked adequate control of its subcontractors, along with "poor cost-reporting, difficulties with producing and meeting schedules, and weaknesses in purchasing system controls." These were among the earliest signs of far greater troubles to come. Ultimately, officials would identify or question vast amounts of unsupported Iraq costs, estimating that the lack of competition alone cost taxpayers $3.3 billion just on LOGCAP. Overstaffing, as in the Balkans, would lead to official estimates that almost $400 million had been wasted through "underutilization" of workers in just a single category of labor, vehicle maintenance. Corruption also thrived. A Kuwaiti company had started paying kickbacks to KBR managers during the run-up to the war in 2002, yielding awards of more than $700 million for dining facility services.

One day after the release of a 2004 GAO report, Neffgen and three other senior KBR Halliburton executives came to Capitol Hill in what would be the first hearing of the war in which Halliburton's leadership testified. Neffgen and his fellow executives came prepared to mount a vigorous public relations defense for all the heat the company had endured in the sixteen months since the invasion. It started with one small accessory in their attire: each wore a yellow ribbon on his lapel. As Neffgen made a point of explaining to the cameras and members of the House Committee on Government Reform, the ribbons were meant to signify that their "colleagues," as he called employees and contract workers, "are on the front lines, putting themselves in harm's way to support U.S. soldiers in a war zone." Among those already killed were ordinary, average Americans, he said, "truck drivers, construction workers, and food service personnel," people who had "made the ultimate sacrifice to support American troops." In fact, very few of the estimated forty-two workers killed up to that point had been "ordinary Americans"; the vast majority comprised foreign nationals working for KBR through contractors such as Daoud and Partners.

Neffgen then detailed the tremendous pressure his company faced in Iraq from the start. The LOGCAP contract's already demanding requirements to rapidly deploy in support of up to 50,000 troops had been shattered. He counted 211,000 personnel in more than sixty camps. "The pace of new requirements and changes to ongoing missions greatly exceeded the original plans of both the government and of KBR," Neffgen said. The company had to "build an extensive network of subcontractors, and assemble the people and systems to supervise them." He also said that "it was difficult to find subcontractors in the Middle East who were knowledgeable about, and could comply with, U.S. regulations. It took time and effort to bring them up to standards." Facing such realities, he asked himself rhetorically, "Did KBR make mistakes? Without question, we encountered difficulties in mounting such a large enterprise in a hostile, dangerous environment . . . our business and subcontract management systems were stretched." Still, he maintained that one thing never wavered. "All the while, we worked within army rules and regulations, supplemented by our own checks and balances and our Code of Business Conduct, which requires employees to conduct business honestly and ethically."

On that very day, as Neffgen and the other KBR Halliburton executives were testifying, Jeet and his compatriots were inside the house at No. 58 Malfuf Street in Amman.

We needed to determine how much company executives and U.S. military personnel on the ground at Al Asad Air Base knew about the men who were being held in that room, and their awareness of Daoud's operations for KBR Halliburton. Once Madhani had finished at Camp Liberty in Baghdad, we had planned for him to embed with U.S. forces at Al Asad, where dozens of Nepalis from the same convoy had made it through. Madhani would use the embed to search the invisible faces at the base for Nepalese workers, and then try to find some of the other men who had been in the same convoy with our twelve, to provide some living, breathing testimony to an investigation that was, by the fact of the men's deaths, still circumstantial. But his experience at Camp Liberty had rattled Madhani, and we feared he might be a marked man. As the plan seemed too risky, we decided to call it off.

On two consecutive days in October 2005, the *Chicago Tribune* published an almost ten-thousand-word investigation covering a total of six pages. The main story appeared as a two-part serial narrative, revealing the larger system of exploitation by retracing the twelve men's journeys to their deaths. For the sake of clarity, we stuck mostly to what had happened to the men and those involved at every stage of the journeys. We chose not to focus on those on the command side who had tried to cover their trail or obscure their role in the invisible army that kept the war running.

The specifics of what had happened at Al Asad—what senior military commanders there might have known; what
senior KBR officials knew, not just about the treatment of
foreign workers, but also about alleged corruption involving
Daoud and KBR managers—still remained beyond our grasp
in 2005.

8

2005
Kathmandu

Above the wooden door of a workshop on the campus of the Tulsi Meher Ashram hung a dictum from the founder, hand-painted in white lettering across a small blue placard. It embodied the Gandhian philosophy underpinning life on the campus: "Labor Is Religion. Work Is Worship." Approaching the workshop, Kamala could hear the day's devotion in the gentle metronomic ticktock of the wooden looms where the women of the campus wove the cloth they used to make their own saris. Kamala would sit on a narrow bench in the center of a loom, rocking slightly left, then right, to alternately depress two long paddles with her feet, while simultaneously using her hands to weave together hundreds of threads intersecting lengthwise and crosswise on a wooden frame. Gandhi and his Nepalese disciple, Meher, believed that people found dignity in work, in addition to the Zen state induced by the repetition of spinning thread and weaving cloth, but the two also believed that everyone could gain independence by making the very fabric in which they clothed themselves. The cloth Kamala and the other women made for their saris was sky-blue with wide navy-blue borders. Making cloth was among the first skills each woman had to master at the ashram, but it held significance beyond engendering self-sufficiency and a kind of mindfulness. It was a first step in each widow's deeper liberation.

Women came to the ashram still wearing the white saris of their widowhood, if not literally upon their bodies, then internalized from the stigma each of them faced. Kamala had not understood the full extent to which she had rebelled against millennia of subjugation when she listened to her father's plea to remove her white sari so soon after donning it. Yet she continued to feel intimidated by the power of what the white sari represented in her life. Historically, at least in some ethnic groups in Nepal, a widow was expected to burn herself alive upon the funeral pyre of her dead husband, and could be forced onto the flames if she refused to go willingly, a practice known as sati, or suttee. In some parts of Nepal, sati survived into the twentieth century and exemplified, in a very literal way, the idea that a wife existed primarily as a piece of her husband, in his life and in his death. Even within ethnic groups and regions where sati wasn't practiced, the white sari was ubiquitous for widows, a kind of shroud marking their sexual and social deaths. Because they were blue, the ashram's saris represented a subtle but deliberate act of defiance, made as they were from fabric woven by the women's own hands.

One of the most difficult days for any widow is a nationwide public holiday in late summer called the Teej, in which married women are expected to worship their husbands and pray for their long lives. The women dress in all red, including in the red saris they wore on their wedding day, and cover their arms with red bangles and their necks with red beaded necklaces. Thousands upon thousands of wives parade en masse along the pathways of public parks and around the streets of Kathmandu's neighborhoods, which look from above as if they were cut by crimson rivers. Kamala's first Teej as a widow would come just a few days after the anniversary of Jeet's execution. She faced its coming with deep trepidation, but on the day before the holiday, the ashram's staff loaded Kamala and the other women onto microbuses, handed them each some cash, and sent them shopping in the noisy markets not far from a bridge that crosses the city's sacred Bagmati River. After husbands die, some in-laws ceremoniously smash red bangles off the arms of the widows, literally, with rocks or other bludgeons. Now the ashram's staff directed Kamala and the other women to buy as many red bangles in the market as they could afford. The women poured back onto the buses, smiling and laughing, extending their arms and showing off their bangles to one another. They spent the holiday itself at a carefully organized party, with songs and dances that carried on during the bus ride home.

The ashram's struggle against millennia of discrimination dovetailed with a growing movement across the country. The nation's civil war had left scores of widows in communities that had never known such widespread loss, especially in conservative areas where the culture of the white sari seemed deeply entrenched. War meant that young widows suddenly had strength in numbers, and in some communities, they began organizing themselves into a kind of loose resistance against the injustices born of their individual but collective tragedies. In 2005, the same year Kamala joined the ashram, a handful of well-intentioned international charity groups started recognizing this movement, and earnestly tried to push it forward. But although awareness of the discrimination, and the resistance against it, was growing, the stigma ran deep. Even Kamala's ashram, perhaps the most enlightened place for widows anywhere in the shadows of the Himalayas, was not without practices that could be seen as judgmental toward the very women it worked so thoughtfully to empower. Upon admission, each widow was given a physical examination by a doctor, which included a test for sexually transmitted diseases. Any woman who tested positive was expelled.

The crying Kamala had heard in her room during her earliest nights at the ashram, which made her feel alone and afraid, began to fade over time, but even when another woman's weeping kept her awake, Kamala's unease dissipated, too, turning toward something else. Feeling another woman's sadness made her less afraid and lonely than it had during her first couple of months. Every woman around her was visible to every other woman in a way none of them could have been on her own, in the same way Kamala and Heera had found strength by doing little more than gathering leaves together on the horseshoe ridge. The women of the ashram also explicitly shared tales of their own struggles, especially at impromptu gatherings in the evenings. The "senior" women, those in their second and final year of the ashram's two-year program, were the most open. They often took the lead when the women would gather in one of the dormitories after dinner, crowding onto straw mats spread across the plaster floor, to speak of how it was that they had arrived at this moment.

A woman named Ganga, who came from a district called Kailali, in the far-western corner of Nepal, had lost her husband to a mining accident in India, where he was a migrant worker. His employer promised to pay workers' compensation to the family, but they had to travel to India to claim it. Ganga told the women how she had crossed the border into India and then boarded a train with her father-in-law bound for the company's headquarters in Himachal, near Kashmir. From nowhere, a group of men in the train car swarmed Ganga, grabbing and molesting her in concert. She screamed out to her father-in-law, but he stood still and silent as the train chugged forward. Ganga burst into a fury, clawing at every man she could reach, slapping their faces, punching, doing whatever she could, until the men, too pained or too frightened to continue their attack, backed off almost as suddenly as they had swarmed. In the immediate aftermath, everyone in the car stared at Ganga in shock, including her father-in-law. All were aghast at her behavior, as if she somehow were to blame for her own molestation and should have endured it in silence. Kamala and the other women were spellbound. So many of them also had felt hands, or worse, upon their bodies, while standing on crowded buses or in street markets, but most had never dared do what Ganga had done, fearing the consequences.

After they returned to Nepal, Ganga's father-in-law and the rest of his family immediately rejected her, casting her out. Before long, she lost her children to an orphanage because she could not house, care for, or feed them on her own, as she was without any means of support. She eventually found her way to the ashram, but only after enduring severe suffering on a cross-country journey. Kamala was inspired by Ganga's bravery and emotional courage, not just in fighting off her attackers, but also for facing the costs, and then finding a way to overcome despair by moving into the ashram. Ganga told the women that she was there to gain the independence that would allow her to regain custody of her children after she graduated. Kamala determined that she must live up to Ganga's courage.

Some nights, the women did more than share their experiences in the dormitories. They would sneak out of their rooms,

walk through the gate from the courtyard to the back of the
ashram's main buildings, and share a cigarette on the rickety
balcony beneath a blanket of stars. Senior women paid particular attention to Kamala, seeming to take special care of
her. Maybe that was because of the public spectacle of her husband's death, and the way it had enraged the country against
its growing economy of exploitation; or because it had been the
first national mourning of its kind beyond the royal family;
or perhaps because Kamala's pain was more evident than that
of the other women in her class. Kamala also likely gravitated
toward these older women because she had been raised and
cared for by elder sisters. Whatever the reasons, their support
helped her develop a growing sense of ease, about her plight
and about Kritika, too. The day care and kindergarten inside
the ashram were so well respected that the campus also took
in the children of tuition-paying parents from the community
beyond its walls. The high quality of Kritika's care and education allowed Kamala to focus on gaining the skills that could
give her independence.

The daily rhythms of life at the ashram were not so different
from those on the farm. Kamala rose at five each morning,
walked out of her room, slipped on her flip-flops, and made her
way down to the far side of the ashram's long, low dining hall,
where four taps spilled water into a stone basin. She cleaned herself and then quietly lined up with the other women at a small
statue of the ashram's late founder, in the center of the courtyard, where each pressed her palms together beneath her chin
and offered a brief prayer and a slight bow. The women then
filed into the main campus building, which held workshops

and classrooms, to do yoga for about ninety minutes, before breaking for morning tea and biscuits. They then split themselves into small groups for the morning's chores, each group carefully configured to keep women from the different castes and strata of the society bound together. The ashram held what was in essence a small working farm on a spread of land at the back of the campus, where the women grew vegetables for their own meals and tended to chickens and a couple of cows. Other women swept and cleaned, or worked with the campus's chef, a wiry old man who sometimes flirted playfully with them, to do the prep work for the day's meals. By nine, they were uniformly dressed in their blue saris and filing into the workshops at the back of the main campus building, a two-story brick edifice with large windows across the front. An open-air gate built through the center of the building served as a passageway from the courtyard to the back, where rickety wooden staircases and balconies hung from the building's exterior. The entrance to each workshop or classroom was at the back, too.

Half the women learned spinning, knitting, and weaving, turning out thread, yarn, tapestries, and fabric. The other half learned to tailor, taking seats at rows of desks, two by two, each desk topped with a vintage-looking treadle sewing machine made in India and etched with silver swirls or vines and flowers. The sewing rooms smelled of dust and linen and oil, and were illuminated by sunlight pouring in from the large windows extending nearly floor to ceiling across the side wall, which faced the courtyard. Each woman powered her machine with her own two feet, rocking the cast-iron treadle like a seesaw and filling the room with a symphony of gentle mechanical rhythms, broken only by the women's banter and laughter. Patterns and fabric were spread across low-slung worktables at the front of the room, weighted down by scissors nearly as long and heavy as garden shears. Over the course of a year, the women learned to make simple things, such as saris, as well as more complex garments, including dresses and men's jackets. The focus that tailoring required, the attention to minute measurements and details, the art and pride of creation—all these drew Kamala to this new craft, but it was something about the rhythm of the treadle that really captured her. The machine she worked on, an Indian-made Luxmi, had been a gift to the ashram from India's foreign ministry, in honor of the connection between Gandhi and Meher, as were all the ashram's machines. It was also Kamala's own machine to keep. Photos of bygone graduation ceremonies were pinned to a bulletin board in the front of the administration building. They showed women lined up in the courtyard, displaying their diplomas for the camera, each woman standing proudly behind her sewing machine. Kamala, like every woman at the ashram, knew that when and if she graduated, she would get to take her machine with her. The ashram also sold and carefully tracked everything each woman made, and put profits from each garment into a fund for her, which she also received upon graduation.

The connection between sewing and healing was something the ashram's chief seamstress, a woman named Shakuntala Basnet, pondered over her years teaching class after class of grieving women. Basnet knew from the start that Kamala would struggle, simply because the widows with children faced a more difficult path, but also because everyone in every corner of the country knew about the twelve men killed in Iraq. The public nature of Kamala's pain would make it harder for her to escape her metaphorical white sari in the eyes of the world. When Basnet saw how hard Kamala worked to learn sewing and tailoring, and how eager the young widow was to advance, she was heartened. Yes, Basnet believed there was something about the rhythm of the sewing machines, the way the sound of the treadles and the rapid pounding of the needles filled the building, but she also knew how comfort comes with the intense focus required to learn something difficult and new, giving rest to a worried mind through escape. She knew that Kamala's hard work would yield rewards that had nothing to do with the garments she made.

Kamala's family believed that the ashram would be good for her, but it was hard for them to envision her life there. Every few weeks, Maya would find a reason to be in the village of Taksar (about a two-hour walk from the horseshoe ridge) with a little money in her purse. It was the nearest village with a public telephone, the one kept by the Kunwar family inside the one-room convenience store they ran from their home beside a narrow road choked with buses. Whoever was on duty would pull the phone out for Maya and place it on a glass display case at the shop's front and dial the ashram. A runner at the administrative office in Kathmandu would fetch Kamala, and the two sisters would reconnect across the long-distance line for twenty to thirty minutes. In the earliest days, as Kamala remained bowed by shock and sadness, Maya would do much of the talking. She caught her sister up on family news and gossip from the horseshoe ridge. She managed to get Kamala talking by asking after Kritika. Perhaps because they spoke only about once a month, it didn't take many of these chats for Maya to start noticing a change that seemed both rapid and marked. Kamala began speaking not only more, but also with excitement, telling Maya about everything she was learning, about the other women she had grown close to, and about potential ideas for her future, which, till then, she had thought about only with dread. Now Maya heard something in Kamala's voice that she had not heard for a couple of years, not just a sense of hope but also a hint that Kamala was getting back to herself, gaining strength and becoming grounded. She sounded confident, even happy at times.

Kamala also wanted to stay connected with Jeet's family back on the horseshoe ridge, at least for the sake of Kritika, but they never called her at the ashram. Just a few weeks after the first anniversary of his murder, and following the waves of red crimson in Kathmandu marking the Teej holiday, Nepalis celebrated the most auspicious holiday on their calendar, the two-week-long Dashain festival. Kamala took Kritika back to the village on the ledge to see Jeet's family, as they had requested of her, but she found that little in the farmhouse had changed. Despite their invitation to her and Kritika, Jeet's family had not prepared any of the traditional gifts normally given to a daughter and granddaughter on Dashain. Kamala had expected little, if anything, for herself, but for Kritika, who was now nearly four, it would be like a grandchild not getting any gifts at Christmas. Kamala returned to the ashram saddened that her relationship with Jeet's family remained so distant and cold, despite the gains she was making in her life.

Not long after, a call came into the ashram's administrative office from a man who said he urgently needed to speak with Kamala. A runner summoned her to the phone, and when she answered, the man on the other line introduced himself as Ganesh Gurung, an academic who ran a small institute in Kathmandu. He told her he was working with a group of American lawyers who believed she was entitled to compensation from the U.S. government because of what had happened to Jeet. Kamala was shocked, if not skeptical, but Gurung seemed both kind and authoritative, so she agreed to come to his office and hear him out.

PART III

"More Vile Than Anything the Court Has Previously Confronted"

9

2005–2006
Washington, DC

Matthew Handley sat down behind the conference table to face two men who had more power over his life than any others. Handley's annual review as a junior lawyer at the Washington law firm of Cohen Milstein Hausfeld and Toll could be make or break. A bad one—filled with euphemisms along the lines of "Needs improvement"—might precipitate a serious diversion from the road to partnership. Becoming a partner is what it's all about at a big firm. It's where the money is. It's where lawyers can earn the freedom to pursue cases they care about. Other paths end at a wall. Handley's review took place in the office of Steve Toll, the firm's managing partner. His immediate supervisor, a senior lawyer named Daniel Sommers, was there, too. Sommers ran the firm's securities group. His cases paid a lot of bills at Cohen Milstein. They also paid Handley's salary.

The firm ran a vigorous class-action practice not unlike that of other large law firms across America. The securities practice group sued major corporations on behalf of allegedly aggrieved shareholders, getting a slice of settlements with the corporations, or from verdicts won at trial. High-profile accounting scandals that roiled financial markets starting in the 1990s, and involving the likes of Enron, Waste Management, and WorldCom, sent share prices plummeting. The farther they fell, the greater the potential reward from a lawsuit on behalf of defrauded shareholders. Such cases might not have turned the pages of legal thrillers by John Grisham, but they did mint millionaires in the wood-paneled offices of Cohen Milstein and partnerships like it across the country—as did the firm's other staple: antitrust lawsuits.

The two partners conducting Handley's review offered some praise. Warm and genial, the young lawyer was impossible to dislike and worked as hard as anyone in the firm. He also competently executed the kind of junior lawyer schlepping that filled most of his days, such as scouring through Securities and Exchange Commission filings of a company called LeapFrog Enterprises, an educational-toy maker whose share price fell 34 percent in a single day on news of questionably booked revenues. Corporate malfeasance could be intellectually engaging for Handley, but injustices to shareholders didn't stir the passions that had sent him to law school. So he dedicated his free time and other stolen moments to working on the firm's pro bono cases, especially those involving civil and human rights. Cohen Milstein had an international reputation for its work on cutting-edge human rights litigation. Its commitment was a big part of what had drawn Handley to the firm in the first place.

This side of the firm's practice came via the outsize personalities of two of its four named partners, both brilliant, both tenacious, both difficult: the firm's late founder, Jerry Cohen, and his leading protégé, Michael Hausfeld. Cohen had been a firebrand. In the 1960s and early '70s, he served as staff director and chief counsel to the antitrust subcommittee of the U.S. Senate's Judiciary Committee. His private practice was animated by an intense suspicion of corporations—a suspicion born of his insider's view from the Senate. He was colead counsel in suits against Exxon following its catastrophic oil spill off Alaska's Prince William Sound, in which he won a $5 billion punitive damages judgment.* He had also sued Union Carbide on behalf of hundreds of thousands of Indian citizens exposed to pesticides in Bhopal following one of history's worst industrial accidents in 1984. His work on sexual harassment established it as a core violation of federal civil rights laws, an outcome he achieved by targeting workplace harassment within the hallowed corridors of none other than the U.S. Department of Justice. Like his mentor, Hausfeld also pushed cases involving causes. In 1996, one year after Cohen's death, Hausfeld secured what was then the largest race discrimination settlement in history, with Texaco paying $141 million. Ostensibly, he headed the firm's antitrust practice. He gambled on high-stakes cases, which could yield huge fee awards or serve as money pits. He spent the firm's vast resources on spec, hiring a team of Holocaust scholars to inch through five thousand cubic feet, or nearly ten million pages, of World War II–era records in the National Archives. They unearthed troves of evidence implicating Swiss bank executives in collaborating with the Nazis, and they found documents showing that European and American corporations had profited from the Holocaust through Nazi-supplied slave labor. In December 1996, Hausfeld launched his assault on the alleged beneficiaries of the twentieth century's biggest crime by suing the Swiss banks on behalf of Holocaust survivors, arguing that the same banks doing business in New York had committed gross human rights violations six decades earlier by handsomely profiting from their collaboration with the Nazis. Critics accused

* The U.S. Supreme Court ultimately cut it to $500 million.

him of being history's version of an international ambulance chaser, but such criticism did not withstand scrutiny. Hausfeld did the case pro bono. To many, he seemed more like an activist who used the law rather than a lawyer with a healthy streak of activism, but by the time the Swiss banks settled for a whopping $1.25 billion, Hausfeld had moved into the side of the litigation that could yield more significant rewards for the firm, suing companies that had allegedly profited off the backs of concentration camp slaves. A vast new area of the law for class-action lawyers opened up, with Hausfeld, a small, soft-spoken, bespectacled man with a penchant for bow ties, among the handful leading the way. He started regularly landing atop lists of the nation's most feared litigators.

By 2005, a younger partner named Agnieszka Fryszman, originally hired by Hausfeld to do antitrust cases, was handling a lot of work for the firm on the human rights side of the practice, and Matthew Handley did much of his pro bono work by volunteering for her. Increasingly, these cases devoured Handley's focus and energies. He helped Fryszman represent detainees at Guantánamo Bay, a daunting legal challenge encased in Pentagon red tape. He plunged into the Bhopal litigation, still pending long after Cohen's death and by then approaching the Dickensian scale of *Jarndyce v. Jarndyce* in *Bleak House*. He worked on lawsuits brought against construction firms for ignoring the Americans with Disabilities Act. And thanks to his time a decade earlier as a Peace Corps volunteer in Nepal, he landed the asylum case of a Nepalese author living in Maryland.

The two partners conducting Handley's review couldn't have been farther away from Hausfeld's side of the practice and wondered aloud if Handley had spread himself too thin, especially regarding the time he spent with Fryszman. "Wow, you're really involved in a lot of things here," one of the partners told Handley. "We think it might be better for you to focus a bit more on some of the core practice areas." The partners were not scolding, but they were firm. Perhaps the hardest part for Handley was this: his bosses were right. He worked at a pace that would have crushed many other lawyers, young or old, billing close to 2,400 hours for a single year. That added up to working full-time, without a vacation or a single day off, for an entire calendar year—and then squeezing in an extra two months of full-time work after hours. And that was just the time he tracked formally. He was less assiduous about clocking the time he spent on the cases he cared about most, such as Fryszman's. The harder it became to devote time to the pro bono cases, owing to the demands of the securities practice, the more Handley worked after hours. Circles darkened the flesh beneath his eyes. His waistband tightened. His marriage frayed. The more difficult his marriage became, the more he stayed late in the office to devote himself to the work that gave him a sense of purpose. Rumors about Handley's personal life made the rounds at the firm. The two partners conducting his review may not have known what was going on at home, but they knew enough about his office presence to be concerned. "They thought I was going to get burned out," Handley would later recall.

Still, he gently pushed back during the annual review. "I'll certainly be more mindful about trying to make sure I'm focusing on important matters," he told the partners, "but these other cases are important to me. I want to continue to make them part of my practice here." The men assented but made it clear they would keep close track of him and see how things progressed in the months ahead. Handley kept his word, but rather than diminishing his work on the pro bono cases, he merely worked on them as quietly and with as little fanfare as possible. Lawyers whom Handley helped on these cases, especially Fryszman, aided and abetted his effort to keep a low profile, owing to their desperate need for assistance on cases that rarely paid for themselves, let alone paid the firm's partners. Sometimes, however, they simply couldn't avoid detection. On one such occasion, Toll, the managing partner, learned at the last minute that Handley would soon board a plane with Fryszman bound for Guantánamo Bay. The detainee cases and others like them made up Fryszman's full-time job, but not Handley's. Toll called Handley's cell phone, saying he felt blindsided by the associate's absence and demanded to know why he had not been informed. "I'm sorry that somehow you were kept out of the loop on this," Handley told his livid boss, "but that wasn't the intention." Handley argued that his presence at Gitmo would be vital to the firm's handling of the detainee cases, at least this time; the Pentagon had given security clearance to Handley before Fryszman, so Handley had met the detainees on an earlier trip without her. He needed to go with Fryszman on this occasion so he could show her the ropes and properly hand things off. At least, that's what he told Toll. In the end, Handley talked the firm's managing partner into letting him board the plane, but just barely. Things seemed to get harder after that.

Fryszman had read the *Tribune* investigation soon after its publication in October 2005 and asked to meet me. We arranged to meet for lunch at a café equidistant from our offices in

Downtown Washington, a few blocks east of the White House. Her résumé was impressive. She worked on lawsuits targeting multinational corporations and others for alleged human rights abuses abroad. She had been a lead lawyer in a suit against the Japanese government on behalf of the estimated two hundred thousand women from Korea, China, and other Asian nations who were forced into sexual slavery for Japanese soldiers during World War II. She had taken on the lead litigation role in a case against ExxonMobil, alleging the company's complicity in the Indonesian military's torture and murder of civilians living near the company's natural gas fields in Aceh Province. She represented victims of the 9/11 attacks and the detainees held at Guantánamo Bay whom she had gone to see with Handley.

For someone who grew up without a passion to practice the law, Fryszman had taken to it with a dedication that, to colleagues, sometimes seemed to border on the obsessive. She could, without hesitation, remember the citations for cases stemming from an obscure law enacted by Congress in 1789 but just as often forget personal dates such as her wedding anniversary. Once, her husband took her on a romantic getaway to Paris for Valentine's Day, but she had forgotten it was Valentine's Day until it was announced on the flight. For court appearances or important meetings, she always wore the same outfit, a black pantsuit and a French-blue blouse. She could afford more clothes, but she didn't want to suffer the burden of choice on days when she had to appear in court. She wanted her head clear for the job at hand: the arguments she would need to muster and the strategies she would need for those she wanted to shoot down. Keeping only one nice outfit hanging in the closet seemed to her to make that easier.

At lunch, she sat across from me on a bar stool at a high

table in a quiet corner by a window, speaking at times like a tommy gun. She rattled off acronyms, citations for laws, and cases stemming from those laws that she saw as potentially triggered by my investigation, putting it all into the context of other cases the firm had handled. I could not keep up with the dizzying speed of her words and her intimidating grasp of international law, including the relatively new federal statute on human trafficking. Fryszman said she wanted to see if my investigation could be pursued further, sensing that KBR Halliburton might be more than just the beneficiary of the system I had written about, and more directly involved in its operation than I had been able to learn before my deadline. She asked for contact details for the families of the twelve Nepalese men.

Generally, journalists do not share with lawyers unpublished materials stemming from their investigations, unless compelled to do so by subpoena. Even a slam-dunk legal case could grind on for years, if not a decade or more, especially against a company with the vast resources of KBR Halliburton. I made clear that I could not help beyond what had been published in the *Tribune*, but I did ask if she had ever heard of two related statutes, called the War Hazards Compensation Act and the Defense Base Act, which required contractors and their subcontractors in an American war zone to provide compensation to surviving family members of those killed. The theory behind the World War II–era law was simple: a contract worker risking life and limb to support the American war effort mattered as much as a full-time government employee doing the same, and should therefore get the same protection, regardless of his or her employment status or nationality. Any company doing business with the United States, including the lowliest subcontractor, needed to carry an insurance policy for the compensation program, but it could charge the costs of the premiums to taxpayers. In the case of payouts for what had been deemed deaths or injuries due to "war hazards," taxpayers made the insurance companies whole. The federal government administered and regulated the system through the Department of Labor.

The legal rights of the families of the twelve Nepali men to the compensation drove my frustration with efforts by those involved to cover up their connection to the tragedy as much as the exploitation of the system that had delivered them to their deaths. Based on even limited research, it seemed clear that contractors and subcontractors in Iraq widely ignored the compensation law, and the U.S. government did little, if anything, to enforce it. If she wanted to help them get the compensation demanded by law, I suggested that Fryszman get in touch with someone who could connect her to the families. The case seemed cut-and-dried and would make a material difference for the families I had met in Nepal. She said she would look into it.

A strong student of math and science, Handley had earned his undergraduate degree in engineering at Princeton. He believed that engineers could make a decent living while also having a positive impact on the world. That latter instinct drew Handley into the Peace Corps, a service that treasured engineers because they could deliver what people in the poorest corners of the world often needed most: the separation of uncontaminated drinking water from sewage through basic sanitation. Handley was sent to Nepal by lottery, knowing little about the country beyond the fact that it was home to the world's highest peak, Mount Everest. His main focus would be designing and building pit latrines to help spare rural villages from the deadly ravages of cholera and other diseases.

Nepal's people captured his heart almost instantly. Crushing poverty paradoxically bred boundless generosity. So many had so little, yet they would give it all to a stranger in need. The language also captured him, as even the illiterate seemed to speak in poetry. The spirits of many Nepalis he met seemed as grand as the landscape climbing into the heavens all around them. Yet near the end of his first year in the Peace Corps, Handley grew disillusioned. American volunteers in Nepal were required to work beside officials from the government's Ministry of Federal Affairs and Local Development. The chief development officer for Handley's district, a politician, told the young engineer that what the district needed most was a central amphitheater. The development officer wanted to spend vast sums, and all Handley's expertise, building a venue for his own political speeches. Meanwhile, local villages in the district were desperate for sanitation. Handley feigned ignorance of how to design or build an amphitheater, but it was difficult for him to do his job in the shadow of this self-serving official and others like him. Time after time, Handley saw how warped political priorities, outright corruption, and the absence of the rule of law held back the country far more than a dearth of technical expertise. While many government officials in Nepal only compounded their people's woes, Handley also saw how little benefit came from the private sector, in the form of major international corporations doing business there. Western breweries and soft drink manufacturers are often the biggest private employers in places such as Nepal, because they produce and bottle their products locally, through indigenous business partners. Yet their plants were surrounded by some of the most desperate shantytowns Handley had ever seen. That's where their workers lived.

Midway through his Peace Corps service, Handley decided that a law degree would help him have a bigger impact on the world than he could have as an engineer, equipping him with the skills needed to tackle the kinds of injustices he saw in every city and village of Nepal. He spent his free time studying for the American law school entry exam and then piecing together applications by candlelight, or beneath the glare of a battery-powered lamp. Once his Peace Corps service ended, he enrolled in the law school at the University of Texas.

A decade later, Handley's Peace Corps experience brought Fryszman to his office with a proposal that he assist her with the case of the twelve Nepalese men killed in Iraq. Who better to help her than a young, idealistic associate who worked tirelessly, knew Nepal, and just happened to speak its language? As 2006 dawned at Cohen Milstein, Handley believed the case had the potential to marry everything that had driven his life up to that moment: tackling exploitation, and more specifically the exploitation of a people he loved; wresting justice from faceless international companies thriving off political clout; and using the law to improve the lives of people who needed it the most. Everything he'd done in life seemed to coalesce around a single purpose. This one case could make sense of the strange and highly unlikely path he had followed to a job at a top Washington law firm. It would also bring him back to one of the happiest and most formative periods of his life. Handley had met his wife, a fellow Peace Corps volunteer, in Nepal. Maybe this case could somehow bring them closer together.

If it was a dream case for the young lawyer, it also came at the worst possible moment. His bosses had agreed to let him help Fryszman, but wary of the time he devoted to such non-core areas of their practice, they placed him under the cover of a no-fly zone. He would not be allowed to travel to Nepal. How on earth could he even begin without being able to go to Nepal to meet the families, or to Jordan, or anywhere else?

No one above Fryszman at the firm had heard of the obscure wartime compensation laws; nor was there a good understanding of what benefit the claims might yield for the partners. Yet Fryszman convinced Hausfeld to let her and Handley pursue compensation claims for the twelve families. The claims case could serve as a vehicle for investigating a potential federal human rights suit and could lead to evidence tying KBR Halliburton and its subcontractor more directly to specific abuses, or to specific knowledge of them. Because of his background and language skills, the claims case fell to Handley.

Handley stared down at a blank U.S. government form, called an LS-201. Across the top, it read, "Notice of Employee's Injury or Death." The form is supposed to be filed with the government within thirty days of a contract worker's death in a foreign combat zone. It was the first step to getting compensation. Yet, nearly two years after the murders of the twelve men, no one had filed it. On the face of it, the form looked simple: nineteen questions for each man, covering a single page. Instructions came on an attached sheet. Yet given the nature of the case, the obfuscation following the men's deaths, and the fact that an entire world separated Handley from the people he represented, even the simplest questions seemed challenging. "Name of supervisor at time of injury"? Which KBR Halliburton boss could that possibly be, and how on earth would he find out? Some basic facts, including even the full legal names, dates of birth, and addresses of the dead, were unknown to Handley. A separate form called the LS-262, to claim the mandatory death benefits, demanded detailed information about the dependents of each murdered man, including the level of dependency for parents of the dead men who had left behind no widows or children, and sources and amounts of income. These were all simple enough questions for a civilian worker in Iraq whose family was in Texas, but daunting for someone from the shadows of the Himalayas whose loved one had been bought and sold into firms that would not acknowledge their connections to him—and for Handley, the answers, each multiplied by twelve, lay scattered across one of the most remote and disconnected places left on earth.

These realities made a mockery of an identical mandatory statement appearing at the bottom of the instruction sheets for both U.S. government forms, the kind that seems designed by federal agencies to show Congress that they are not overburdening taxpayers with too much red tape. "We estimate that it will take an average of 15 minutes to complete this collection of information," it read. For all twelve men, that was supposed to add up to just six hours of work.

Handley made a list containing twenty-six items needed from each of the twelve families. Knowing Nepal as well as he did, he understood it could take weeks, even months, to physically track down everyone, assuming it could be done at all without his own presence on the ground and without the serious full-time help of a small staff. Handley's only plan was to connect by phone with my contact in Nepal. If the two agreed on a plan together, that man could follow my trail back to the families and serve as a sort of bridge across the world for Handley.

Even assuming Handley could get everything he needed by working remotely, other basic challenges inherent in the case might prove more significant, if not fatal. Because the men had been kidnapped en route to the base where they were supposed to work, the U.S. military might not have even a single piece of paper establishing their employment in the KBR Halliburton chain—not a sign-in sheet from the base, not a duty roster, not a contract, not a witness in the form of a supervisor or coworker. And at each link in the chain, from agents in Nepal up to and including KBR Halliburton, people had dissembled, obfuscated, or refused to cooperate. It took pieces of evidence from all of them, and beyond, to create a mosaic of what had happened. If Handley could not muster proof beyond stories published in the *Tribune*, the compensation claims might quickly crumble upon a challenge. He also faced a more bracing reality: if the logistical obstacles to launching compensation cases in which the law clearly demanded that the men's families be paid were this great, what would it look like if the firm tried to take on KBR Halliburton and an army of well-paid defense lawyers in a complex human rights case?

Assisting Handley was Molly McOwen, a young woman with degrees from Harvard and Columbia. McOwen easily could have made her way up the lucrative partnership ladder at almost any firm in the nation. Instead, she chose a relatively low-paying job in a human rights fellowship at Cohen Milstein, one the firm had established to give Fryszman full-time help from a lawyer without having to give McOwen the benefits of a fully paid associate. The salary barely covered the costs for a recent graduate to live in Washington and muster student loan payments, and there was no chance to get on even the bottom rung of Cohen Milstein's ladder. Yet, for McOwen, the job represented the opportunity of a lifetime. How many lawyers in America get to focus full-time on international human rights, and do so right out of law school?

Before the end of 2005, Handley and McOwen connected with Ganesh Gurung, the Nepalese academic and expert on foreign migration whose staff had helped me crisscross the country.

Early one morning, as he waited by the phone in the ground-floor office of his Kathmandu home for a phone call from an American lawyer whom he had never met, Gurung braced for an oncoming wave of culture shock. The traditional Nepalese greeting is one word, *Namaste*. Its translation, "I bow to your spirit," is familiar the world over, thanks to the modern ubiquity of yoga studios, but it carries a deeper meaning in Nepal. Despite the rigidity of the caste system, an educated or wealthy Nepali can literally bow to the spirit of the poorest farmer he meets, and vice versa. Mutual respect often is the default. In such a culture, dealing with Westerners, especially Americans, can be a jarring experience. The American straight-to-business, command-driven style can seem coarse to even the most Westernized Nepali. This can be made worse by the inherently transactional nature of business, and by the dynamics of someone from a very wealthy country speaking to someone from a very poor one. However, educated in the United States, Gurung understood the cultural divide thanks to years of dealing with Americans and Europeans.

So, when Handley called to outline his purpose and the complexities and difficulties of the task before them, Gurung was guarded. Yet Handley deferred to Gurung on how best to proceed, asking questions and then listening thoughtfully to all Gurung's replies. Once Gurung agreed to help, Handley also made it clear that he would accommodate Gurung's schedule as they dealt with each other across the nearly eleven-hour time zone divide even if it meant rising in the middle of the night. It was the first time a Westerner, let alone an American, had ever shown Gurung such deference. It would have been natural, and even expected, for Handley to speak some Nepalese on the call, in an effort to forge a closer bond. He not only avoided doing this but also never even mentioned that he had lived in Nepal as a Peace Corps volunteer, or his familiarity with the country. In short, Handley made Gurung feel every bit in charge of what needed to be done on his end. Gurung's worst fears immediately melted.

Gurung set about relocating and recontacting the families of the twelve dead men. Some who had moved to Kathmandu in the wake of the massacre had run out of the small amount of money they had been given from the onetime charitable payment made by their own government. Hunger had driven some of these families back to their farms in the rural expanses of Nepal. Few had phones, so to reach those beyond Kathmandu, Gurung drew a bull's-eye on a map around villages where he thought they resided, and then made concentric circles reaching out to the nearest regional government offices. He recruited officials at these offices to help hunt the families down. When this method failed, he would send a member of his own staff to a family via cross-country expedition—by plane, then by bus, then on foot.

Kamala and the other families scattered across Nepal had no way of knowing what had happened in the United States in the many months since I had ever so briefly appeared to interview them about their dead sons, brothers, and husbands. So, when Gurung tracked them down, many were uncertain about him and his claims. The farmers had never heard of Gurung. Most still had no idea what had really happened to their loved ones, or what role the system that had delivered them to their deaths played for the United States and its prosecution of the Iraq War. The idea that they were entitled to money from the U.S. government had never occurred to them.

In a country still divided by its own civil war, their other relatives, friends, or local elders sowed doubts about Gurung's intentions. Who was this bigwig from Kathmandu asking them to cross the country and come to his office, bearing copies of birth and marriage certificates, passports, citizenship cards, and every other piece of paper they had? Could they really believe his claim that he worked with American lawyers who wanted to help them? Some cautioned that Gurung was out to manipulate the dead for his own ends. Complicating matters further were the basic questions Handley needed answered on the forms, some of which violated cultural taboos in Nepal. Requests for seemingly intimate information fueled distrust.

Gurung found himself in the confounding position of having to convince and reassure the people he was trying so hard to help that he meant them no harm. "There is nothing lost in simply filing these papers, but if you don't file, then it's finished," he would tell them over and over again. "If you don't file, what hope is there? If you withdraw, there is no chance." Because of the nature of what had happened to the men in Jordan and Iraq, because of the tragedy of their shared endings, Handley wanted to file all the cases together, believing there was strength in numbers. That meant that no case could proceed until Gurung had pulled all the families together and elicited all the necessary information. Foot-dragging by one family delayed them all.

In imploring some of the more reluctant families to move forward, Gurung found himself in the role of not just interpreter and assistant to Handley, but also social worker, therapist, priest, chief persuader, and family counselor. In desperation, he would remind them that they all needed to be together in order for any one of them to stand a chance.

Kamala never seemed to doubt Gurung's intentions. Her ashram was not far away from his offices, and she visited several times, carefully listening to his take on what Handley was trying to do, and how she might benefit. She questioned him about the process, but always with the aim of figuring out what else she could do to help. Gurung seemed to be wise and kind, almost avuncular, so she trusted him. On September 10, 2006, less than two weeks after the second anniversary of Jeet's murder, she sat down in Gurung's office and signed Handley's forms.

Weeks turned to months as the forms for the families made their way back and forth across the world by courier service, and between Gurung's office and Handley's. They were accompanied by supporting documents and their legally certified translations. As 2006 came to a close, the forms were all signed and delivered to Washington. Handley inspected them immediately, checking that everything was in order. Reaching the form for Ramesh Khadka, Handley noted that the date of birth listed for him meant Khadka was nineteen on the day of his murder. At the bottom of the claim form, where signatures were commanded from his parents, two lines instead contained their thumbprints. They were pressed onto the U.S. govern-

ment form so close to one another that they had overlapped
at the edges. Flipping through the rest of the forms, Handley
would see that paperwork for three other families also carried
the dark swirls, loops, and arches left by ink-stained fingers. He
had never before represented clients unable to sign their own
names.

John R. Miller, the U.S. ambassador-at-large in charge of the
State Department's recently created Office to Monitor and
Combat Trafficking in Persons, had also noticed the *Tribune*
series and wanted to investigate. Miller and his staff had already been placing key Iraq War allies on the top tier of the
U.S. watch list for human trafficking, without knowing that
the Pentagon relied so heavily on those same nations to channel
tens of thousands of workers into Iraq. He had never imagined
that his post would require him to investigate his own government, and he felt genuine outrage, even as he was unsure
whether he had the statutory authority to do anything about
it. His remit was to hold foreign governments accountable, not
the U.S. government. And the only real power flowing from
his office was the ability to publicly name and shame those
governments through the annual watch list. Even this power
could be greatly diluted. Just weeks before the *Tribune* stories
appeared, President Bush had waived the rules for the White
House's Iraq War allies on Miller's list, sparing them from potential sanctions and citing "national security" concerns in the
cases of Kuwait and Saudi Arabia.

Still, as Handley and Gurung worked across the world in
2006 to file compensation claims for the families, Miller had
pulled whatever levers he could in Washington. Although the

issue of human trafficking had first come onto the radar of the U.S. government largely through the work of conservative Christian groups fighting sex trafficking, what was happening in Iraq had opened Miller's eyes, and those of many other American leaders, to the far wider world of forced and coerced labor. The United Nations' International Labour Organization would estimate that 68 percent of the twenty-one million people trafficked worldwide were trapped in situations of forced or coerced labor.

As an economist, Miller knew that market forces drove human trafficking as much as depravity and indifference, and he could see the extraordinary demand created by the privatization of war. He wanted to force the Washington bureaucracy into action, not just on what had happened to the twelve men, but also on the system behind the invisible army running the war effort. Miller also had been a four-term Republican member of the House, so he understood the pressure Congress could bring to bear on the bureaucracy. He quietly worked with allies in the GOP-controlled House to push the Pentagon for an investigation. One of those whom Miller leaned on was Representative Christopher H. Smith. The New Jersey Republican had sponsored legislation that became the cornerstone of the U.S. human trafficking law that President Bill Clinton signed in October 2000, less than four years before the twelve Nepali men were executed. Smith's law had also created Miller's job.

Smith was the vice chairman of the House International Relations Committee, and he chaired a subcommittee with oversight for human rights. It did not, however, have oversight of the Pentagon. Smith therefore needed to team up with the House Armed Services Committee, where the appetite for taking on contractors wasn't always so strong. Together, Miller and Smith nudged the bureaucracy. Ultimately, however, it would move only so far. The two men had pressed the Bush administration's undersecretary of defense for an investigation. He, in turn, got the Defense Department's inspector general to launch an inquiry in conjunction with the inspectors general of the armed services in Iraq.

The resulting memorandum verified the *Tribune* investigation but also reached some other startling conclusions, including that KBR Halliburton was under no obligation to make sure the companies supplying its massive force of foreign workers in Iraq complied with U.S. antitrafficking laws inside the war zone or en route. "To date, there are no clauses in contracts between [the U.S. government and] KBR Halliburton that make them responsible for labor fraudulently procured by independent contractors or subcontractors," it read. Because there were no such accountability clauses in the contracts, and because regulations requiring such clauses still had not been finalized by the federal government, the memorandum concluded that "there are no potential criminal violations to be investigated or DoD contracts that can be legally terminated." The official who wrote the memorandum presumed that the contract language had greater force of law than the laws against human trafficking themselves.

He appeared to go even further in offering cover to KBR Halliburton. "While it would appear that some foreign based companies are using false pretenses to provide laborers to KBR Halliburton subcontractors in Iraq, we must note that none of the allegations in the *Chicago Tribune* articles are against U.S. persons or U.S. contractors."

General George Casey, the U.S. commander in Iraq, had determined that widespread passport seizures by contractors and subcontractors clearly violated U.S. laws against human trafficking. He issued orders to everyone under his command demanding that all workers' passports promptly be returned. His orders contained a host of other reforms, including banning illegal or excessive fees for workers. It was unclear how any of these orders, beyond passport returns, might be enforced. Still, the actions amounted to enough for Smith to get a hearing on the issue before Congress, but since his human rights subcommittee lacked jurisdiction over Pentagon contractors, he could do so only by persuading the Armed Services Committee to hold a joint hearing. Lawmakers and witnesses in attendance read statements condemning the practices, to varying degrees. An air force colonel overseeing efforts to implement Casey's orders said that getting contractors to return passports was harder than the proverbial pulling of teeth. No one from KBR Halliburton was forced to testify.

Still, the inspector general's memorandum leaked out, along with Casey's orders and other records. The memorandum specifically corroborated accounts that the twelve men had been working for the KBR Halliburton contractor Daoud and Partners. In so doing, it offered Handley evidence beyond the *Tribune*, from no less than the Pentagon's investigative arm, if anyone were to challenge the compensation claims.

One family simply wouldn't cooperate with Gurung. As for the rest, only siblings survived two of the murdered men, and were not entitled to compensation under U.S. law, even though they had lived together as a family unit, had paid for their brothers' jobs, and were dependent upon them for survival. When, in 2007, Handley sent the claims and supporting documents to the New York offices of an obscure division of the U.S. Department of Labor with responsibility for running the compensation program, the twelve cases had, by law, been whittled down to just nine.

Almost immediately, the insurance company for Daoud and Partners declared the claims invalid and said it would not pay them. It told the government that the contractor had no record of ever employing any of the Nepalese men and brought in Roger Levy, a California-based lawyer, to fight the claims. Nearing retirement, Levy had literally written the book on the obscure wartime compensation law, a legal *textbook*, and his decades of specialty practice made him one of the foremost experts in the nation on such cases.

The Department of Labor office overseeing the program also had responsibility for federal workers' compensation programs and cases. Its chief was a curmudgeonly New Yorker named Richard Robilotti. In his fourth decade on the job, he had dealt with countless battles between employers and insurance companies on one side and workers or their families on the other. He'd also dealt with legions of lawyers. To Handley, it didn't seem that Robilotti liked any of them. He would call Handley and leave terse, gruff voice mail messages, sometimes half barking, almost always commanding some action, such as "Call me!"

Ambassador Miller's office at the State Department worked behind the scenes to encourage compensation for the families. Handley got his hands on the Pentagon memos, but he had no clue from his dealings with Robilotti what position the U.S. Department of Labor would take. A key part of Robilotti's job was to try to press the two sides into resolving cases without having to go to court. He had little power, but his long experience gave him the gravitas to wield considerable influence, such as when he advised an insurance company lawyer to pay a claim because otherwise he would get his ass handed to him by a judge, or when he told a worker's lawyer to drop a claim for the same reason. His New Yorker's forcefulness didn't hurt, either.

Handley was nervous about his first conference call with Robilotti and Roger Levy, but his anxiety melted quickly when Robilotti lit into Levy over the long-distance line. "How on earth can you be objecting to these claims?" the gruff New Yorker declared. The more Robilotti pressed Levy, the more Levy pressed back. The defense lawyer said that Daoud had never employed the Nepalese men. Not only that, but the company never even did the kind of military support services claimed in the case. Daoud wasn't even in the business. Robilotti did not relent, but Levy had far too much experience to get riled. He knew he simply had to hold his ground. If Handley and the families wanted compensation, they would have to take their case to a judge. Levy just had to keep saying no.

Insurance companies make their money in two ways: by taking in more cash from the premiums paid by policyholders than they dole out in claims, and by earning cash off those premium payments through investments. Even if it ultimately has to pay a claim, an insurance company has an incentive to hold on to the money for as long as it can, because holding money buys more time for the company to earn interest on its investments. This is why insurance companies find ways to delay paying claims even when their policyholders are clamoring for payment, as in the case of someone who has had a car accident. But in the case of foreign workers for wartime contractors, the policyholders were the contractors, not the workers or the survivors meant to receive the payments. And the contractors were hardly clamoring for the insurance companies to pay claims from foreign workers or survivors they were likely never to see or hear from again, especially in cases where the contractors were trying to avoid any paper trail legally connecting them to the workers. This reality created that almost unprecedented moment in the history of the insurance business, when the interests of the policyholder and the interests of the insurance company serendipitously aligned to create an incentive for failing to pay claims.

On July 27, 2007, Handley filed a motion demanding a hearing before an administrative judge for the families. This was the initiation of the inevitable court case born of the insurance company's resistance, and it meant that Handley could formally seek "discovery" (private, internal records) from Daoud and its insurance carrier. Just after the third anniversary of the twelve men's deaths, Handley demanded reams of evidence from the companies, related not just to the murdered men, but also to Daoud's work for KBR Halliburton in Iraq. In reply, Levy sent Handley just one document, and he waited until the day of the deadline two months later. It was a copy of the insurance policy Daoud had taken out on April 14, 2004, in order to comply with the wartime compensation law. The policy specifically listed coverage for "Third Country Nationals" working at U.S. military bases in Iraq. This meant that the first and most basic set of denials—that Daoud simply could not have had anything to do with these murdered men or this case, that Daoud wasn't even in this line of business—had been pierced. Yet so much effort, spanning a year and reaching across the world, had gone into just getting the case to the point where Handley could prove the most basic facts about

Daoud: that it worked for KBR Halliburton in Iraq and employed men *like* the twelve Nepalis, but not necessarily that it employed *those* twelve Nepalis. Levy and the company continued to dispute Daoud's connection to the twelve. "Daoud steadfastly denies that any employer-employee relationship or prospective employer-employee relationship existed," Levy said in a motion filed after he handed over the insurance policy. The hardest thing to grasp was this: Any payouts ultimately were unlikely to cost the companies involved or the insurer a dime. In fact, they could even yield a healthy profit. Because the men had died as a result of a "war hazard," the insurance company's payout and its costs were 100 percent reimbursable under the War Hazards Compensation Act. The U.S. government, by law, would also give a 15 percent bonus to the insurance company after it paid the claims, along with reimbursing all its reasonable costs, including Levy's fees.

Still, Levy fought on. The insurance company remained steadfast in its refusal to pay. Handley prepared for court.

10

2 0 0 7
Washington, DC

Establishing the truth is one thing. Satisfying the rules of evidence in a court, especially against a well-funded adversary, is another matter entirely. Matthew Handley grew keenly aware of this as he faced the intransigence of KBR Halliburton's Iraq contractor and that of its insurance company. The State Department was on his side. The Defense Department's inspector general was on his side, at least on paper. The truth and the law were on his side. But a newspaper investigation and a corroborating three-page document from the Defense Department would not be enough to win the day before a judge, and two years of effort might yield nothing for Kamala and the other families, now more than three years after the deaths of their husbands, sons, and brothers. The case was strong but still circumstantial. Handley and Ganesh Gurung were desparate to find any other men who had made it to the Al Asad Air Base via Jordan, had worked for the KBR Halliburton contractor, and had returned to the Himalayan kingdom. One living, breathing witness could be enough to bring home the overwhelming nature of the circumstantial evidence for anyone willing to consider it. But finding a returnee in Nepal more than three years after the massacre seemed beyond even the wildest needle-in-a-haystack fantasy, given the challenges of just finding the families. Gurung might have been a brilliant academic, but he wasn't much of a detective, and Handley remained grounded in Washington, unable to travel to Nepal, Jordan, or Iraq for the case, as he continued to face the daily demands of his firm's core work on shareholder class-action litigation.

Gurung put out feelers all over the nation. His best chance, the only real one he had, was to locate someone from his own ethnic group in the area close to where he had grown up, in the hills near the city of Pokhara. There he had the deepest connections and the most respect, and it's also where the tradition of working overseas had first taken root in Nepal, thanks to the region's history of filling the ranks of the elite Gurkha Brigade for the British. Gurung called and visited influential people across the region, imploring them to see if anyone could locate the needle in the haystack. It was a long shot, but it was the best idea he could come up with.

One day in late 2007, after more than a year of searching, Gurung got a call from a trusted friend in Pokhara. He had located someone who had been driven into Iraq on the Amman-to-Baghdad highway in the same convoy as the twelve, but in one of the vehicles that made it through to the base unmolested that day. Daoud had employed the man at Al Asad. Gurung's friend suggested that the former Daoud worker, whose name was Buddi Gurung (no relation), wasn't the most reliable Nepali he had ever met, given the man's apparent penchant for alcohol, but he said he believed the story. He also confirmed the source's details with others who had contemporaneous knowledge.

With the deadline for filing court papers fast approaching, Ganesh Gurung phoned Handley to share the exciting news. Handley told Gurung that even a sworn statement from the former Daoud worker might not prove sufficiently credible, and he needed a copy of the worker's Daoud contract or some other documentary evidence clearly corroborating his story. A contract or pay stub also would help Handley overcome one other significant procedural challenge in the case. By law, compensation for the families was to be based on how much the men were supposed to be paid under Daoud's contract with KBR Halliburton, and for this, Handley didn't have a shred of evidence. Handley feared there would be no compensation, and his attempts to wrench loose pertinent documents via discovery in the case had yielded only a copy of the insurance policy.

In February 2008, Handley filed a motion with an administrative judge demanding compensation for all nine families and arguing that the evidence was so strong that the judge should order the insurance company to pay the claims without even holding a hearing. Exhibit A was the *Tribune* investigation. Exhibit B was the inspector general's report. There were twenty-one exhibits in all, and Handley attached a declaration to the court attesting to his own phone conversation with Buddi Gurung. "Counsel for claimants discovered another Nepali citizen who had been employed in Iraq at the same time as claimants, had traveled to Iraq in the same caravan as claimants, and has since returned to Nepal," Handley wrote. In the declaration, he said, "I spoke to Mr. Buddi Gurung via telephone . . . Mr. Gurung said that the [twelve] were also with him in Amman at that time and that he traveled in the same caravan from Jordan to Iraq . . . Mr. Gurung told me that he was not in the vehicle in which [the twelve men] rode and which was ultimately stopped by insurgents." Handley also gave the judge a copy of

Buddi Gurung's contract with Daoud at Al Asad, showing he was paid about $112 per week, or just under $16 a day, which included the always demanded overtime. Ganesh Gurung gave a statement attesting to and detailing the dependency of each surviving relative on each murdered man prior to his death. In the case of Kamala and the other widows, there was nothing to prove, beyond the fact that they had been married to the murdered men and had had children with them. For those who left behind only parents, however, the sociologist detailed the integral role each son had played in providing for their security.

Two weeks later, Roger Levy finally conceded that the Nepalese men had in fact worked for Daoud when they were driven into Iraq, kidnapped, and executed. Buddi Gurung and his contract meant that reality could no longer be denied and had elicited a remarkable concession coming from the attorney formally representing the contractor. Then Levy shifted his ground again, in an effort to deny most of, but not all, the claims. While he conceded that Kamala and the other two widows should be paid, he argued that Handley had not provided enough evidence to show that the six sets of surviving parents had been sufficiently dependent upon their sons to warrant compensation, referring instead to their "alleged dependency." The sworn statement of Ganesh Gurung, a sociologist and expert in foreign migration who had interviewed each of the families about their circumstances, didn't cut it, Levy said. "Interestingly, in the Hindu religion, one of the best known and most-worshipped deities is also named 'Ganesh,'" Levy wrote to the judge. "The deity 'Ganesh' is known to and worshipped by Hindus as the 'Remover of Obstacles.' The 'Ganesh' in this case, unlike the deity who bears his name, has not removed all obstacles impeding claimants."

Levy flew to New York and checked into Le Parker Meridien hotel, in the heart of Midtown Manhattan. He had asked Handley to meet him there on the morning of March 20, 2008, insisting on a telephone deposition of Ganesh Gurung from his hotel. Handley wasn't sure why this couldn't have been arranged on a conference call from their offices, but he flew to New York anyway and met Levy in person for the first time. A court reporter was in the hotel room, too, with her stenography machine. Handley sat awkwardly on a swivel chair next to Levy's bed in the somewhat cramped quarters, with the telephone, on speaker mode, on a side table next to them. They called Ganesh Gurung at about 10:15 a.m., 8:00 p.m. in Kathmandu, and Gurung answered in the ground-floor office of his home. The power was out at his home in Kathmandu, as usual, so Gurung sat at his desk and gave his deposition by candlelight. One of the six families Levy was fighting was that of Bishnu Hari Thapa, the eighteen-year-old who had left the clipped, haunting message "I am done for" just before he was driven into Iraq, and whose mother had survived in their village as a stonecutter. In his questioning, Levy asked for a general understanding of the socioeconomic structure of farm life in rural Nepal. Gurung did his best to convey intellectually what Bishnu Hari's mother had so viscerally conveyed to me three years earlier: why she had prayed so hard to have a son, why she had so often heard the blessing "May you be the mother of a hundred sons," and then why she had been so grateful after he was born. "We do not have any kind of insurance system in Nepal," Gurung said through the speakerphone. "That is why we prefer to have many sons, which are taken as a kind of social security in parents' old age. Sons are very important in Nepalese society because they are the insurance, they are the social security." Levy spent about forty minutes questioning Gurung on a call that likely cost thousands of dollars from a hotel. At the end, Levy made it clear to Handley that he remained unconvinced, which infuriated and exasperated the young lawyer, but Handley kept cool as he walked out of Levy's room.

• • •

About one month before the first anniversary of Kamala's entry into the ashram, the head seamstress and other members of the staff started noticing a change across the campus, one that arrived as reliably each year as the onset of the monsoons. Women in the senior class began crying openly as they faced the reality that their time behind the walls was coming to an end and they would soon have to return to the outside world. Kamala and others in her class who had grown especially close to the seniors also found themselves struggling. The singing and dancing parties they held almost every Friday night inside their dorms got a little louder, a little more joyous, and went on a little later. They performed a traditional style of Nepali folk music known as *dohori*, in which two sides engage in a sort of Bollywood-style call-and-response battle. One side sings a question, often about love, and the other must sing back a witty reply, not too dissimilar from the way Kamala sang with her sisters when they worked in the hills. In the world outside the ashram, the opposing forces in a *dohori* battle are almost always divided by gender, so some of the women had to play male roles, which they relished with flashes of comedic oafishness.

Graduation day for the seniors came, and the women, dressed in their identical blue saris, stood in unbroken lines across the courtyard where the giant crows bowed the tree branches near the statue of the ashram's founder. Kamala cried silently with pride and sadness as she listened to reminiscences and speeches filled with hope and watched each woman receive her diploma and then pose for a photo behind her sewing machine. By nightfall, an unfamiliar quiet fell over the campus.

In the days ahead, Maya began to notice that Kamala had turned a corner, not through some significant moment of self-awareness shared over the long-distance line, but simply through the stories of daily life her younger sister relayed during monthly phone calls to the shop by the side of the road in Taksar. In the days before the peaches or apples ripened fully on the campus trees, Kamala would sneak into the yard, survey the ground for perfect stones, and whip them at high-hanging fruit, knocking them to the earth so she and Kritika could snack. She told Maya how wayward stones occasionally ricocheted near the guard-house, which was manned by the campus warden, who would burst out and chase after her, but she either got away or feigned remorse, promising she would never do it again. She also told Maya of the other small rebellions she led against some of the ashram's rules, such as how she had stopped going to yoga in the mornings so she could spend more time with Kritika, and even sleep late with her; or how she would occasionally rally the other women into demanding extra free time or larger rations at meals; or how she would sneak out of her dorm in the night darkness and onto the balcony of the main classroom building to gaze at the stars above the emptiness of the airport at the edge of town. Maya realized that her sister was regaining the spirit of her childhood, a time when she could never resist the challenge to scamper up the tallest tree on the horseshoe ridge.

As the new class of women moved into the ashram to re-place the graduates, Kamala recognized the shock and fear and mourning she saw on many of their faces, and she found herself offering the occasional unobtrusive word of encouragement. When they gathered at night on the straw mats spread across the plaster floor to speak of the past, Kamala found herself slipping deeper into the role of a senior woman, sharing openly her feelings on the sudden isolation she had felt in the home of a family that had previously embraced her so warmly. Like their predecessors, every woman in the new class knew the story of the twelve men, so there must have been some extra sense of connection as they heard that the pain behind a moment that had bound the nation together in grief and anger was no different from their own.

Not everyone in the ashram, however, appreciated that Kamala's struggle had been as painful as her own, if not more so, given how difficult it was for Kamala's grief to find anonymity within the infamy of her husband's murder. Over their time together on the campus, Kamala and Heera, the other widow from the village on the ledge, had grown apart. Whenever the two women began to discuss anxieties about the future, or the pain of their pasts, Heera would tell Kamala that she was more privileged than the other women, that she was not like them. She told Kamala that she had nothing to worry about, thanks to the charitable money Jeet's family had received in the wake of the nationwide riots, money that largely had been locked away from Kamala by her in-laws. As she regained her confidence, Kamala had at first pushed back gently in these moments, but Heera persisted, out of resentment perhaps or from a sincere belief that Kamala had no cause for pain or worry. Yet, as the women moved deeper into their second year at the ashram, Kamala was increasingly upset by Heera's dismissal of her grief. One day, after a particularly stinging refrain from Heera, a shouting match erupted between the two women, in front of the others. "Money means nothing to me!" Kamala said. "My husband's life cannot be compensated by any amount of money. I lost him and I lost my family, and no amount of money can fill the gap in my life! My in-laws got that money because my husband died in a place and at a time he wasn't supposed to!" But Heera would not relent. Unleashed, Kamala screamed through her tears: "Yes, the government and the people were with me after my husband died, but no one cared about your husband!" Kamala's words tore into Heera, and as the crying and shouting between the women escalated, a teacher from the ashram came rushing over to intervene. Kamala was instantly ashamed, but there was little she could say to undo the pain she'd caused Heera in that moment. The two women apologized, assuaged some of their hurt, and were civil to each other, but were never close again.

When the Dashain festival came around that year, the fourth since Jeet's death, Kamala and Kritika fought through the crowds at Kathmandu's transport terminus to squeeze into a hot, tightly packed bus bound for Gorkha. Little had changed in the village on the ledge. Kamala's in-laws remained distant, but she cared far less now. She watched with joy as Kritika took to the freedom of the hills, where there were no walls or streets, running barefoot with her young cousins up and down the dirt tracks worn into the hillsides. During the two-week holiday, Kamala made her way back around the length of the horseshoe, spending as much time as she could with her aunts and uncles and with Maya and her family. It was the first time Maya had seen Kamala since she left the ashram, and she marveled at how confident and contented her *nani* had become.

Kamala also had struck up a friendship with Surya Bhujel, a man she had known for years from another village in the horseshoe. He had started a business ferrying passengers in a microbus along dirt roads from the bottom of the horseshoe ridge to the nearest towns, where they could shop or catch buses to the bigger cities, and he sometimes took villagers all the way to Kathmandu. He always checked on Kamala whenever he heard she was en route back home, and made sure he was available to take her anywhere she needed or wanted to go. He was waiting when her bus from Kathmandu arrived, and drove her and Kritika toward the horseshoe ridge. Sometimes he would take them on his motorcycle after the point where the road was too narrow for his microbus to continue. In just the three years since she donned the white sari at the well below the village, Kamala had come far, but some inequities surrounding widowhood remained unshakable. Some villagers from all around the ridge, even friends of hers, could barely mask their disdain when they saw her and the driver in each other's company, and some members of Jeet's family openly chided her, saying that she should never think of remarrying. Kamala appreciated Bhujel's many unconditional kindnesses to her and Kritika, but she decided to maintain a certain distance from him, for everyone's sake.

Kamala had met the families of the other men murdered in Iraq a few times when they came together for special functions, but the families of the twelve stayed fairly guarded in such moments, mostly because their grief was on public display. Although Kamala was keen to get to know them, especially the other widows, such opportunities never seemed to avail themselves. At one event, held in a hotel ballroom, she was hounded by television reporters as she tried, for the first time, to share a private moment with the other women. The families also had gathered together a few times for meetings at the offices of Ganesh Gurung and the small think tank he ran on the north side of Kathmandu. They grew somewhat closer on these occasions, and sometimes even had the opportunity to share memories and speak of their pain, but most of these meetings were dominated by the administrative tasks at hand, as Gurung managed all Handley's long-distance paperwork demands. It had been some time since Kamala had heard from Gurung when, in mid-2008, she got a call commanding her to come to an emergency meeting at the Shangri-La Hotel along the busy Lazimpat Road in Kathmandu, just north of the Royal Palace. Gurung told her he could not speak over the phone about why they needed to meet, which worried Kamala.

Kamala walked past the glass doors leading to the lavish gardens of the Shangri-La Hotel, up the stairs from the ground floor, and into a small conference room with a sign that read "NIDS," the acronym for Ganesh Gurung's think tank, the Nepal Institute of Development Studies. Gurung was just inside the door, standing with a tall, smiling, slightly heavyset foreigner dressed in a business suit and tie, along with a woman by his side. They all greeted Kamala and the other family members as they came into the room. Gurung and the foreigners were beaming, which slightly unsettled Kamala, still unaware as to why she had been called to the hotel with the other family members. Gurung thanked everyone for coming and then turned to the foreigner. "This is Matt Handley," he said, and then also introduced Handley's wife. It was the first time the couple had returned to Nepal since finishing their service in the Peace Corps more than a decade earlier. Handley rose and started speaking Nepalese for the first time in ages, although he quickly realized he didn't know the Nepalese word for "lawyer," and had to ask for Gurung's help. Handley told the families that he had come to Kathmandu to inform them in person that they had won their compensation case. The judge, a former judge advocate for the U.S. Air Force, had found the evidence so compelling that he had rejected all the arguments from the attorney representing the contractor for KBR Halliburton and its insurance carrier without even holding a hearing. The judge had restated Handley's evidence as his formal findings in a dispassionate, matter-of-fact five-page order and had commanded the payments, which were calculated from the copy of Buddi Gurung's contract, in two final words: "So ordered."

There was a sense of relief and gratitude in the room, but nothing approaching joy. Soon it would be four years since the massacre, but the pain clearly remained raw. Gurung invited anyone who wanted to speak to stand and do so. The mothers of the dead rose first, without allowing their husbands to say anything and without seeking even so much as a nod of permission from them. Each woman looked at Handley and told him about the moment she had learned that her son had died, and the devastating impact that it had had on her life since that day. Bishnu Maya Thapa, the stonecutter who had prayed so hard for a son, said that she had wanted to die when she first learned of his murder, and that she would have done anything to have him by her side again. She looked at Handley from across the room and began weeping as she profusely thanked him, saying that whatever compensation she received would mean nothing compared with the fact that Handley, a foreign man whom she had never met, had shown such concern. "Just the fact that people so far away have worked so hard to keep my son's memory alive for these years, this is the greatest comfort to me," she said. It was the first time the families had been so open with one another about their experiences, because it was the first forum in which they had had any real opportunity to do so.

Handley and Gurung met with the families one on one to discuss privately how much each would receive, since the awards were all different. Each was built on the cold calculus of actuarial tables generated by the insurance industry, with such factors as the level of dependence for each family and each man's age at the time of his death among the most important. The awards ranged from a low end of about $60,000 to a high end of about $200,000, a sum that would have seemed trifling in the United States for the value of a young life lost, but almost unimaginable in Nepal, especially for farmers. Gurung found that, after their conversion into the local currency, the compensation amounts were so large that there was virtually no translation in Nepalese for their values, at least not one that any of the farmers had ever heard in their daily lives. Kamala received one of the largest awards because she was a widow and had a child.

Looking at Handley, she thought he had a kind face, but as the two men explained how much she would be paid, Kamala could not help but feel sad, as the money, and the entire occasion, served to remind her of what she had lost, and how that loss now was being calculated in cash. Still, she felt grateful that someone would be paying a price, any price, for what had happened to Jeet, grateful that his death had not been forgotten, and thankful that a prayer had been answered, one she had made during her worst days in Jeet's farmhouse following his death—that she would gain enough independence never to have to rely on anyone else again. For many of the families, Handley's surprise appearance that day seemed to be the answer to a prayer.

Handley also explained to the families that the compensation came from a program administered by the U.S. government, but having already worked with Gurung to corroborate the circumstances behind each man's journey to Iraq, he also told the families that they could pursue a broader civil action in the American courts for human trafficking against the companies involved—KBR Halliburton and its Jordanian contracting company Daoud and Partners. It would be up to them, he said. Each family, including the sets of siblings who did not receive the compensation payments, wanted to know more. The families understood that the second case would be about accountability and justice, as opposed to simply compensating them for a lifetime of lost income. If a case got filed, Handley told them, it would inevitably be a far more difficult journey than anything they had faced to date, and could be a source of pain in their lives for years to come, potentially delaying any hope they might have for closure.

Beyond questions of compensation and closure, the American lawyers believed a successful action for human trafficking against one of the largest U.S. government contractors in history, one with sway over tens of thousands of at-risk foreign migrant workers in a war zone, could deal a powerful blow against forced and coerced labor at a critical moment. It also could bring accountability for multinationals operating in a globalized age squarely into an American courtroom. At a minimum, Handley told the families, a lawsuit filed on their behalf would include a demand against KBR Halliburton that nothing like this would ever happen again for any of the men and women like their husbands, brothers, and sons in its supply chain. Each family wanted Handley to move forward. Kamala felt especially committed to the notion of accountability for what had happened to Jeet.

By the end of the day, Handley felt both exhausted and exhilarated, especially given the wrenching words of the mothers. He knew this was one of the most fulfilling moments of his life, certainly professionally, most likely personally, and that he had used the law to achieve justice in a concrete way for people who needed and deserved it more than any others he had ever met, and in a way few lawyers ever got a chance to accomplish. That night in the Shangri-La Hotel, his wife did not seem to share the depth of his feelings about the day, though. By now, their marriage had become irretrievably broken, and it was clear to both that returning to Nepal was not going to fix it, a hope Handley had, perhaps naively, subscribed to before they left for Kathmandu. Within a few days, she told Handley she was leaving him.

• • •

Handley returned to Washington, paradoxically buoyed by a sense of purpose and bowed by heartache. He and his wife had struggled for what seemed like ages, but the pain of their unfolding breakup gripped him just as he felt new meaning and urgency in his vocation. The hours he had poured into his work since joining the firm surely hadn't helped settle his marriage, and at a minimum, they helped blind him to its approaching end. Still, they at least represented something in his life that would give him hope and pride. His victory in the compensation case also vindicated his decision to carry a heavy load of pro bono matters despite the overwhelming demands of the firm's shareholder class-action practice, and despite the concerns of its partners. Cohen Milstein's top lawyers seemed pleased by the victory, and the firm garnered positive national publicity from being the first to fight and win such a high-profile battle emerging from the war, and in an area of the war's prosecution that few knew about. The U.S. government even reimbursed Cohen Milstein for its costs and fees, meaning that the partners got paid for what initially had been a pro bono venture.

Agnieszka Fryszman, the human rights lawyer at Cohen Milstein who had pulled Handley into the case, had been working in parallel on investigating and crafting the broader potential human rights lawsuit against KBR Halliburton and Daoud that Handley had discussed with Kamala and the other families in Nepal. Even without the victory in the compensation battle, there seemed to be momentum for broader action. By 2008, human trafficking in U.S. contracting operations in Iraq had become widely acknowledged at the highest levels of the executive and legislative branches of the U.S. government. At the Pentagon, General George Casey's order following the inspector general's investigation specifically cited violations of the U.S. antitrafficking laws and "evidence of illegal confiscation of worker passports by contractors/subcontractors; deceptive hiring practices and excessive recruiting fees, substandard worker living conditions at some sites, circumvention of Iraqi immigration procedures by contractors/subcontractors, and a lack of mandatory trafficking in persons training." Although the actions of the U.S. government were beyond its purview, the State Department took the unprecedented step of citing the abuses in its annual compendium on global human trafficking, doing so in a special section titled "Department of Defense (DOD) Responds to Labor Trafficking in Iraq." The report, published as a book and unveiled by Secretary of State Condoleezza Rice at a press conference, said that a "DOD investigation . . . identified a number of abuses, some of them considered widespread, committed by DOD contractors or subcontractors of third country national (TCN) workers in Iraq," and went on to specifically cite "low-skilled workers from Nepal." In March 2007, a subcommittee on human rights of the Senate Judiciary Committee followed the House of Representatives action of the prior year by holding its own hearing on the issue. The subcommittee chairman, Senator Richard Durbin of Illinois, declared for the record that the government needed to "find a way to make sure that our contractors, these companies that our tax dollars sustain, are held accountable, and understand the economics of their decision, if not the criminality of their decision."

This was precisely the sentiment Fryszman seized on as she argued behind the scenes at Cohen Milstein for a second case, one that she saw as continuing the firm's proud tradition of seeking accountability for multinationals. But if momentum and awareness were gathering behind the issue of human trafficking across official Washington, the appetite for such actions seemed to be diminishing inside the walls of Cohen Milstein. The firm's highest-profile partner, Fryszman's boss, Michael Hausfeld, had led the way nationwide on Holocaust litigation, dating back to his case against the Swiss banks. Despite the massive commitment of time and resources that went into the complex, research-intensive international effort, Hausfeld had fought it on a pro bono basis. On the second wave of Holocaust cases he brought, the firm's partners had earned a financial pittance compared with the 15 to 22 percent slice they, or any of their counterparts, usually received from class-action settlements. Even so, public controversy dogged the lawyers for their accepting anything at all, given the modest payments that were then passed on to survivors of the Nazi system of slave labor. Then Hausfeld suffered total defeat on the next front of his World War II–era litigation initiative, the case spearheaded by Fryszman against the Japanese government on behalf of women from Korea, China, and other Asian nations who had been forced into sexual slavery for Japanese soldiers during World War II. The case was dismissed, without a lifeline from appellate courts, before there was ever enough pressure for a settlement. Also, Hausfeld had opened, at significant expense, a London office of the firm, believing that the future of class-action litigation was in Europe, as Republicans in Congress and judges increasingly squeezed the space for them in American courtrooms. The expansion came as the financial crisis hit without warning, devastating the legal business around the world.

By mid-2008, Hausfeld had become increasingly isolated among partners in the firm, some of whom were quietly organizing a putsch. How much would they be willing to invest at that same moment in yet another international human rights and war slavery case—one headed by the less experienced Fryszman, along with Molly McOwen, the junior lawyer serving in a fellowship, with only occasional help from Handley, who was still just an associate in the shareholder class-action group? Deciding how much to spend out of pocket to develop a case like this is always a delicate matter at any firm.

On August 27, 2008, Cohen Milstein filed a federal lawsuit in the U.S. District Court in Los Angeles against Daoud and Partners and KBR, which Halliburton had spun off as a separate company during the height of its Iraq War controversies. In the corporate divorce, which was finalized in 2007, KBR had agreed to accept full freight for any liabilities resulting from its work in the war. The suit was filed on behalf of Kamala, Kritika, Jeet's mother, other family members of the twelve, and Buddi Gurung, the worker who had been in the same seventeen-vehicle convoy the day the men were kidnapped. The suit said:

> This is an action for damages brought by the family members of twelve men who were victims of trafficking in persons and one surviving laborer. All of the men were illicitly trafficked across international borders to provide menial labor at a United States military facility in Iraq for defendants, which are United States military contractors. The men were recruited in Nepal to work overseas. Most of them left their homes believing they were going to work at a luxury hotel in Amman, Jordan. Their families went deep into debt to arrange the jobs, which they hoped would lift them out of poverty. Instead, they were transported to work as laborers at a military base in Iraq. Twelve of the men were killed.

The body shops and labor brokers, from Kathmandu to Amman, were named as coconspirators but not defendants. As often happens in a case like this, the firm threw the book at KBR and its contractor, hoping that just one of the listed causes of action would stick. In the process, its forty-eight pages accused one or both of the defendants of violating a laundry list of statutes—everything from human trafficking and racketeering down to vanilla negligence due to the clear risk of sending

Jeet and the other men along the Highway Through Hell. The amount of damages sought was not specified. Yet the calculus of valuing a life in a case such as this, given the horrific way in which the men had died, the global public spectacle around their deaths, and the exploitation that had led them to their own massacre, could easily reach vast multiples beyond what had been paid in the compensation claims. Invoking the laws against racketeering also allowed for a potential tripling of any damages. In short, it was a fiercely aggressive lawsuit, and it could cost KBR significantly, in terms not just of damages but also perhaps of future business for the largest wartime contractor in U.S. history. From a business perspective at Cohen Milstein, it also was not inconceivable that the case could yield fees in the neighborhood of those from Hausfeld's Nazi slavery case, and all for a greatly reduced up-front investment by the partners.

Victory in the compensation case had been a vital prerequisite to filing the lawsuit, but it also took a toll. Even though Handley won the claims without a formal hearing, the insurance company's delays meant that the case had dragged on for so long that there was little time left within which to prepare and file their lawsuit. The federal court filing in Los Angeles came within hours of the five-year anniversary of the massacre and, depending on how it was calculated, either just before or just after the statute of limitations expired. That had put extraordinary pressure on Fryszman and her small team in the weeks leading up to the deadline. In the end, it meant that the lawsuit's accusations were powerful but its details slender.

Fryszman had largely crafted the suit, but in the end, it needed, and received, Hausfeld's authorization. The main signature page listed his name first, followed by those of Fryszman, Handley, and McOwen. Giving Hausfeld's name pride of place was critical to attracting attention in a case where publicity might make a difference, and to letting the defendants know they were in for a serious fight. Including Buddi Gurung in the lawsuit was a gamble. His path into the convoy that day was completely different from that of the other twelve. Yet, on balance, the potential downside seemed limited compared with the obvious benefits. His presence had a noticeable and profound effect in the compensation case, as he provided a direct, living connection to the mountain of circumstantial evidence regarding what had happened to the twelve dead men. It was possible, with the help of an investigator on the ground in Nepal, that they might find other former Iraq workers with closer links to the twelve, but as the clock on the filing deadline expired, Buddi Gurung was all they had.

Picking a jurisdiction in which to file a case like this was in some senses irrelevant, but one thing seemed certain: the relatively young federal statute on human trafficking was at the core of the lawsuit, and had never been tested like this, meaning that KBR would be likely to fight each and every significant battle up to a federal appeals court and perhaps to the U.S. Supreme Court. The court that would hear any appeal in California was likely to be the friendliest in the country for plaintiffs making international human rights claims, because some of the most progressive appellate judges in the nation sat on the bench of the U.S. Court of Appeals for the Ninth Circuit, based in San Francisco. Defense lawyers had a derisive name for the most blatant exercise of this strategy: forum or jurisdiction "shopping." While, strictly speaking, it is not allowed, it is often worth a roll of the dice, hence the filing at the federal courthouse in Los Angeles.

KBR's lawyers immediately pounced on the obvious opening,

demanding that the case be moved to Houston. "This case has been filed in the Central District of California for no apparent reason other than Plaintiffs' counsel's desire to forum shop," they told the judge in one of the first substantive filings of the case. "It has no link to the Central District of California or any other place in California. The operative facts occurred in Nepal, Jordan, Iraq, and perhaps Texas, but not anywhere within 1,500 miles of California . . . KBR is the only defendant that has been served. Its principal place of business is in Houston, Texas." Not only would bringing the lawsuit from the Pacific Coast to the Gulf Coast give KBR home court advantage, but the federal district courts in Texas, and the U.S. appeals court above them, are widely viewed to be among the most conservative and business-friendly federal benches in the country. Every appellate court also has a Supreme Court justice assigned to oversee it. The justice above Texas's Fifth Circuit was Antonin Scalia, one of the most probusiness, anti-international jurists in the modern history of the Supreme Court. In this regard, Texas and California were night and day for a case such as this one.

KBR's arguments to move the case were both obvious and strong, but its lawyers didn't take any chances. They heaped evidence into their motion and offered declarations about witnesses who might possibly have a connection to the twelve dead men in order to show that the case had absolutely no conceivable connection to California, but did to Texas. Perhaps no KBR Halliburton executive was more significant in this regard than a former manager stationed at the Al Asad Air Base named Robert Gerlach. He was "KBR's Procurement Manager in 2004, and handled KBR's subcontracts with Daoud & Partners," the company's lawyers wrote. That authority extended across Anbar Province. "Mr. Gerlach executed subcontract number GU84-VC-SB10005 with Daoud on behalf of Kellogg Brown & Root International, Inc. The subcontract with Daoud, as all other subcontracts with foreign entities, specifies it shall be construed and governed by the laws of the State of Texas." The declaration regarding Gerlach closed with these words about the man who had played the most critical and direct role for KBR in overseeing the firm that had brought the twelve into Iraq, along with countless other workers like them: "Mr. Gerlach is no longer with KBR and his last known address is in Corpus Christi, Texas."

The California federal judge assigned to the case, U.S. District Court judge R. Gary Klausner, a U.S. Army veteran and appointee of President George W. Bush, quickly agreed that it should be sent to Texas. By then, the partners at Cohen Milstein Hausfeld and Toll had voted their international human rights titan, Michael Hausfeld, out of the firm and its chairmanship. The move tore the firm apart, with several lawyers from the antitrust practice siding with Hausfeld, and heading out the door with him. He also took his biggest cases with him, but not the case of the twelve, which belonged to Fryszman, Handley, and Molly McOwen. With their law firm in chaos, the trio prepared to take their fight to Texas, to argue what would likely be one of the most significant motions in the case right at its very start, and facing one of the nation's most powerful companies on its home turf.

11

2 0 0 9

Houston

George and Herman Brown, the brothers who made their fortune building the world's largest construction company, may not have erected the cathedrals of steel and glass filling Houston's modern skyline, but their influence remains inescapable across the city's landscape, even long after their deaths. The Cohen Milstein lawyers checked into their hotel the day before the first hearing in their case against the Browns' legacy corporation, KBR, just a few blocks away from Houston's mammoth George R. Brown Convention Center, which covers ten city blocks Downtown. George Brown himself, albeit cast in bronze and perched atop a stone plinth, watches over conventioneers and the city from a park across the street. The trio's hotel was within walking distance from the site of their battle with KBR—the Bob Casey Federal Courthouse, named for a Texas congressmen who no doubt had benefited from the Brown brothers' political largesse, at least via Lyndon Johnson's hold over the Democratic Congressional Campaign Committee. The brothers' legacy also reached inside the courthouse, where the jurist assigned to the trio's case, U.S. District Court judge Ewing Werlein Jr., had listed dividend payments from Halliburton stock as his first and second sources of outside income on his annual federal ethics report. Werlein recused himself from the case, but his stock portfolio made clear how the fortunes of KBR and Halliburton remained knotted up with those of Houston and its ruling elite.

After dropping their bags and freshening up, Fryszman, Handley, and McOwen prepared to huddle for an overpriced work dinner inside their hotel, where they would discuss some last-minute refinements to their arguments for the next day. Virtually anyone who can cover the $350 filing fee is entitled to bring a federal lawsuit against anyone they want. That part was easy. Now came the real test. The judge would consider KBR's motion to dismiss the case, detailed in thick briefs and replies that had piled up from both sides over the previous months. As Fryszman had thrown the book at KBR in the forty-eight pages of allegations that made up the lawsuit, the motion to dismiss gave KBR its chance to throw it back.

During their dinner, the red lights on their BlackBerry phones started flashing, portending perhaps the greatest nightmare that can prey upon a lawyer on the eve of a major hearing. It was an e-mail from the chambers of U.S. District Court judge Keith P. Ellison advising them of questions the judge wanted addressed the next day—not just any questions, but "a list of questions that have concerned me" about the lawsuit, the judge would say. Not only was the e-mail highly unusual—judges usually ask their questions in the courtroom—but its queries seemed to attack the very heart of their case, a job most judges usually leave to lawyers from the opposing side. In it, Ellison raised questions about the procedural viability of the case, but focused most ominously on what lawyers call its "factual sufficiency." By alleging that KBR had run a racketeering enterprise involving human trafficking, Fryszman had invoked a law originally passed to dismember organized crime families across the United States. In so doing, she also had set an incredibly high bar for herself in Texas, where such allegations required meticulously detailed and specific facts even in the initial pleadings of a case. The standards in this regard are far more stringent in Texas than they are in California, and that's not necessarily unwarranted, as the law had become a favorite tool of plaintiffs' lawyers in the decades since its initial deployment against organized crime. Some of its popularity in this regard was rooted in the trebling of damages it allowed.

Ellison would also question whether their lawsuit, even on its face, alleged enough specific acts of coercion to amount to human trafficking. The judge focused on Buddi Gurung, the laborer who had been in the same convoy with the twelve but who had not suffered the same fate. The details in the lawsuit surrounding Gurung's alleged ordeal were thin compared with those of the twelve men who were murdered, and yet Gurung was alive to provide all the details that could be had. Had he at any point faced physical restraint or any other specific acts of coercion? Had he even requested to leave the U.S. military base in Iraq? If so, what had happened? And what was the true nature of the relationship, on the ground, between KBR and the contractor that had brought Gurung and the other twelve into Iraq? Did KBR have control over, or even knowledge of, what its contractor was up to? Answers to those questions could be vital to whether the case could survive under the stricter scrutiny of Texas. The judge had given the lawyers less than twenty-four hours to prepare their answers.

The trio divided up Ellison's questions. The hardest of them largely fell to Handley, as the answers lay with Buddi Gurung. He frantically started e-mailing and then calling Ganesh Gurung so that he might reach Buddi Gurung immediately to clarify important details. Handley prayed he could even get through to Kathmandu on the telephone, and then that Ganesh Gurung could reach their client in the rural village where he lived. The trio worked feverishly together, and then separately in their hotel rooms, well into the night, keeping in frequent touch on their room phones. Although still worried, an exhausted Handley finally fell asleep near midnight.

The streets and sidewalks across Downtown Houston are eerily empty, even at the height of the workday, as if the city were plagued by some postapocalyptic nightmare. The real reason is that almost everyone who lives there uses a network of subterranean walkways twenty feet below the streets, a series of climate-controlled tunnels linking nearly one hundred city blocks in cool, dry comfort. On Thursday, October 8, 2009, near the height of hurricane season in the Gulf of Mexico, Handley, a native Texan, led his two colleagues on a trek through the tunnels from their hotel to the Bob Casey Federal Courthouse. They left excessively early, perhaps owing to their nerves, and when they emerged across the street from the courthouse into thirty-mile-per-hour wind gusts and ninety-degree heat, they were more than an hour ahead of the hearing's scheduled start.

Built in 1962 as offices for U.S. government workers, the courthouse is a box-shaped concrete slab just eleven stories high. Risibly small, square windows poke uniformly from its face in seventeen perfectly spaced rows across all ten stories above ground level. The windows are designed to protrude noticeably away from the building's exterior, like portholes on the side of a ship; this gives the courthouse the look of a box cheese grater resting on its side. The building spends much of the day in the shadow of a fifty-six-story postmodern skyscraper complete with Dutch Gothic gables, rising on the other side of Smith Street. The proximity emphasizes the federal building's appearance as a forgotten old box left at the feet of Houston's glass-and-steel giants, which were erected across Downtown during the massive Texas oil and real estate boom that stretched into the 1980s, an era of excess exemplified by the television show *Dallas* and its ten-gallon-hat-wearing antihero, J. R. Ewing.

The three sat beneath the institutional glare of fluorescent tubes in the building's cafeteria to speak again of the judge's key questions. They had readied a sort of lifeline in case it seemed the divide between the standards of California and those of Texas was too wide for Ellison. Handley would volunteer that they could file an amended complaint to add enough specificity about the alleged acts of coercion against Buddi Gurung, or on whatever other aspect of their case the judge might require. It wasn't ideal, but it was the best they had been able to come up with in less than twenty-four hours.

The trio headed upstairs to Judge Ellison's chambers with plenty of time still to spare. Antique furniture and modern art filled the reception area outside the judge's courtroom and office, along with dozens of framed family-style snapshots, making it seem as if Handley, Fryszman, and McOwen had just stepped into the living room of Ellison's home. Oil paintings from the judge's modern art collection hung on walls up and down the corridors. The familial warmth was in sharp contrast to the coldness of the rest of the building, or any other court chamber any of them had ever seen, but it did little to set the lawyers at ease.

With about twenty minutes to go, the team representing KBR emerged from the elevator.

KBR had a substantial in-house legal team, but nowhere near the firepower needed to defend it against the torrent of challenges it faced in federal courthouses nationwide as a result of its actions during the Iraq War, including lawsuits leveled at it by the U.S. government. The Justice Department alleged massive KBR overbilling from its active business as the war's biggest contractor. Other cases against the company were pending, from Washington, DC, to the Pacific Northwest, and of course as far south as Houston. Litigation was such an enormous part of KBR's business that when the human trafficking lawsuit landed on his docket, Judge Ellison alone already had two other major cases against the company pending before him. The bigger of Ellison's two cases had nothing to do with Iraq, but it did little to burnish the company's reputation. Standing before the judge in the same courtroom just a few months earlier, representatives of KBR and Halliburton had agreed to a record $579 million fine to settle criminal and civil charges for bribing Nigerian officials for more than $6 billion in contracts, all orchestrated through KBR while it was Halliburton's subsidiary. Sham consulting agreements with shell companies had hidden the bribes. The rot did not involve a couple of "bad apples" at the bottom of the proverbial barrel, either. Albert Jackson "Jack" Stanley, the former KBR chairman, president, and chief executive officer, was awaiting sentencing before Ellison after personally pleading guilty in the case. On the day the company itself had pleaded guilty, KBR's new chairman, president, and CEO, William "Bill" Utt, told reporters on a conference call, "I would like to state that KBR in no way condones, nor tolerates the illegal and unethical behavior that led to the settlement announced today."

Utt, an oilman and engineer, then repeated the line the company seemed to pull out every time it faced trouble over abuses: "KBR has developed and implemented a code of business conduct, and an active code-of-business-conduct training program, to drive the standards to which we hold ourselves, as well as our many stakeholders accountable." The other KBR case pending before Ellison had gained even more publicity, becoming something of a nationwide cause célèbre. Jamie Leigh Jones, a young woman who had gone to Iraq for KBR, alleged that she was drugged and gang-raped by coworkers after arriving in Baghdad and that company officials had locked her in a trailer after she reported the rape. The conservative Fifth Circuit U.S. Court of Appeals had just rejected KBR's bid to throw out her lawsuit, clearing the way for a trial in Ellison's courtroom.

For cases such as these, KBR kept a raft of top lawyers on retainer in Houston and at white-shoe firms across the country. The not insubstantial job of the in-house legal team was to manage the live cases and assist the outside lawyers when necessary. To fight the human trafficking lawsuit, KBR had hired a team from Baker & Hostetler, a prominent defense firm with offices in Houston and nationwide. But rather than being headed by a corporate defense specialist that day, the team was headed by David Rivkin, a Washington lawyer who was among the highest-profile conservative legal ideologues in the country. A firebrand who would sue President Barack Obama on behalf of Republicans in Congress and bring a nationwide challenge to the president's health care law on behalf of conservative attorneys general, Rivkin was born and raised in the former Soviet Union. His grandparents and parents survived Joseph Stalin's reign of terror, a history that seemed to have imbued him with a kind of convert's zeal, akin to that of Ayn Rand. He was bespectacled, could often be seen wearing a seersucker suit, and had built the kind of legal career that seems possible only in Washington. His reputation as a leading conservative legal thinker was based not on a successful record of high-profile court cases, or even on writing articles for law reviews, but on penning opinion pieces for the *Wall Street Journal*, the *National Review*, and the Heritage Foundation. He also regularly promoted his views in cable and broadcast television news programs, reliably making himself available to bookers as a ready and willing on-air proponent of the Iraq War, and specifically of the Bush administration's legal strategy for justifying torture, along with defending the White House's legal arguments for indefinite detentions at Guantánamo Bay. When the Supreme Court ruled in 2008 that those detentions had violated the U.S. Constitution, Rivkin declared during a television appearance that it was "one of the worst decisions by the Supreme Court I've ever read, on par with the Dred Scott decisions [*sic*] and Plessy versus Ferguson." Those infamous nineteenth-century decisions had left slavery and racial segregation, respectively, intact.

Despite their polar opposite political views, Fryszman and Rivkin shared oddly similar backgrounds. She had been born to Soviet scientist parents in April 1964 beneath the gray wet skies of Warsaw, Poland. Just before she turned four, her family was forced to flee an anti-Semitic purge targeting professionals, academics, and intellectuals. Although they both lived and practiced law in Washington, Fryszman and Rivkin met for the first time when Rivkin stepped off the elevator that day into Judge Ellison's reception area, accompanied by the rest of his team. They were early, too.

Rivkin greeted members of the trio, and Handley took immediate notice of his erudite yet staccato manner of speaking. Rivkin spaces his words in an unnatural-sounding way, as if trying to carefully avoid revealing any traces of his native tongue. What emerges is an accent that Handley found distinctive but hard to describe, a bit like that of an Eastern European who had learned English at a Swiss prep school or a villain from a 1960s James Bond film. If not for this slightly jarring feature, the clever and ever-persuasive Rivkin would speak with a tongue cast in pure silver.

The hearing had been set for 2:30 p.m., but seeing that both sides were waiting, Ellison had them called into the courtroom about fifteen minutes early. Draped in his black robe, he entered from the right-hand side of the court, stepped up onto the slightly elevated platform that holds his bench front and center in the courtroom, and sat down in the red leather chair. Perched on the wall behind him, a giant bald eagle, clasping thirteen arrows in one talon and an olive branch in the other, watched silently from a bronzed copy of the Great Seal of the U.S. government. "Good afternoon and welcome to each of you," Ellison said. "Let me say at the outset that I feel very fortunate—any judge would feel very fortunate—to have such superb lawyers in front of him. Thank you all very much."

Fryszman stood at the head of the plaintiffs' table on the left side of Ellison's courtroom and spoke into the thin black microphone snaking out of the lectern before her. "Agnieszka Fryszman for plaintiffs, and I'm here with Matthew Handley and Molly McOwen," she said.

"David Rivkin, Your Honor, for defendants. I'm here with Lee Casey and Billy Donley." Casey was Rivkin's longtime friend, collaborator, and law partner, and had coauthored many op-eds with him, but he seemed far more camera shy. Donley, who was wiry and bald, worked in Baker & Hostetler's Houston office and focused largely on representing carmakers in disputes with their auto dealerships. Rivkin inexplicably skipped over introducing another member of the defense team, a veteran Houston corporate lawyer named Michael Mengis, who had recently joined Baker & Hostetler from one of the nation's preeminent firms, where he'd focused on oil- and gas-related litigation, which was bread and butter for Houston corporate lawyers.

Ellison immediately drew a personal connection to Rivkin, one that could have been perceived as the judge either cozying up to the conservative lawyer or attempting to emphasize his own worldliness. "I remember now," Ellison announced to Rivkin, out of the blue and as if the thought about to pass his lips had just come into his head. "Many years ago, I think—did you go on a tour of western Europe with the Council on Foreign Relations?"

"I most certainly did, Your Honor," Rivkin said.

"I haven't seen you in twenty years, I guess," the judge replied.

"You have not changed," Rivkin said, without missing a beat. "I wish I could say the same about me."

"There's many signs of mileage on me," Ellison demurred.

The judge abruptly ended the pleasantries with an introduction of the great unpleasantness looming since red lights had flashed on BlackBerrys the night before. "We sent out a list of questions yesterday that have concerned me," Ellison said. He told the lawyers he wanted them to address first the questions of the law and then the questions of fact. Because KBR's motion to dismiss the case was the reason they had all come to his courtroom in Houston that day, he invited Rivkin to go first.

Most likely because of Judge Ellison's e-mail and its seemingly favorable attitude toward his case, Rivkin spent little time
on questions of the law. Instead, he hammered away with the
very same fundamental line of attack launched by everyone
involved in the case from the start, and the same one Handley
had seen in his fight with the contractor and the insurance
company: the key witness in each and every man's journey to
his death was, of course, dead. The death of the key witness is
an inescapable fact in every murder committed across human
history. Even Cain, after murdering his brother Abel, tried to
use the silence of the key witness for his defense, replying to a
question from God about his victim's whereabouts with "Am
I my brother's keeper?" Because they hadn't even made it to
their jobs on the base, it was difficult to ascertain what, if any,
role KBR played in the machinery behind their ordeal. In the
minds of those who shared responsibility across the world, from
Nepal to Washington, either directly or indirectly, it made a
defense that is often difficult to employ much more plausible:
deny, deny, deny. Rivkin was the latest in a long line to try
to leverage the missing witnesses for his defense, this time on
behalf of KBR.

Rivkin acknowledged Judge Ellison's request to focus first on the
law, but he made it clear from the start that he would go the other
way. "I actually would like to focus my remarks on the fundamental factual deficiencies of the complaint, but I would weave
in several points about the law," he said. The weaving didn't take
long, as Rivkin moved quickly through a procedural question.
Then he paid momentary respect to the dead. "Let me also begin
by making clear that we understand the nature and the depth

of the personal losses suffered by the plaintiffs," he said. "We extend our condolences. Moreover, we also understand and acknowledge that the problem of human trafficking is a very grave one. That said, I want to underscore that KBR was not associated with the trafficking enterprise, as claimed by plaintiffs, nor was it responsible for the murder of their loved ones or any of their other claimed injuries."

The overall standard the trio of human rights lawyers needed to meet by the end of their case was to win by a preponderance of the evidence, which is to say that they needed to prove that the allegations in their lawsuit were more likely to be true than not. Yet, on that day in Texas, they did not have to prove their entire case. To defeat KBR's motion to dismiss, they faced a much lower bar. They simply needed to show that what they had alleged in their lawsuit was factually "plausible." Still, Ellison's e-mail worried the trio: perhaps he wasn't buying even that much, at least when it came to some core elements of their case, including KBR's involvement in a racketeering enterprise.

Rivkin argued that Fryszman and her team needed to put the fingerprints of specific KBR executives on a human trafficking enterprise in each and every one of the twelve victims' individual cases, and in a detailed way, because the allegations contained in the lawsuit amounted to "claims based upon newspaper or government reports, or about individuals who are not party to this suit, that provide little or no information about the individual experiences" of the twelve dead men. "Indeed, Your Honor," said Rivkin, "virtually all of the facts alleged in the complaint, regarding how plaintiffs' relatives came to be in Iraq, appear to have come from a three-page Defense Department memorandum dated April 14, 2006, which was cited in the complaint, and two *Chicago Tribune* stories dated

October 9 and 10, 2005, upon which these documents relied."
There was plenty of information from the U.S. government
"in the wake of the murder of the plaintiffs' relatives in 2004
[about] how workers were recruited in Nepal and transported
into Iraq. [But] they do not significantly provide information"
about each of the twelve men at the center of this case, Rivkin
said, "except to the extent that they may have been Nepali—"

"Let's just pause for a moment," Judge Ellison said, cutting
Rivkin off and taking stock of the dilemma the families faced
in bringing their suit and of the "dead men tell no tales" defense. "What other sources of information are they likely to
have, given that these horrific acts were committed the way
they were? I mean, how else do they get facts about that?"

"Well, Your Honor, they certainly had opportunities to interview the plaintiffs or relatives of the deceased victims," Rivkin
said. "They've done that in the context of preparing for this litigation. Significantly, they've done it much earlier in the context
of preparing for their DBA, Defense Base Act, hearings at the
Department of Labor, because there is at least some overlap between the plaintiffs in that case and the plaintiffs here. And,
most importantly, they had opportunities to interview at length
Mr. Gurung, who is indeed alive."

Ellison intervened again, trying to steer Rivkin toward a
discussion of the law by asking him about the leading court
precedents that mattered most in weighing KBR's motion to
dismiss the case, but Rivkin would not yield in his campaign
to raise doubts about what had happened to each of the twelve
dead men. He launched into a man-by-man accounting of the
lack of specificity cited in the lawsuit for each individual dead
man, in terms of who, exactly, had promised what to each man,
where, and when, at each step in his journey across the world

and into the convoy. Some of these details would never precisely be known, which Rivkin obviously knew, but the lawyers representing the families certainly had more granular detail than they had put into their lawsuit, and they would use the suit and the discovery process to gather even more. The question was: had they included enough to survive this motion, especially given how the move from California to Texas had opened a door for Rivkin?

Rivkin turned his attention to the dramatic video in which, one by one, each man, knowing his death likely was imminent, stood before the terrorist's black banner, faced the camera head-on, and offered his final words in Nepalese. Many of their statements had been included in the lawsuit, and they would surely constitute a powerful piece of evidence at trial. Some of the men said they had been held in Jordan and sent into Iraq against their will, while others lashed out at the brokers who had taken their families' life savings or bought and sold them across the world, while others used words such as *trapped* to describe their ordeal. Even here, Rivkin took issue with the lack of unanimity and the lack of detailed specificity in the men's final words to their families and the world. "These include allegations that at least *some* of the men in the video—and I have to say the word 'some'—stated that they were held captive in Jordan, and that all stated on television that they were forced to go to Iraq, also without saying who was responsible." He then asserted, "Such statements were, of course, routinely coerced by insurgents from their captives in Iraq."

Rivkin's argument about the statements being coerced was implausible in two important ways: the odds were close to astronomical that the Iraqi insurgents even had a vague comprehension of what the men had said into the camera in their native tongue, let alone that they had coerced them into saying it. Nepalese is one of the most obscure languages in the world, and it was estimated that only two out of Iraq's twenty-five million people spoke it at all. Even if the insurgents had miraculously managed to find and capture those two people to act as interpreters for them, and then had scripted these clearly unscripted statements, the argument also made no sense on another level: the point of such a coerced statement would be to deter other contract workers from *willingly* joining the "Crusader" army. Coercing the Nepalis into saying they had been tricked and forced to come would not have been a very logical way to serve such a goal. A different video released by the insurgents, the very first one, in which the farmer who later had his throat slit tried to read out a mangled, unintelligible statement in broken English, clearly fit Rivkin's bill of a coerced, false statement. The video containing the men's final words in Nepalese did not.

The nearly limitless possibilities offered to a defense lawyer by the principle of "dead men tell no tales" seemed so irresistible to Rivkin that even though the dead men in this case had told their tales, and those tales had been recorded for posterity, he couldn't resist trying to skate past them. Before finishing his line of attack on the twelve, he pretended that the words in the video had never been spoken, had never been recorded, had never been broadcast. "There were no allegations that any of the plaintiffs' relatives attempted to escape or even demanded to be returned home before they joined the convoy into Iraq," he told the judge.

Ellison let Rivkin go on from the start of the hearing for eighteen straight minutes and gave Rivkin so much deference throughout the afternoon that not only were the three human rights lawyers worried, but one of Ellison's own clerks privately warned the judge that he had afforded Rivkin way too much time.

Rivkin devoted the biggest chunk of that time to Buddi Gurung, the thirteenth man. Gurung served some important functions in the case for the plaintiffs. By virtue of his inclusion in the same convoy that day with the twelve, but in a car that had made it through, his very existence offered a powerful connection between the dead men who could not speak and the reality of what had happened to them. He gave their story flesh and breath and voice. *I was there*, he could say. *The road was long and we were terrified*, and so on. He also served another important role in the case. The fact that he got through to the Al Asad Air Base irrefutably proved the function that the convoy served, along with the function of the entire transnational pipeline of cheap labor behind it, which ended at, and fed, KBR's operations at the base for the U.S. military. He and the other men who made it through that day not only went to work under KBR's contract but would be supervised by KBR managers.

Yet, for all that Gurung's presence added to the case of the twelve, the differing details of his own journey to Iraq could also significantly detract from it. If the trio of human rights lawyers were to try to reap the benefits of including Gurung, KBR's lawyers would try to exploit his weaknesses and wrap those back around the twelve. Judge Ellison had sensed some of these potential weaknesses, and so had raised questions about Gurung in his e-mail to the lawyers the night before. Perhaps Rivkin's best chance to dent the plausibility of the trio's lawsuit was through Gurung.

"Now, again, in answer to your question," Rivkin told the judge, referring to the e-mail from the night before, "I mention the theory that one could have gotten a lot more out of Mr. Gurung, who is alive; but the complaint is even less informative with regard to him. There are no factual allegations regarding who recruited him in Nepal, what he may have been told there, how he arrived in Jordan. And the complaint merely states—and I quote—'Plaintiff Gurung's journey to Iraq was similar to that of the deceased victims,' except, Your Honor, that it was not. Mr. Gurung was alleged to have been recruited in Nepal by an unidentified party and first traveled to India, which is not an allegation made in regard to any other plaintiffs, where he stayed for three weeks before going on to Jordan. There's no allegation he had any contact with either Moon Light or Morning Star, the supposed gateways into this whole enterprise, or that he expected to work anywhere but in Iraq."

Rivkin had done some truth stretching throughout his presentation on the twelve, but there wasn't much stretching needed with regard to Gurung. Rivkin noted that, according to the lawsuit, Gurung had signed a contract in Jordan, although that was not a fact the suit offered up about any of the twelve. "And then he was assigned to the same caravan as the plaintiffs' relatives. [There are] no other facts that would link him to any trafficking scheme—alleged trafficking scheme. Once he's in Iraq, he's alleged to have worked for Daoud and KBR and to have been supervised by KBR representatives. He was allegedly told by Daoud, quote, 'He could not leave until his work in Iraq was complete.' That's an ambiguous statement that does not manifest intimidation or physical coercion. Certainly, it does not necessarily do so. And actually, in answer to Your Honor's question on this point, no facts are alleged showing any kind of physical harm, coercion, or intimidation directed at plaintiff Gurung or, for that matter, any of the deceased victims. There's no allegation that Mr. Gurung attempted to leave or that he demanded his passport upon arrival in Iraq. It's simply alleged that his passport, quote, 'had not been returned until he was returned to Nepal upon completion of his contract.' There are no allegations regarding who may have held Mr. Gurung's passport, under what circumstances it was taken, and why."

Rivkin concluded by wrapping all the doubts he had elaborated about Gurung's experience back around the twelve: "We believe, Your Honor, that although the complaint certainly presents a skillfully woven narrative, allegations regarding the experiences of one plaintiff, or plaintiff's relative, or the experiences of workers in general, cannot serve to make plausible the claims of another. Each plaintiff must independently meet" the plausibility test, he said. "We, as defendants, are entitled to know the factual basis of each plaintiff's claim."

Conveniently for his client, Rivkin concluded by informing the judge that "in response to another one of your questions, we are unable to ascertain the frequency at this time of the contacts between Daoud and KBR." Then he suggested something that his client knew was not true: maybe these twelve men were not even headed to work under KBR's contract when they were driven into Iraq. "Daoud was a subcontractor not only for KBR, but for other prime contractors in Iraq, as well as [being] a prime contractor in its own name, both in Iraq and elsewhere in the region," he said. There was no evidence even in the allegations, let alone plausible evidence, he argued, that the two companies had formed a human trafficking enterprise in violation of the racketeering laws.

Perhaps even more conveniently for KBR, Daoud was a ghost.
The plaintiffs' lawyers had hunted from Switzerland to Amman,
Jordan, hiring attorneys around the world, and still had not been
able to serve their lawsuit against the KBR contractor. Perhaps
it was even more of a fly-by-night company than anyone had
imagined.

Handley began his opening remarks by reminding the judge
that the human rights lawyers actually had very little they
needed to do in order to keep their case alive in court that day.
Even if there were two plausible interpretations of the facts presented in the lawsuit, the plaintiffs' interpretation and KBR's
interpretation, the judge was compelled by law at this point to
stick to the plaintiffs' side, Handley asserted, quoting an opinion from U.S. Supreme Court justice David Souter: "Plaintiffs
merely have to nudge the claim across the line from something
that's conceivable to something that's plausible." Handley then
turned to the strongest evidence of plausibility on the weak-
est part of his case: that KBR was culpably involved. He cited
much of the evidence, also cited in the lawsuit, that KBR knew,
or reasonably should have known, what was going on behind
the invisible army of tens of thousands of workers fundamental
to keeping the war running under its contract with the U.S.
military, the biggest in the Iraq War. These included press accounts in the *New York Times* and the *Washington Post*, among
others, alleging coercion and deception (even regarding Daoud
forcing men to Fallujah) that had been brought to the attention
of KBR executives at the time. In addition, Handley said that
the lawyers had continued their investigation since originally
filing the case and could file an amended complaint before

Ellison that offered more specificity. "We learned that it was the practice at Al Asad Air Force Base, which is where these men were to be taken, for KBR employees to threaten to expel third-country nationals from the protection of the base if they complained about their conditions of assignment or their work conditions," he said. He added that KBR officials themselves met the Nepalis at the Jordanian-Iraqi border on August 19, 2004, "and that those men were wearing KBR badges, and that KBR badges were then given to the deceased workers and to Mr. Gurung at that time."

Handley wove Buddi Gurung into these arguments, noting that the lawsuit specifically alleged that after his car got through that day Gurung was supervised by KBR employees—who told him that he could not leave the war zone until his work was completed. "And I believe one of your questions, Your Honor, was—that you had sent—was 'Did Mr. Gurung attempt to leave or request that his passport be given back to him when he arrived in Iraq,'" Handley said. In fact, the lawsuit clearly stated that Gurung and the other men had their passports taken from them. And then, not intimating any of the stress Ellison's e-mail had induced the night before, Handley added, "And I was able to confirm last night through our liaison in Nepal, who was able to contact our client Mr. Gurung, who lives in a very remote village outside—"

"I hate to put you through all that," Ellison interjected. "I'm sorry."

"No, no," Handley said, "It was, it was actually—normally it's actually quite difficult, but this time he was able to reach him quite quickly." Handley then said, "Yes, he did request the passport several times, wanting to leave, but was told on each of those times that he requested that, 'No, he could not have it,' and must continue to work until the contract was complete." Handley concluded by making clear that they could amend the suit to make it friendlier to the standards of Texas, but he believed it was already sufficient.

By the time the hearing was over, it had taken nearly two hours, which was twice as long as the human rights lawyers had anticipated. Even so, they had barely touched on the bevy of procedural arguments KBR's lawyers had lodged, ranging from their contention that the U.S. anti–human trafficking laws did not apply to KBR's conduct overseas in 2004 to a shameless argument over the statute of limitations. In essence, KBR's lawyers had said that the clock on the four-year deadline to file a lawsuit started running when the men were kidnapped, on or about August 19, 2004, not when they were executed about two weeks later. According to KBR's clock, the Cohen Milstein lawyers had missed the deadline by a matter of days. The fast-talking Fryszman had addressed some of these arguments, but earned an instant admonition from Judge Ellison. "Slow it down a little bit. Slow down a little bit," he said, less than one minute into her presentation. As she commenced to rattle off the citations in the U.S. code that applied to her case, Ellison interrupted again. "Section numbers are especially hard for the court reporters," he said. He similarly had asked Rivkin to slow down, urging the lawyers to have some sympathy for the court stenographer. What Ellison had not told them was that, nearly three decades earlier, a surgical procedure had left him completely deaf in one ear.

As he drew the hearing to a close, Ellison then took the unusual step of descending from the bench to shake the hand of each lawyer on both sides, offering each a personalized version of "Thank you very much."

The trio from Cohen Milstein left the courthouse, their luggage already in hand, and got in a cab headed to the airport. There was a collective sense of relief among them that Judge Ellison had not been completely hostile to their lawsuit, but they had no idea what he ultimately might do. At one point, Ellison had made it abundantly clear that he was concerned about how the conservative Fifth U.S. Circuit Court of Appeals would scrutinize his first big decision in the case on KBR's motion to dismiss, a statement he made with the full expectation that the losing side might appeal each major ruling at every step of the case. "I'm directly answerable to the Fifth Circuit, so their concerns have to be my concerns," he had told Handley. Then, moments later, Ellison had added, "I don't know how I'm going to rule. I don't know."

12

2 0 0 9
Houston

Keith P. Ellison was born April 29, 1950, in New Orleans, Louisiana, to churchgoing parents, a prosperous Southern businessman and a mother who had ventured abroad as a foreign correspondent long before such postings at big-city newspapers were open to women. Despite his hometown's world-famous fusion of ethnic diversity and progressive vibrancy—Tennessee Williams said New Orleans held "the last frontier of Bohemia"—racial conflict lit by white opposition to desegregation seared Ellison's childhood. Indeed, it burned as fiercely in New Orleans as it did anywhere else in the American South, if not more so. State law had mandated the cleaving of students into black-only and white-only schools, with predictable results: poverty born of a paucity of resources and opportunity for the former, and the wealth of the state for the latter. Efforts to force desegregation began in earnest in 1952, when an African American father filed a federal lawsuit demanding an equal education for his children under the guarantees afforded him by the U.S. Constitution. The case was assigned to U.S. District Court judge J. Skelly Wright, also a native son of New Orleans.

Wright's work dominated the local headlines and riveted the young Ellison, as it took the judge forty-one separate rulings over the next decade to break down the racist institutions of New Orleans and Louisiana enough to enforce the Constitution and desegregate the schools, with his rulings following on the heels of the Supreme Court's 1954 decision in *Brown v. Board of Education*. In so doing, Wright waged a one-man battle against virtually every power center in the state, from the attorney general to the Louisiana National Guard. He put federal court injunctions into force against them, and also against the governor; the superintendent of education; the Louisiana State Police; and every local district attorney, mayor, police chief, sheriff, and anyone acting on their behalf. He also enjoined the entirety of the Louisiana State Legislature, whose lawmakers had attempted to take over the city's schools in order to maintain the black-white divide. Wright would strike down more than sixty laws as unconstitutional. Then, in 1960, after papering the city and state with injunctions, he handpicked a group of U.S. Marshals to escort four African American girls through a gauntlet of screaming and spitting white parents amassed to try to keep them out of primary school. Norman Rockwell's painting of Wright's men marching the pigtailed Ruby Bridges to school, which the painter titled *The Problem We All Live With*, remains one of the most enduring images of the era, and hung in the White House during Obama's presidency.

Eighty percent of white parents had voted in a referendum to shutter the schools rather than integrate them, a sentiment that fueled reactionary white violence in New Orleans, often led by the White Citizens Council and other racist groups. They publicly derided the judge as "Judas Scalawag Wrong," instead of J. Skelly Wright. The Louisiana State Legislature lynched an effigy of Wright on the floor of its chamber, where it had enacted the segregationist laws that he struck down. One night, someone planted a wooden cross in his front yard and set it ablaze. One morning, a group of men tried to throw him in front of oncoming traffic as he headed to work at the federal court-house. Despite all this and more, Wright won with his wits, his fierce tenacity, and his patience. President John F. Kennedy soon elevated him to the federal appeals court bench in Washington, DC, in part because the U.S. Marshals did not know how much longer they could keep him alive in New Orleans.

The battle over desegregation consumed the young Keith Ellison, first because his parents were ardent supporters of the cause, which had riven them from lifelong friends in the pews of their church, and then because Wright had singlehandedly kept the young Ellison's primary school open. He adopted Wright as his childhood hero, and from there forward nurtured only one true aspiration: to become a federal judge. Only much later would Ellison understand the full force of Wright's bravery and the full measure of his sacrifice. "What he endured," Ellison would say of Wright in a speech many years later, "can scarcely be imagined." After amassing an impeccable academic pedigree—he graduated summa cum laude from Harvard, attended Oxford as a Rhodes Scholar, and earned a law degree from Yale, where he edited the *Yale Law Journal*—Ellison was accepted as Wright's law clerk in 1976. One day, the young clerk made a reference to their shared experience as New Orleanians, and sheepishly asked Wright whether faith had led him to see the world so much differently from the vast majority of their fellow whites. "No," Wright said, "I'm a bad Catholic." Instead, he said his views were born as he looked out the window at an office Christmas party when he was a federal prosecutor in New Orleans. Across the way, he could see the New Orleans Lighthouse for the Blind, which was having its own holiday party. He saw blind white children and blind black children gathering together on the steps, and then he saw someone separate them by race; the white children were taken through the front door, while the black children were led around to the back of the building. Blind children could not segregate themselves, Wright told Ellison, adding, "It had an effect on me." The sight and its memory slowly began to eat away at Wright, making him rethink the segregated world he had taken for granted because it was ever-present throughout his life. "It eats at me even now," he told his young clerk.

Ellison's desire to follow in Wright's footsteps only grew stronger under his tutelage, and he saw how the gravity of the judge's work never elevated him above the people over whom he held such enormous sway. Wright once borrowed from the children's author Theodor Geisel, better known as Dr. Seuss, to state his judicial credo: in the eyes of the law, "a person's a person, no matter how small." It was the kind of wisdom that made Wright so influential among great jurists, including U.S. Supreme Court justice Ruth Bader Ginsburg. After Ellison clerked for Wright, he landed an even more widely coveted and prestigious role, as law clerk for U.S. Supreme Court justice Harry Blackmun, who had authored the majority opinion in *Roe v. Wade*. After serving with Blackmun, Ellison spent the next two decades in private practice as a corporate attorney in Louisiana, Texas, and Oklahoma, learning firsthand that some judges could be tyrants. Walking out of a courtroom following one particularly brutal savaging from a jurist, an older colleague turned to Ellison and said, "Every time you go into court, they take a little piece of you that you never get back." The experience and the words stuck with him forever. Ellison was a good litigator, but he never seemed to love litigation. Instead, he continued to yearn for a federal judgeship.

In 1999, President Bill Clinton appointed Ellison to fill a vacancy in the U.S. District Court for the Southern District of Texas. Ellison sat on the bench at a satellite federal courthouse in Laredo, Texas, along the border with Mexico. Although Laredo's tallest building is just twelve stories high, Laredo's status as the nation's busiest inland border crossing means the very worst troubles between Latin America and the United States get funneled into the small city. With just one other judge, Ellison shared one of the busiest criminal dockets in the nation, a baptism by inferno for any new jurist. The pair got nearly three thousand criminal cases a year, many with multiple defendants, and most related to drugs and immigration, usually in conjunction. Sentencing defendants whose crying families filled his courtroom sometimes kept Ellison awake at night, especially given how little discretion federal judges then held in setting prison terms. When he transferred to Houston in 2005, his caseload got flipped upside down: more than 80 percent of his time would be spent on civil rather than criminal cases, and almost always business-related lawsuits. Even scoundrels within the Laredo bar, of which there were more than a few, could be passionate, elegant, and nimble on their feet. For the most part, the lawyers he faced in Houston were much better on paper.

The judge's experience with tyrannical jurists led him to intentionally cultivate the habit of shaking hands with every lawyer, and even criminal defendants, at the end of a hearing. He shook hands with men moments after he sent them away to prison, along with the very few he set free. This gentility made it virtually impossible for the lawyers appearing before him to have any idea how he might rule after he had walked out of the courtroom and back into his chambers to begin drafting his opinions.

On November 3, 2009, a little more than three weeks after they had flown out of Texas, the Cohen Milstein lawyers got a call from Houston: Judge Ellison had ruled on KBR's motion to dismiss the case. Fryszman tore through the opinion, finding cause to nod and smile on each of its thirty-two pages. Ellison had tossed out almost every argument Rivkin had mustered. Questions of factual sufficiency, which had dominated Rivkin's presentation and the hearing, were dealt with almost brusquely, while Ellison tackled all the procedural questions in great depth. The most significant was KBR's claim that the anti–human trafficking statute first passed by Congress in 2000 under the sponsorship of the New Jersey congressman who held a hearing about the twelve men from Nepal, could not be used to sue the company. Rivkin had argued that the version of the law in effect when the men were killed in 2004 did not explicitly state that it applied to human trafficking outside the territorial boundaries of the United States, a legal principle known as "extraterritoriality." Fryszman argued that the law did not need to explicitly state that it applied internationally given that the very nature of human trafficking was that it was a transnational crime, and that the antitrafficking law had been passed, in part, to fulfill the U.S. government's obligations under several international accords it had signed, including those specifically calling for the eradication of *international* human trafficking. Judge Ellison agreed, writing that the entire thrust of the federal trafficking law "would be severely undermined" if he were to rule that "defendants who gained a commercial advantage in this country through engaging in illegal human trafficking were free from liability, so long as the trafficking acts themselves took place outside of American borders."

Even if the human trafficking law could not be applied overseas when the men were killed in 2004, another law, more than two hundred years old, existed explicitly to allow foreigners to bring lawsuits in American courts for violations of U.S. law if the alleged abuses were deemed to be "violations of the laws of nations." The intent was to include transnational crimes, such as piracy, that otherwise could not easily find a jurisdiction somewhere in the world, under the principle that perpetrators should not be able to use the United States as a safe harbor against liability after they have committed great wrongs in international jurisdictions. The law was named the Alien Tort Statute because it allows "aliens," as in "foreigners," to bring injury lawsuits, or "torts," in U.S. federal court. The underlying abuses they could raise in such lawsuits were not unlimited; they had to be for crimes that were considered *hostis humani generis*, a Latin phrase that means "enemy of all mankind." In addition to piracy, the transgressions that courts recognized as fitting under this principle included torture, war crimes, and the slave trade. The idea was that jurisdiction was universal for such crimes. This was the ground upon which Michael Hausfeld, the former chairman of Cohen Milstein, had built his cases against those who profited from the Holocaust. Not surprisingly, it also was an area of the law that significantly expanded during the modern era of globalization.

Agnieszka Fryszman had crafted her lawsuit for the families of the twelve to include a cause of action under the Alien Tort Statute, one that probably had never been tried before. She said

that human trafficking was a legitimate tort under the law because slavery already was included, and human trafficking simply was the modern-day form of slavery, as defined by Congress
and legal scholars. Ellison agreed, rejecting KBR's efforts to
throw out that piece of the case, too.

Finally, KBR had tried to get the case dismissed by arguing
that the lawsuit had been filed a few days too late. The statute of limitations was four years for all but the simplest claim,
the one involving negligence. By law, the clock starts running
when a plaintiff knows, or reasonably should have known, that
he or she has been injured by the defendant's actions. KBR's
lawyers argued that for Kamala and the other surviving family members, that day came no later than August 24, 2004,
while the insurgents were holding the men in Iraq but before
they had murdered them. Under this interpretation, the lawsuit, stamped by the court clerk in Los Angeles on August 27,
2008, had been filed three days too late. But to expect that the
families could reasonably have known on August 24, 2004,
that KBR had injured them was absurd, given that they had no
idea what was happening, and given that the mystery of this
human supply chain would not begin to be unraveled for more
than a year. Ellison dismissed KBR's claim on this basis, but he
did throw the company one bone: the statute of limitations on
negligence was just two years in Texas, not four, so by the time
the suit got filed in California, that single claim in the lawsuit
was more than two years past the statutory deadline.

Ellison's decision on negligence seemed just, but it also removed from the case what would likely have been the easiest
victory. While the bar to proving human trafficking might have
been high, it was hard to imagine any jury failing to recognize
how Jeet and the other men had been delivered into Iraq. On

this score, the delays Handley had faced, inside the firm and in dealing with the intransigence of the insurance company, seemed to haunt the quest for justice. But as Fryszman and Handley read Ellison's ruling that day, it became apparent that KBR's decision to bring the lawsuit home to Houston had likely backfired, given that the judge weighing the case had embraced the judicial philosophy that every person is deserving of the full protection of the law, no matter how small they are in the eyes of the world. That most especially included a young widow from Kathmandu and her daughter.

The plaintiffs' team in Washington savored the moment. Far tougher battles lay ahead, likely for years to come, and the company surely would throw its considerable weight behind each one, but for the first time it seemed Kamala and the other Nepali families stood a chance of achieving the impossible.

. . .

Women such as Kamala and widows from the Maoist war fighting for dignity in communities across the country might have pushed the culture of discrimination in Nepal onto its back foot, but they still faced centuries of tradition that needed to be ground down in order to secure their gains and achieve more. Beyond the cultural discrimination they faced, significant structural barriers also needed breaching, including property and probate laws akin to those on the books a century and a half earlier in Victorian England and the United States, laws that denied widows the right to inherit property from their dead husbands. Because such was still the law of the land in Nepal, a small national controversy erupted after Kamala and the other Iraq War widows started receiving American compensation payments from Matthew Handley's victory in their case; the in-laws were entitled to absolutely nothing, as U.S. law stipulated that if there was a sole surviving spouse, only she and her children were the legally entitled beneficiaries. Clearly, this was poetic justice for Kamala and the other widows who had suffered so greatly, but Ganesh Gurung, the academic who had helped secure victory in their case, quickly found himself at the center of a personal, political, and media uproar in Nepal, where the American system appeared to be punishing the dead men's parents, at least when viewed through the Nepalese lens.

Angry in-laws or their representatives called Gurung at all hours to scream about having been robbed, and prominent politicians and government officials soon joined the chorus. Gurung did his best to try to explain that American law, not Nepalese customs or law, controlled destiny in the case, but the in-laws were livid, and many Nepalis were on their side. For religious and political conservatives in Nepal, it became something of a cultural rallying cry, as they suggested that important traditions were under threat. Almost without exception, however, the widows resisted the pressure to share the award money with their dead husbands' families.

Although they had spoken to the press, Kamala didn't hear from Jeet's family right away. Receiving the compensation payment might have been a cause of celebration for some, but it simply reminded Kamala of her loss and pain, and the actual transfer of the funds drove home the reality she had lived with since Jeet's death, a reality that could not be wiped away by cash. After consulting with Ganesh Gurung and her sisters, she decided to use her money to buy some land on the northern edge of Kathmandu, not too far from one of her sisters, and to construct a small building on the site with some commercial space on the ground floor and a few apartments above. Like a lot of Asian cities, Kathmandu was booming, and its real estate market probably represented the safest investment in Nepal. A building would give Kamala a place to live with Kritika, a small space for a dress shop, and some other commercial and residential spaces to rent out, providing her a small but steady income. A distant relative from Gorkha who had a small construction concern in Kathmandu offered to run the project for her, but like contractors the world over, he squeezed her for more and more cash as construction languished well into 2009. Kamala knew that the man, who saw only a young woman alone with a large stash of cash, had taken advantage of her, but she felt helpless and got sucked into paying him more and more to try to get her house built. Then, one day, she met by chance with another distant relative from the horseshoe ridge, a man with a reputation as a sort of tough guy, if not a small-time hood. He was livid over Kamala's treatment, and not long after, he had what might euphemistically be called a heart-to-heart conversation with the builder. More of the work got done, but even then, Kamala found herself doing some of the painting and other odd jobs to finish off her own flat on the second floor.

Once she was settled into her new home, Jeet's family came knocking. The insurance company in the United States had agreed to pay the families in lump sums, instead of trickling out payments over many years, and Kamala's in-laws wanted half of what she had received. Kamala couldn't believe that after all she had been through that they wanted money from her, but she also felt in her heart an obligation to consider their request. She believed in a Nepalese version of the saying that you should treat people who are unpleasant to you by killing them with kindness. She stood ready to forgive and help them, something she also thought would be important for Kritika's future. Her mother-in-law's second-youngest son had been killed in India, so the family felt as if their home in the village on the ledge had somehow become cursed with the painful memories of two lost sons. They asked Kamala for money so they could build another house and leave their own past behind, as she had done.

Kamala told her mother-in-law she could keep all the money in their joint bank account back home in Gorkha, which had been created with the small payment the Nepalese government had made in the wake of the killings. Later, Kamala spoke to her sisters about whether she had done the right thing. They were somewhat sympathetic to Jeet's family, and one even suggested that Kamala give them more. "You lost a husband, but they lost their son and brother," the sister said to her. So Kamala sold another piece of the Kathmandu land she had purchased as an investment and gave the money to Jeet's family, going well beyond what other widows had done for the families of their deceased husbands. Yet Jeet's family never showed any gratitude; nor did they invite her to visit or make her feel welcome on the occasions when she returned to the horseshoe ridge with Kritika. Even so, Kamala believed that honoring Jeet's family in this way also honored his memory.

Kamala opened her dress shop on the ground floor of her new building and rented out the adjoining shop as a convenience store. She also leased a couple of sewing machines to use in the shop. Her Luxmi from the ashram would stay in her flat on the second floor, in the living room, where the sight of it each day filled her with a sense of pride and warmth. She felt she had finally secured a future for herself and her daughter.

• • •

Any sense of accomplishment for Fryszman and Handley after the initial victory over Rivkin and the rest of KBR's defense team in Houston quickly dissipated as the lawyers took full measure of what was ahead. If taking on the company was akin to scaling a peak, they had simply survived KBR's effort to block them from reaching the first base camp. From her other battles with powerful defendants, Fryszman knew the real climb remained, and the air would get thinner with each step.

Even the most basic steps required in a lawsuit could leave the lawyers feeling frozen in place. Consider their civil action's codefendant, Daoud and Partners. The contractor was nowhere to be found and had not even been served with a copy of the court papers, though not for lack of trying. It was as if the company did not exist. Molly McOwen, the young human rights fellow on the Cohen Milstein team, was in charge of investigating Daoud, including locating any and all of its offices throughout the world. She discovered that the company had listed its total revenues as $10 million per year when it had been awarded a small U.S. Navy contract in 2009. Piecing together virtually every U.S. government spending record available connected with Daoud, she found more than a dozen other contracts with U.S. military entities, valued at a total of about $8.4 million. However, the real game was in Daoud's work for the U.S. military via KBR, and publicly available records on payments to subcontractors were incomplete at best, making it impossible for her to get a good handle on that side of its business. Her best guess, based on fragmentary evidence, was that it probably amounted to about $50 million over a roughly five-year period before the suit was filed.

Physically serving papers on the company proved maddening. After finding a business registration address in Geneva, Switzerland, Cohen Milstein paid to have all its documents in the case translated into French, so they could be processed properly and served under Swiss law. But by the time the firm got all the necessary paperwork together, the company had either changed its name in Switzerland or liquidated its registered office there. (It was listed on a leafy residential street in Geneva, which suggested that the address had existed only on paper, perhaps to facilitate a Swiss bank account.) After more than nine months into the case, Cohen Milstein's lawyers had to ask Judge Ellison to formally request the assistance of a Jordanian judge to try to serve the papers in Amman, where Daoud had another office. The human rights lawyers had everything translated into Arabic, hired a Jordanian lawyer, and went through an even more cumbersome process than they had undertaken for the Swiss address. Ellison signed a letter to court officials in Jordan on June 1, 2009. After nothing happened, he signed another request almost two months later. Still nothing.

Around Christmas 2009, Fryszman received a call out of the blue from a partner at a major Washington, DC, law firm. It was a man she vaguely knew, and vaguely knew to be associated with various national security apparatuses of the U.S. government. "The following is completely off the record," the lawyer told her, "but you will soon hear from a firm which will be in a position to accept service for Daoud and Partners." About a week after New Year's Day in 2010, a Hollywood lawyer, a partner at one of the nation's leading white-shoe law firms, filed an appearance with the federal court clerk in Houston saying he represented Daoud and Partners.

Before becoming one of Hollywood's most noted defense attorneys, Christopher Tayback had been a prosecutor in the Los

Angeles County District Attorney's Office, and then a federal prosecutor. He worked at the firm Quinn Emanuel Urquhart Oliver and Hedges, and would later serve as the lead defense attorney for Bill Cosby. Some of his success perhaps owed to his Hollywood bona fides. Tayback looked just like his father, the late Vic Tayback, a character actor who played the eponymous owner of Mel's Diner in the long-running television series *Alice*. Before long, an even higher-profile partner at the firm, Susan Estrich, also filed an appearance in the case for Daoud. Estrich, one of the most noted legal commentators in the country, had been the presidential campaign manager for Michael Dukakis in 1988. Perhaps not coincidentally, she shared a deep bond with Judge Ellison, also having served in a clerkship for J. Skelly Wright before going on to clerk at the U.S. Supreme Court, and she had remained in contact with Ellison.

McOwen and Fryszman could not be certain why their longtime prey finally emerged from the shadows, but McOwen believed that the tree shaking they had done through the Jordanian courts, although seemingly futile, had likely created local pressure on Daoud that the company felt it could no longer ignore. Beyond that, however, virtually everyone, including some of KBR's lawyers, wondered how a small fly-by-night firm from the Middle East, one that no one could even find, could afford a top-flight defense firm, not to mention lawyers with the star caliber of Tayback and Estrich.

Almost as soon as Daoud came into view, however, it sought to retreat back into the shadows. Tayback demanded the dismissal of the lawsuit against his client, arguing that Judge Ellison had no legal authority to weigh a case against the firm. Daoud, Tayback wrote, "is a foreign company based in Jordan that does business exclusively in the Middle East." It does not conduct, and has never conducted, any business in Texas or elsewhere in the United States, he said. It did not have employees, agents, offices, or property in America; nor did it have U.S. bank accounts or any assets inside the country. "Daoud's involvement in this lawsuit arises solely from its work in Iraq as one of many KBR subcontractors," Tayback argued. He proceeded to list, in great detail, all the things his client had never done inside the United States throughout the history of its existence. No Daoud entity ever had "an office, a telephone number, a postal delivery location, or a bank account in Texas or anywhere in the United States . . . No Daoud entity is (or ever was) registered or licensed to do business in Texas or any other U.S. state, nor does any Daoud entity have a registered agent for service of process anywhere in the United States. No Daoud entity has ever owned or leased any property in Texas or anywhere in the United States." In case that wasn't enough, Tayback also made clear that none of the alleged wrongdoing by Daoud had taken place "in Texas or anywhere else in the United States" and the families' "alleged injuries were incurred in Nepal, Jordan and Iraq." Kamala and the others who were suing Daoud, along with all their dead husbands, sons, and brothers, were or had been citizens of Nepal, not Texas, and not even the United States.

Tayback then made a claim on behalf of Daoud that had been defeated time and time again over the previous five years, proving once again the irresistibility of the "dead men tell no tales" defense. "Daoud never employed or entered into any employment agreements with the twelve deceased Nepalis whose families have brought this action," he told the judge in one filing. Each body shop broker in Jordan working for Daoud, or in its human supply chain to KBR, had made one version or another of the very same claim during the *Tribune* investigation in 2005, and in each and every case, either they eventually confessed that it wasn't true or their lies were debunked. The same basic defense was repeatedly attempted and debunked again throughout the two years that the compensation case was pending with the Department of Labor. And after the human trafficking lawsuit was filed, David Rivkin had danced around a similar claim at the first major hearing in the case in 2009. Now, in April 2010, this timeless defense was back again. Tayback based his assertion on the very last statement listed in a six-page declaration he filed with the court, which had been signed by Yazan Banna, Daoud's manager. "Daoud did not employ, and therefore did not have employment agreements with, any of the other individuals" named in the lawsuit, a reference to Jeet and his eleven murdered compatriots. The next line in Banna's declaration was this: "I declare under penalty of perjury under the laws of the United States of America that the foregoing is true and correct."

Beyond the dead men not being available to testify, one other thing clearly made this defense possible, and even plausible, each and every time it had been attempted in the six years since the men's deaths, and it got at the very heart of the case. It was the fundamental nature of modern human trafficking. There is no single villain pulling strings from the top, but instead, several individual actors who make up an overall chain of conduct. It is an inherently transnational enterprise that utilizes a global supply chain extending across multiple countries, and it requires an extensive transnational network of recruiters, contractors, subcontractors, parent corporations, and subsidiaries crossing jurisdictions, countries, and continents. The sheer number of actors involved allows each to point a finger somewhere else—to someone below him in the supply chain, or to someone above—or simply to deny his own individual piece of responsibility. But as one climbs higher in the chain, two things undeniably accrue: financial benefits and the potential knowledge of the wrongs below that delivered them.

Despite Tayback's lengthy catalogue of all the things Daoud had never done, he let slip a couple of interesting tidbits about some of things it had done. For starters, the company began working for "U.S. Army personnel located in Jordan, and the United States Embassy in Amman" starting in 1996. None of these contracts or payments had turned up in Molly McOwen's scouring of the public records about the firm, but they suggested that Daoud had what is known in Arabic as *wasta*, which means "political clout"; not just anyone in Jordan could get such contracts with the U.S. government. KBR would later admit, through a declaration from one of its executives, that unnamed "officials of the U.S. government" had introduced Daoud to KBR prior to the U.S. invasion, helping facilitate the contracts for the Jordanian company. Daoud's lawyers also admitted that there were actually two firms run by the same men called Daoud and Partners, at least on paper. Although it was founded in Amman, Daoud had created in March 2004 a new and separate corporation that was registered in the British Virgin Islands, one of the world's premier tax havens. Its previously existing contracts with KBR, and every existing contract it had related to the U.S. war in Iraq, were transferred to, and exclusively channeled through, the version of Daoud registered in the Caribbean. This company paid no taxes in Jordan, where its offices were located and from which it substantially ran the Iraq business. For Molly McOwen, these facts meant the once ghostly qualities of Daoud and Partners were beginning to take a more tangible form.

The true nature of Daoud started coming into view as KBR's lawyers launched an assault on the subcontractor, attempting to shift responsibility for the case onto Daoud's shoulders. Daoud had agreed through a clause in its Iraq contract, known as an indemnity clause, to assume responsibility for any liability that resulted from its work for KBR, and now KBR wanted to force the issue. But first, KBR's lawyers made it clear this was no tiny fly-by-night operator.

"Since 2003 Daoud & Partners has entered into over fourteen-hundred contracts worth nearly $500 million with various KBR entities," KBR's lawyers wrote in one of their first salvos. Through an order from Judge Ellison that followed, Fryszman and McOwen got access to internal Daoud records. What they found was jaw-dropping: between 2003 and 2008 alone, the actual payments to Daoud reached a total of $641 million. The human rights lawyers also learned that these funds made up at least 98 percent of Daoud's total revenues, while the remainder came directly from the U.S. government itself. That meant the Jordanian company received an average of almost $130 million per year from American military contracts, awarded by and performed through an American company—and for work carried out on a military base occupied and run by Americans. It also meant that 100 percent of Daoud's corporate revenues came courtesy of American taxpayers. Now this same company was arguing that Kamala and the other families had no right to sue it in an American courtroom for what had happened to their husbands, sons, and brothers.

Rivkin's role for KBR receded somewhat as the battle with Daoud began. The man charged with leading that fight for KBR was the seasoned and skilled corporate defense attorney

Michael Mengis. Mengis started dribbling out important revelations about the twelve Nepalis in the motions and briefs he filed, and in the attached documents. In one, KBR revealed that it had evidence showing that Jeet and the other eleven men were, in fact, headed to work for Daoud under one of its contracts with KBR at Al Asad. It said that "the twelve Nepalese men who were killed by insurgents in August 2004, and whose relatives are plaintiffs in the instant action, were recruited by Daoud and were scheduled to work in the laundry facility under the Laundry Contract." That contract was "for the operation of a laundry facility at Al Asad Air Base in Iraq between December 2003 and December 2004," Mengis wrote, naming it specifically as "Subcontract Number GU84-VC-SB10005."

Although this marked the first time KBR had admitted knowing specifically that Jeet and his compatriots "were recruited by Daoud and were scheduled to work in the laundry facility," it was not the first time that KBR had singled out that very contract. In fact, KBR, when it made one of its first substantive motions in the case, the one it filed to transfer the lawsuit from California to Texas, had specifically flagged the relevance of the laundry contract without revealing that it knew that the murdered men had been recruited by Daoud to work under it. (KBR had pointed out then that the man who had executed the deal, along with other contracts it had with Daoud that year, was then-KBR procurement manager Robert Gerlach, who was a resident of Texas, not California.)

The battle over whether Daoud could be sued in an American federal courtroom, along with KBR's battle to make it responsible for defending the entire lawsuit, dragged on before Ellison for an astonishing two years. Fryszman didn't mind watching her two defendants fight and sap each other, but this meant that most of the overall progress of the case stalled. Ultimately, Ellison rejected Daoud's efforts to dismiss the case based on jurisdiction and KBR's attempt to place the liability on Daoud's shoulders. On the latter front, Ellison ruled that no one can contractually agree to assume liability for a business partner's share of "future criminal misconduct." By the time all these battles were settled, however, it was Christmas 2011.

The only other real movement in the case during those nearly two years of fighting was the Cohen Milstein lawyers' discovery process against KBR, but it would prove to be movement without significant progress. Discovery gives each side the ability, in the words of the Supreme Court, to "compel the other to disgorge whatever facts he has in his possession" about the case, based on the principle that mutual "knowledge of all the relevant facts gathered by both parties is essential to proper litigation." Lawyers gather these facts through demands for internal records, except for those that are deemed to be privileged communications between an attorney and his client, and through cross-examining witnesses or key litigants from the other side in depositions. Adversaries also can demand that their opponents answer written questions. Claiming the other side is merely on "a fishing expedition" does not offer relief from the investigation, and willfully withholding relevant documents or facts is a most serious offense, given how important the discovery process is to reaching a just resolution of disputes in an adversarial legal system. Short of that misconduct, the process can, at times, get rather bloody, but more often than not, it unfolds in a manner satisfactory to both sides, with a rhythm like this: a plaintiff's lawyer asks for the moon, the defense balks and then makes a fairly reasonable counteroffer, and the deed is done. Getting KBR's internal documents was the top priority, as it would enable Fryszman and her team to properly prepare to cross-examine and confront KBR executives during depositions.

KBR's lawyers told Fryszman that the company's documents had all been moved to an electronic retrieval system. She shot for the moon in seeking access to a vast trove, but the defense team balked. Its initial counteroffer was to search a limited number of terms for documents generated by, or about, ten out of KBR's more than twenty-seven thousand employees, which did not include employees for its former parent company, Halliburton. It offered to include search terms about its operations at Al Asad, such as *mess hall* and *laundry*, and specific terms about the allegations in the suit, such as *trafficking in persons*. Fryszman thought a search term such as *mess hall* was so broad it would be a waste of time for KBR, likely to return tens of thousands of irrelevant e-mails about overcooked hamburgers and stale potato chips. And, she suspected, a search for terms such as *trafficking in persons* would yield an utter paucity of anything valuable, as an employee or contractor complaining about or even participating in such abuses would never type anything akin to the lawyerly phrase "trafficking in persons" into an e-mail. Despite these concerns, she agreed to KBR's initial proposal, believing this was just the first round. Perhaps she also was feeling a bit overconfident, given that her team was on a roll, winning on virtually every front thus far in the more than three years the case had been pending. In addition, Fryszman was keen to get a look at KBR's internal documents sooner rather than later. The ten current or former employees on KBR's list included at least one name that already was familiar to her team: Robert Gerlach, the KBR manager at Al Asad responsible for the laundry contract with Daoud under which the twelve men had been brought into Iraq.

13

The receiving line started almost half a mile outside the village, along the narrow trail winding up from the riverbank and into the hills. Virtually every boy and girl, every man and woman, every living person of every age born in the village of Garang stood beside the trail, shoulder to shoulder, to welcome the three arriving Americans, covering each in garlands of marigolds and purple trumpet flowers, and unleashing applause that thundered into the hills as they approached and passed. Matthew Handley, Molly McOwen, and McOwen's fiancé, an architect named Craig Cook, had had no idea any of this awaited them. They had trekked all day to reach Garang after their four-wheeler could take them no farther. The receiving line curled in behind the trio as they stepped up the trail, creating a cheering crowd all around them as they entered the village like champions at the end of some epic race. Handley and McOwen's success in the compensation case of another Iraq worker's widow had changed the woman's life, and had helped transform the entire village of Garang, making Handley something of a miracle worker to the people there. Handley had done most of the work on her case, which had become an area of expertise for him following his initial experience with Kamala and the other families of the massacre. The widow in Garang had established a charity to provide scholarships for girls, and her newfound wealth had benefited the lives of those near her in countless ways. Handley beamed silently, feeling somewhat overwhelmed as he stood drowning in marigolds. Cook also was overcome if sheepish, telling nearly everyone who draped a string of flowers over his head, "Really, I had nothing to do with this!" until the applause brought him to tears. McOwen offered the villagers her own bit of self-deprecation: "I only did ten percent of the work!" Someone put white and lavender trumpet flowers in her hair.

In the four years since he had won compensation for Kamala and the other families, and his marriage had simultaneously collapsed, Handley had made partner at Cohen Milstein, and then, not long after, sought a one-year leave of absence. Handley wanted to travel and also wanted to explore the potential to build his own practice around international human rights litigation, one anchored largely in what he assumed was an ocean of compensation cases from the wars in Iraq and Afghanistan. These cases might not carry anything remotely close to the potentially massive attorney awards offered by class-action litigation, but they could pay the bills. Other partners at Cohen Milstein didn't seem happy with Handley's demand for leave, arguing that it was financially unsound for both him and the practice, but he was unbending. He was also burned out, just as his bosses had feared years earlier. It was remarkable he'd lasted so long, given that the grind of the shareholder class-action cases hadn't relented while his devotion to the other side of his practice had only grown. As strongly as he felt about his part-time role in the lawsuit against KBR and Daoud, he also felt frustrated by the snail's pace at which the litigation was moving toward an unknown resolution, in contrast to the compensation cases, which had all concluded so much faster, and successfully. Those cases gave him a deep sense of pride and accomplishment, as tangible as standing in one of the world's most beautiful landscapes and drowning in marigolds. Moments like this, and his victories in these cases, would stay with him forever. They had a narcotic effect, furthering his desire to bring his practice of the law as close as he could to actual human beings who had been denied justice, versus entire classes of faceless shareholders.

McOwen and Cook were on vacation, and had joined Handley on a trekking expedition, which they had routed through Garang so they could meet the widow. McOwen had been inspired by her work on the case against KBR and Daoud to visit Nepal, a land she knew only in black-and-white court filings stuffed in manila file folders around her office. Handley had promised to meet her and Cook along the way. The extraordinary reception in Garang was emotional for everyone, and gave McOwen a needed boost. She hadn't done much work on the original compensation case, but had now been immersed for four years in the lawsuit against KBR and Daoud without even having met the people she represented. Almost six years into her work for the firm, she also remained stuck on a track that didn't offer her much pay compared with that of other lawyers, or even a road to partnership, so she had searched for other ways to stay committed to her job. Garang gave both her and her fiancé a profound sense of what was behind her long hours in the office, which had been an occasional source of tension in their relationship. McOwen couldn't resist hoping that, in eighteen months, this same scene might be repeated with Kamala and the other families of the twelve, not necessarily with the lawyers bathed in wildflowers, but with them all celebrating that some measure of justice had been achieved.

That night the three Americans shared a traditional Nepalese dinner with their hostess and then slept soundly in the mountain air.

As the sun rose over the river valley below Garang, the Americans said their good-byes, bowed gently to the villagers, and then headed back down the winding trail amid the sweet smell of the kitchen fires wafting around them. They trekked deeper into the hills for a couple of days more before meeting Ganesh Gurung. McOwen had agreed with her bosses that she would sit down with the families of the twelve at the end of her vacation in order to assess their abilities, their willingness, and their potential strengths or weaknesses as witnesses in the case. Handley had agreed to help, even though he was on leave. Gurung had arranged an all-day meeting with the families in Kathmandu, but first, he took the trio to the sacred temple in Gorkha called Manakamana. It is Nepal's most famous temple outside Kathmandu, not far from the horseshoe ridge where Kamala was born and raised. Cable cars that glide in the sky above more than a mile and a half of steep terrain, delivering thousands of pilgrims and tourists a day to the top of the mountain, had recently replaced the three-hour trek that used to be necessary to reach the peak. Bleating goats are herded into some cars reserved for ferrying them to the peak, but the goats don't come back down: they are sacrificed in ritual prayer at a blood-splattered stone pillar near the temple's entrance.

McOwen feared she was coming down with a case of dysentery but was determined not to let it ruin their adventure, and she did her best to hold on to the contents of her stomach as she rode back down the mountainside with Nepalis clutching plastic bags filled with the butchered remnants of their sacrifices, which would be used to make goat curries that very night. She and her fiancé then piled with Handley and Gurung into a jeep that bounced them over Nepalese roads for about five hours before reaching Kathmandu, where Gurung had organized a small dinner party at his home with some elite Nepalis. Before dinner was served, McOwen realized quite suddenly that she could no longer maintain a peaceful coexistence with her body, a reality that overtook her while she was speaking to Nepal's former ambassador to Myanmar. She barely made it past the woman and into Gurung's bathroom, where she would spend much of the night.

With some bed rest and the aid of powerful antibiotics, McOwen rose to face her first meeting with the families at the office of Gurung's think tank near the American embassy in Kathmandu. Normally, a law firm such as Cohen Milstein would prepare for days, if not weeks, to assess the witnesses for its side in a case, bringing in an entire team to meet with them and then brainstorm about different facets of their stories, their suitability, their potential weaknesses. McOwen, not even an associate at the firm, let alone a partner, was expected to do this at the end of her vacation and virtually alone, with Handley chipping in only while on leave.

There are always struggles with interviewing through an interpreter, especially in speaking with less educated people and having to parse past, present, future, and pluperfect tenses in an attempt to build a detailed time line—and in litigation, especially a cross-examination, such details are what matter. In addition, McOwen was supposed to sort through any papers her interview subjects still had relating to their sons, husbands, and brothers. Among the Nepalis, there was confusion over the constant plea from the lawyers for "documents," a word they associated solely with the likes of a birth certificate. McOwen not only had to collect any documents that might be relevant, but then had to share them with KBR in the discovery process under way. Combined with her dysentery-addled body, her duties proved overwhelming at times that day.

All twelve families gathered beneath the low ceiling in the narrow room on the top story of Gurung's office, crowding on the floor around a low rectangular table. Handley and McOwen met individually with each of the families. McOwen soon began to feel the accumulating emotional weight of each family's story, with mothers describing how they had watched the executions of their sons, or women explaining the pain of the suddenness of widowhood. She felt the imploring eyes of these same women looking to her to do something about these experiences, and about what had happened to their loved ones. Some wondered how many more times they would have to relive their trauma for the American lawyers, how much longer they would have to engage in a process that seemingly had no end, but hearing of these collective experiences was new to McOwen.

Kamala came into the room from the adjacent rooftop deck and sat down before McOwen and Handley. She was reserved in a way that made her seem almost skeptical of the lawyers. Soon, though, she started to speak with candor and passion about everything she had been through, from the farm to the ashram, the experience of raising a daughter on her own, and even of the rejection by her in-laws. The strength she had regained during her two years with the women of the ashram, and the way she had rebuilt her life, gave her telling of her ordeal a quality that set her apart from others, a kind of steadiness and soft-spoken clarity born of self-awareness. McOwen and Handley both knew she would make a powerful witness in the case—forceful, but with a certain wisdom about everything the Iraq War and its global supply chain of human beings had meant for her corner of the universe in Nepal, and for her daughter. They asked if she would be willing to help, and she pledged to do whatever was necessary.

McOwen and her fiancé flew back to Washington a day later. She was overwhelmed by her experiences with the families and the stress of having such a major task on her hands, but she felt fairly confident Kamala should be at the fore of their case.

As she exited Gurung's office, Kamala was reminded anew of how Jeet had died in a time and a place and a way that weren't meant to be, and a fire started to grow in her. Having shielded Kritika from her father's fate for nearly a decade, Kamala waited for a moment when she was alone in the house and gathered the courage to watch the execution video she had avoided for just as long, feeling, perhaps, that it was finally time for her to know precisely what had happened to her husband in that ditch in Iraq. As the images and the sounds moved across the screen of her phone, they were seared indelibly into her mind in a way she immediately knew she could never unsee, but still, she watched a second time, having been so traumatized upon the first viewing that she hadn't even looked for, or specifically noticed, Jeet, though the camera captured each man as he was shot in the back or the back of the head. Upon watching a second time, she looked just for him, and she recognized the gray shirt on her husband's back as he lay facedown in the ditch, and then she saw his thick black hair, which had smelled of sweet jasmine oil when he held her, and almost instantly a kind of cold that Kamala had never experienced seeped into her heart. Forever after, she would carry a new memory of the last time she saw her husband alive.

En route back to the horseshoe ridge, Kamala made her own trip to Manakamana, flying in a cable car up the side of a mountain she used to climb with her family as a child. She had never had the heart or the stomach to make sacrifices at the pillar of the temple the way other pilgrims did, but she did make offerings of flowers and rice and incense in some of the temple's darkened alcoves. More than just offering prayers that day, she tried using her prayers to speak directly to Jeet, and with the images she had seen on the video seared into her mind, she made him a promise: "I swear that I will do everything in my power to try to bring justice to you."

• • •

While McOwen was in Nepal, Fryszman was preparing to return to Judge Ellison's courtroom in Texas. He had called a hearing on March 12, 2012, to address what was becoming a total breakdown between her and the lawyers from KBR. The company was putting up roadblocks in the discovery process, refusing to search for or hand over anything beyond the initial burst of searches it had conducted on just ten current and former employees. That refusal had now spanned more than a year. Fryszman had originally feared that KBR's proposed search terms were either so broad that they would return everything or so narrow that they would return nothing, but she figured it was the company's time to waste. Now, standing before Ellison, she felt she had stepped into a trap.

Michael Mengis, the KBR lawyer, found creative ways to illustrate for the judge how much money KBR had been required to spend on "a fishing expedition." It had to pay internal costs to do the searches, he said, and then it needed to pay lawyers from Mengis's firm to review the potentially relevant documents. "The initial search terms that we ran on the ten persons of interest kicked back 2.3 million hits," Mengis told Ellison. That sounded overwhelming, but anyone who has conducted the simplest Google search knows that such a big headline number can also be misleading. After all, a Google search on the name "Robert Gerlach" alone returns 527,000 hits, but very few of them are even remotely related to the former KBR procurement manager for Anbar Province who was one of the ten "persons of interest" the discovery focused on. Still, Mengis craftily built on his headline number as he spoke to Judge Ellison. "We believe that the persons of interest right now are costing KBR, on average, $60,000 per person to search and review and produce documents—$60,000," he repeated. He reframed this for the judge: "It boils down to almost a hundred dollars a page for electronic discovery from what we have had to review. And you get lost maybe in what we have produced, but we have reviewed four times what we have produced to determine whether or not something is responsive." He explained that KBR had ceased conducting any more searches or providing any more documents, a position he told the judge he had taken "now for well over a year," because the company believed "that the ten [people] we have looked at is sufficient." The basis of that belief was simple, Mengis said. "We have absolutely nothing from them [the plaintiffs] that would substantiate their claims, yet they want to go on a fishing expedition with our records, and especially our electronic records, that has been costly to date. And we have been very, I think, accommodating when it comes to what we have provided so far, but we are at our end in terms of agreeing to produce more."

Ellison liked Mengis, another native son of Louisiana and a former Catholic seminarian who had also clerked for a federal judge. Perhaps most important, Mengis spoke for Ellison the way genteel Southern lawyers were meant to: slowly, and with a deep breath between each word. Still, Ellison did not appear to be buying Mengis's argument. "It seemed to me, though, that the ten custodians or the ten individuals in these original search terms were never intended to be the limits of the universe of searching," Ellison told him, adding moments later that the law required a judge to consider several variables in determining the scope of discovery allowed. "And of course one of them, is the importance of the issues at stake," he told Mengis, "and here, the issues at stake are highly, highly important." Then Ellison put it bluntly: "Now, we do have, tragically, people who are dead."

Mengis refused to yield. "KBR has spent in excess of $700,000, probably approaching a million dollars now in discovery, on a case that should never have been filed based on the evidentiary support they had prior to filing," he said. He and the other lawyers from his firm, along with KBR's in-house legal team, may have believed even more firmly now that there was not enough evidence of the company's culpability to warrant the lawsuit, but the defense had already lost that fight more than two years earlier. Fryszman, of course, argued that Mengis was completely wrong about the developing evidence, in terms both of what KBR had handed over thus far and of what she was generating on her own without the company's help, but for strategic reasons she said as little about it as possible in court, or at least as little as Ellison would let her get away with, to avoid foreshadowing her strategy. She also suggested that KBR was sitting on the ball. "I think," she told Ellison, "Mr. Mengis is a master at slowdown." The less evidence she had from within KBR's files about the true nature of its relationship with Daoud, and about KBR's potential participation or acquiescence in Daoud's conduct, the harder it would be for her in the next, major battle of the case.

Ellison ordered the two sides to meet over lunch that day to try to resolve their discovery differences, and even offered to pick up the tab, telling them to come back to his courtroom after lunch with a resolution.

That day, and for another year to come, in contentious hearing after hearing, in vitriolic e-mail after e-mail, in motion after motion, there would be little give from KBR. Mengis and the other defense lawyers even took a surprising tone before Ellison on the issue, almost dictating terms to him about what the company would and would not do regarding the handover of its internal records. Taking advantage of Ellison's deferential manner to the lawyers appearing before him, KBR's lawyers tried to muddy the waters regarding the discovery disputes at every turn with extensive presentations rehashing their claim that the case was frivolous, including once when Ellison let them put on a PowerPoint presentation. Perhaps they knew they could continue to refuse to budge so long as the referee was a federal judge who came off the bench to shake their hands after a hearing, and who, by choice, avoided aggressive confrontation. Time and again, Ellison's demeanor worked in KBR's favor, at least in slowing down the critical discovery process. Over the course of a year, Judge Ellison simply did not rule on key discovery questions. Some of the documents the company did hand over—the documents Mengis had said KBR was spending so much money to find—were so obviously worthless that they seemed like schoolboy pranks from the defense team, including when it dumped nineteen thousand pages of Al Asad laundry logs on Fryszman.

Perhaps it was no accident that the defense team's ceaseless arguments about the "very expensive fishing expedition" for a "frivolous" lawsuit came almost immediately on the heels of another years-long case in front of Ellison in the very same courtroom. Before the discovery war erupted, Ellison had presided over the trial of KBR in the Jamie Leigh Jones case. Jones, who had gone to Iraq for KBR as a twenty-year-old in July 2005, alleged that only days after arriving in Baghdad, she had been drugged and gang-raped by coworkers, and that company representatives had locked her in a trailer after she reported the rape. Her lawsuit had advanced, at least in part, on the wings of countless dramatic media appearances, and even the passage of a new federal law inspired by her case. KBR had countered that Jones was a world-class self-promoter—she had already sold the rights to her story for a docudrama—and that her allegations were demonstrably false, but Ellison, backed by the federal appeals court, brought the case to trial over KBR's objections and following years of intense skirmishes. Several important discrepancies about her story, however, emerged during the summer 2011 trial, including some from medical evidence. In the end, members of the jury didn't buy her story, and found in KBR's favor after only a day and a half of deliberations. In the wake of the verdict, the company's lawyers had asked Ellison to force Jones to pay more than two million dollars in attorneys' fees, arguing that her claims had been fabricated and malicious, and her suit frivolous. Ellison rejected the demand, but gave KBR a greatly reduced bill for costs unrelated to attorneys' fees.

Now, only three weeks later, KBR's defense team in Kamala's case used language reminiscent of terms the company's lawyers had just raised before Ellison in the Jones proceedings, as if to remind him of how much his judgment had hurt KBR already: *frivolous, false and unsubstantiated allegations, costing us a fortune*. Advocates for victims of sexual assault saw the Jones verdict as a setback for their cause, with one publication even declaring in a giant, bold headline "Jamie Leigh Jones Probably Lied About Her Rape. That Doesn't Mean Most Women Do." Yet it is unlikely that anyone envisioned its potential to damage the cause of demonstrably clear victims of the war seeking to hold KBR accountable before the very same judge.

When it came to KBR's posture and intransigence, perhaps another moment proved more significant, this one occurring in Washington less than three weeks after Judge Ellison rejected KBR's demand that Jones pay its legal fees. Beyond a small circle of corporate defense lawyers nationwide, few noticed that on October 17, 2011, the U.S. Supreme Court announced that it would hear arguments in a case focused on whether corporations could be sued in U.S. courts for human rights abuses overseas. At the heart of the issue was the 1789 statute that Fryszman and star human rights litigator Michael Hausfeld had employed in Kamala's case and others, including the Holocaust cases. The Supreme Court case involved a lawsuit alleging that Royal Dutch Shell had aided and abetted the torture and murder of Nigerians who had protested against oil exploration and production, and their environmental impact, on ancestral lands in the Niger Delta. It alleged that government military and police forces had responded to those protests by attacking villages, beating, raping, killing, and arresting residents and destroying or looting property. The company was accused of aiding the abuses by providing compensation to government forces, feeding them, giving them transportation, and allowing them to stage attacks from company properties. The lead plaintiff was Esther Kiobel, the widow of a murdered activist, who had fled Nigeria and received asylum in the United States.

The U.S. Court of Appeals for the Second Circuit, based in New York, had found that international jurisprudence in the post-Holocaust world *did allow* people such as Kiobel to bring human rights cases "against states and against individual men and women" in American courtrooms, "but not against" strictly *legal* persons "such as corporations," in this case, Royal Dutch Shell. It was the first time an appeals court had held that companies could not be sued under the law, and so it had the potential to affect human rights cases filed against corporations across the country. A growing body of law in the United States had extended the rights and privileges enjoyed by human beings to corporations, and yet it appeared the the Supreme Court might now protect corporations from some of the attendant liabilities, at least beyond the country's borders.

Mengis and KBR had been waving the appeals court decision out of New York in front of judge Ellison since 2010, but it had no automatic authority in his courtroom unless and until the U.S. Supreme Court blessed it. Now the high court had said it would hear the case, portending potential trouble for Kamala and the other families. As it dug in against them, KBR literally put its money into the pending Supreme Court case as a way to get the families' lawsuit dismissed, paying for

David Rivkin and three other lawyers from Baker & Hostetler to file a friend-of-the-court brief with the highest court in the nation. Rivkin and his colleagues told the Supreme Court justices that KBR condemned human rights abuses worldwide, and then pointed to the company's frequently invoked "Code of Business Conduct." "Despite KBR's record of leadership on these issues, it is a defendant in a lawsuit under the Alien Tort Statute concerning other companies' worker recruitment practices undertaken in the sovereign territories of foreign nations and said to violate the norms of customary international law. Although premised on allegations of KBR's participation or acquiescence in wrongful conduct that, to this day, remain without any support in fact, that lawsuit has dragged on for four years, imposing substantial litigation and reputational costs on KBR." On the very first page of its first brief to the nation's highest court about Kamala's lawsuit, KBR called itself a leader in global human rights, and then repeated the notion that the case was not about its supply chain, its *human* supply chain, but about "other companies' worker recruitment practices" and that there was no "support in fact" that it had acquiesced or participated in those practices.

If there was a discernible moment when KBR first went on the offensive in the lawsuit from Kamala and the other families, it was probably the day after the Supreme Court said it would hear Esther Kiobel's case. The company's lawyers had remained silent for nearly three months about Fryszman's request to expand discovery, but on October 18, the day after the high court's announcement, Mengis fired off a letter to Fryszman. Claiming once again that the case was becoming "a very expensive 'fishing expedition, which appears to be based on nothing more than your suspicions,'" Mengis declared that KBR would not search any additional employees' records as part of the discovery process. He also heaped scorn on Fryszman for an interview she had done that January with the *National Law Journal*, in which she indicated that she had first become aware of the case of the twelve men from Nepal by reading the *Chicago Tribune* investigation. "Having no evidence other than those news reports, you went looking for clients and a lawsuit," Mengis wrote, before adding that Fryszman had not yet produced anything "that would support any of your unsubstantiated allegations against KBR." The defense was digging its trench.

Fryszman did not connect it to the impending arguments before the Supreme Court, but KBR's lawyers even proposed that Judge Ellison hold off on making any major decisions in Kamala's lawsuit until the Supreme Court had ruled in *Kiobel*, confident in their belief that it could make Kamala's case go away. Ellison allowed the discovery disputes to drag on unresolved, but he did not allow the entire case to grind to a halt. That's when a crack in Fryszman's case threatened to deepen, and KBR moved in for the kill.

• • •

On July 20, 2012, Buddi Prasad Gurung raised his right hand and swore he would tell the truth. It had been nearly eight years since he climbed into a vehicle in Amman, Jordan, that was part of a much bigger convoy along the Highway Through Hell charged with delivering dozens of Nepali workers to the Al Asad Air Base, including the twelve who were kidnapped and executed. Today, he sat in an air-conditioned conference room on the tenth floor of a Downtown Los Angeles skyscraper. Featuring a helicopter landing pad on the roof for corporate travelers, the building housed the offices of Christopher Tayback, the LA lawyer representing Daoud and Partners. Over the course of Gurung's two-day cross-examination, at least eleven different lawyers from all sides of the case would be in the conference room, along with two interpreters, a videographer, a court reporter, and a Daoud manager from Amman. Another Baker & Hostetler lawyer, Billy Donley, was there for KBR, and played an increasingly prominent role as the company began to go on the offensive.

From the first hearing in the case, it had been apparent to everyone that Gurung's journey to the convoy had been completely different from that of the twelve dead men, a difference that the defense had used to attack the overall case. Now, in the deposition, Tayback and Donley wasted little time before zeroing in on the most glaring of these differences and weaknesses. With the camera rolling, Gurung said that his journey to Al Asad did not start with "Moon Light Consultants" in Kathmandu or continue with forty-five days inside in a dark room in Jordan. Instead, he had gone through a different Nepali man, someone who seemed to be a friend more than a labor broker, to New Delhi, where he spent nearly three weeks. While there, he and other Nepalis "just stay in a room, sleep in the room, sometimes we just walk around close by, and sometimes we go far with, you know, in a bus, for [a] visit. And it was a very big place." The bus rides took the men sightseeing, Gurung said. Then, after arriving in Jordan, he stayed in a completely different location from the men who would be kidnapped and executed, and testified that he stayed in what he called a hotel. When he was asked, "Were you free to leave your hotel room and walk around whenever you wanted?" Gurung replied, "Yes. We were able to get out of the hotel." At another point, he added that he would "sometimes walk around the park and go back to [the] hotel." It was by no means fatal to the case, but Gurung's testimony in Los Angeles seemed to do little to bolster the plaintiffs' overall portrait of coercion necessary to call his experience "human trafficking." Perhaps most devastating to his credibility, Gurung admitted that he was fired after fifteen months on the job at Al Asad because KBR had found a bottle of whiskey in his duffel bag during a search. Although none questioned that Gurung was in the convoy with the twelve, the defense would use his weaknesses to attack the entire narrative the plaintiffs had constructed around the twelve dead men.

Matthew Handley returned from his leave in the summer of 2012 in shock at the state of affairs that had developed in the case. What had been a relatively professional adversarial proceeding, in which both sides had been fairly civil while still upholding their duties to their clients, had degenerated into something just shy of warfare. Handley reintroduced himself to KBR's defense team with a friendly "Hello, I'm back," as if he were ironing out a seemingly straightforward matter in the case, only to receive a brusque reply from Billy Donley, in essence: *With all due respect, Matt, you have no idea what's been going on here in the last year.* Donley was emerging as the lead KBR lawyer attempting to portray the company as the true victim in the case, a drum he beat ceaselessly following the Jamie Leigh Jones verdict. If Michael Mengis was the Southern gentleman of KBR's defense team, and David Rivkin was its conservative intellectual firebrand, then Donley was its Texas street fighter, at least as far as the plaintiffs were concerned; he had largely made his name working for automobile makers in legal battles against their own franchised car dealerships. Fryszman and Handley got the distinct impression from their dealings with Donley that taking on car salesmen must have been a tough, sometimes bare-knuckle business for a Texas lawyer.

Near the end of the summer, KBR filed what is known as a motion for summary judgment. Lawyers can spend months preparing a summary judgment motion, which offers a defendant in a federal lawsuit its last significant chance to keep the case away from a jury. Mengis's name was first on the filing, and he clearly had taken the lead. When all the exhibits and attachments were included, it reached more than eight hundred pages. The company asked Ellison to find that none of the evidence and pleadings to date showed any genuine issue of material fact for a jury to weigh—that the case was meritless and that Ellison had to give a verdict in favor of KBR. The company's lawyers hammered away at the weaknesses in Buddi Gurung's story, and took the inspector general's report from 2006, which had confirmed that the twelve men were in KBR's human supply chain, and turned it against the families. The report said there were no clauses "in contracts between [the U.S. government and] KBR Halliburton that make them responsible for labor fraudulently procured by independent contractors or subcontractors." KBR now claimed that this conclusion, based on contract language rather than the law, meant the company was free from liability. "The plaintiffs and their counsel based their grave allegations of human rights abuses by KBR on newspaper articles and a government report that cleared KBR of any wrongdoing. And now, after years of discovery and great expense to KBR, the plaintiffs still lack the evidence necessary to establish genuine issues of material fact as to the existence of essential elements of their claims against KBR."

Under the law, Fryszman and her team now had to go much further than they did when they beat back KBR's initial motion to dismiss the lawsuit in the first big hearing in the case. To survive they had to show that Kamala's lawsuit was built on more than "conclusional allegations, unsubstantiated assertions, or only a scintilla of evidence." In some ways, KBR had jumped the gun; a motion such as this usually comes after the discovery deadline expires, but KBR's lawyers didn't wait. In so doing, they put Fryszman's team under significant pressure.

Fearing that her entire case hung in the balance—which it did—Fryszman now saw precisely what KBR's strategy had been. By refusing to budge on any additional discovery for more than a year, the company had filed a motion to kill her case while simultaneously blocking her from obtaining the evidence she needed to prove it. Now she had to fight off KBR's motion for summary judgment at the same time that she would have to meet the company's own outstanding discovery requests to her side. Indeed, KBR sought four hundred documents, answers to sixteen hundred written deposition-style questions for Kamala and the other Nepali family members, and answers to more than five thousand yes/no questions for the Nepalis, which KBR's lawyers knew would require Fryszman to fly to Nepal to facilitate while trying to respond to its motion to kill the case. She had not yet taken even a single deposition of a single KBR employee, because in order to prepare her questions, she needed documents that she believed KBR had not yet provided. She told Judge Ellison that the company had refused to search even for documents containing the name "Daoud," despite how basic the relationship between the two companies was to fundamental issues in the case. She urged Ellison to give her at least a few more weeks, although even that might not be long enough.

Increasingly, Fryszman also was alone in the battle. Handley had been back at the firm only a short time when he received an offer for another job: chief litigator for the Washington Lawyers' Committee for Civil Rights and Urban Affairs. It would mean giving up on the lawsuit, and taking a significant cut in earnings, but given how much his experiences in the compensation case had changed his priorities, Handley didn't hesitate to accept the post.

Under the gun, Fryszman pressed Molly McOwen to dedicate even more ceaseless hours to the case as the pair pushed to meet their deadline to answer the motion for summary judgment. McOwen and her fiancé were to be married in the same window of time, and they proceeded with the wedding, but there would be no honeymoon as McOwen drove toward the finish. After Buddi Gurung's troubled performance in Los Angeles, Fryszman pressed Ganesh Gurung in Nepal to redouble his efforts to find more men who had been in Jordan with the twelve, a seemingly impossible task. She also was trying to bring Kamala and four other witnesses to Washington to sit for cross-examination by lawyers from KBR and Daoud, an effort that was turning into its own logistical nightmare. Shortly after the company's surprise summary judgment filing but before the discovery deadline, Fryszman also handed over to KBR's lawyers additional documents, including translations of what McOwen had collected during her vacation in Nepal. This included the moving letter from Prakash Adhikari to his parents, which had arrived in their village five days after they had burned an effigy of their murdered son. The letter was no secret, as excerpts had been included in the *Tribune* series about the men seven years earlier. In it, the young Prakash had done everything he possibly could to avoid worrying his family, and had also mentioned that he had attempted to call the local *dalal* from whom the family had bought the job, but the agent had not responded. Prakash gave no explanation for his need to reach the *dalal*, but he did write, in a matter-of-fact way, that soon he would head into Iraq after being "in Jordan for a month without work." He also wrote, "I have realized that life is like a flowing stream. Until yesterday I was in Nepal. Now I am in a foreign land. Why? Who knows? Maybe it's the times, or the situation, or maybe I had no choice."

After Fryszman turned over her copy of the translation of the letter before the discovery deadline, Donley almost immediately accused her of misconduct for withholding crucial evidence that he claimed exonerated the company, saying the letter proved definitively that Adhikari and the rest of the twelve men held in Jordan for forty-five days were actually eagerly anticipating their work in Iraq, that they had been well treated, and that Adhikari was even grateful to the relative who had encouraged him to seek work overseas. In phone calls with Fryszman and her team, Donley began threatening to file formal misconduct charges against Fryszman, McOwen, Handley, and almost every other lawyer who had thus far participated in the case on behalf of Kamala and the other family members. The threat of misconduct got deeply under McOwen's skin, and she began to wilt under the pressure. In calmer moments, she almost considered it a badge of honor to be accused of misconduct by a company such as KBR, and accused along with some of the finest human rights lawyers working anywhere in the United States. But when she found herself up against extraordinary deadlines in their effort to keep the case alive—for Kamala and other women from Nepal who had wept before her eyes and implored her for help—she also found herself questioning virtually every document she signed in the case and every move she made, fearing her career could be affected for the rest of her life.

Judge Ellison allowed Fryszman and her team the extra time they had requested to file their response to KBR's summary judgment motion, but by then, the damage had been done, personally, if not legally. When McOwen got home late one night to the apartment she shared with Cook in Washington, she sat on the edge of her bed and told her new husband that she felt she was circling the edges of a nervous breakdown. With a heavy heart for the families in Nepal, she decided to quit the firm.

As Fryszman prepared to meet the deadline to respond to KBR's summary judgment motion, she was informed by its lawyers that they were formalizing misconduct charges against her and the other lawyers who had assisted her in the case, even Handley and McOwen, despite the fact that they were no longer involved. When the written charges followed in early February, they covered nearly five hundred pages, including all the attachments and exhibits, and rehashed many of the same arguments the company had been making for four years. The difference now was that KBR's lawyers had completed their transformation of the company into the victim in the litigation, and personally attacked the attorneys for the families, accusing Fryszman and the other lawyers of manufacturing human rights charges based on nothing more than newspaper stories. Not surprisingly, Billy Donley was the lead lawyer in the effort, and his signature came first. Rivkin had also signed it. Noticeably absent was Michael Mengis, and this seemed to suggest an unspoken acknowledgment of how low the defense had sunk and how much the company itself was dictating the strategy against the counsel of at least one prominent member of the firm it had hired. Mark Lowes, a KBR vice president who was the in-house chief of litigation for the company, added his name to the motion, further signaling the company's direct sanctioning of the effort. Perhaps most brazen of all was that the petition accusing Fryszman and her team of misconduct sought attorneys' fees while the case was still pending, and while Kamala and the other families still might win. It claimed that KBR had spent more than five million dollars defending itself against this "frivolous" lawsuit. At least in the Jamie Leigh Jones case, KBR had waited until after it won a jury verdict before trying to recover costs and fees.

At a minimum, the attack held the potential to serve as a massive distraction for Fryszman from the existential fight she had at hand: trying to prove for Judge Ellison, once and for all, that the case belonged in front of a jury, something KBR seemed desperate to avoid. When the misconduct charges landed at her office she also was preparing to bring Kamala and four other witnesses from Nepal to Washington, where they would face interrogation from KBR and Daoud in depositions. Kamala and the other family members, some barely literate, most having barely ever left rural Nepal, none ever having even been on an airplane, would be under direct fire, just as Buddi Gurung had been in Los Angeles. With his deposition used as a weapon against Fryszman in both the effort to dismiss her case and the misconduct petition, it seemed she had everything to lose from this exercise and virtually nothing to gain—as did Kamala and the other families.

14

Building heights in Washington, DC, are strictly regulated, yielding a skyline where nothing rises more dramatically than the U.S. Capitol at the end of Pennsylvania Avenue. The effect is a curtsy to the ideals of American democracy: nothing is above the people's assembly—not the White House, not an embassy, not a corporate tower. The political realities beneath these visual strictures may be different now, but the zoning laws haven't changed, meaning that architects in modern Washington have a limited bag of tools with which to work, so they lean heavily on the city's historic character: neoclassical structures, Georgian Revivals, and the like. Although located in the middle of the city, the Washington Plaza Hotel is as far removed from this historic aesthetic as possible, resembling an early 1960s vision for the future of Miami, managing to be both retro and modern thanks to a nine-story facade that is glass and beachfront white, and to long curved corridors owing to a boomerang-shaped footprint; hoteliers in the nation's capital need to make up the floor space they lose in height through length and width. Although they may have seen some faux-classical, Empire-inspired buildings in Kathmandu, Kamala and the five other travelers from Nepal had never seen anything like the Washington Plaza, a fact that added to their sense of being in foreign, unfamiliar, and imposing surroundings. But the initial visual shock after the long ride into the city from Washington Dulles International Airport on the morning of February 18, 2013, was mild compared with what they were about to experience.

Joining Kamala were four men from four other families, three fathers and one brother. A young woman from Ganesh Gurung's office named Reena Gurung (no relation), a trained Nepalese lawyer who spoke English, came along as a sort of logistics manager and chaperone. She had made small placards in English to help the four men on the trip request water or whatever else they might need. Kamala was more self-sufficient, and she watched Bollywood films and listened to music during the air legs of their nearly two-day journey via Dubai, but she was anxious about being away from Kritika for the first time. She felt nauseated, and was unsure whether it was the air travel, her worrying about her daughter, her nervousness about what was ahead for them in Washington, or something she had eaten that was gnawing at her stomach.

After a day of settling in, the family members spent a week preparing for their depositions. Assisting Fryszman was a human rights lawyer from New York she had recruited named Anthony DiCaprio. Preparing witnesses is an arduous task, even when the client isn't from a farming village on the other side of the world. But for the Nepalis, the challenges extended well beyond their total lack of familiarity with legal proceedings, the English language, and even the food they were served in Washington, which was as radically different for them as Nepalese food would be for an American staying at a farmhouse in the foothills of the Himalayas. The basics were plain enough, as the witnesses learned everything from sitting upright, to making sure they carefully understood each question before answering, to thinking carefully about their answers before speaking, to answering only the question before them and saying nothing more, to expressing themselves in the shortest and clearest way possible. Other challenges were more deeply and culturally ingrained. Many Nepalis, especially those from rural areas, tend to be extremely deferential to anyone who seems to represent or hold authority, so the witnesses had to grasp that the lawyers from KBR and Daoud had no power over them, nor any benevolent intentions, even if their voices were soft and their manners kindly. Those lawyers, the Nepalis were made to understand now, would try to get them to volunteer information that could be used against them in the case, and they most certainly would ask questions that would upset them and stir up the darkest moments of their families' lives.

DiCaprio perhaps slightly overplayed his role as the tough guy during mock sessions, mainly because Fryszman was expecting the family members to face Billy Donley, whom the plaintiffs' team had come to see as KBR's enforcer. DiCaprio had thick dark hair and a graying beard and was built like a fireplug, possessing a strength beneath his kindness that gave Kamala reassurance and a sense of calm, even as he told her in their practice sessions to imagine him as the most horrible man she had ever known, a man intent on breaking her down. Over several days, and with DiCaprio's help, Kamala's confidence grew, even though at times she found herself overcome by the dual emotional forces weighing on her during the trip: that she was away from Kritika for the first time and that each practice session, by design, dredged up all her sadness, not just about having lost Jeet, but about everything else that had come before and after the moment captured in the video footage, which was now seared into her mind. Of all the witnesses, though, Kamala might have needed the least amount of persuading when it came to seeing the attorneys for KBR and Daoud as adversaries, given her fully formed rebellious streak, from defending herself as a young girl to whipping stones at trees so she could pilfer fruit for herself and Kritika at the ashram.

Adjusting to American food wasn't easy for any of the Nepalis, but Kamala politely ate every hot dog she was offered, while the men gravitated toward instant noodles they had stocked up on at a local convenience store. Before long, they discovered Indian takeout. Reena Gurung did her best to fill their hours with diversions designed to leaven their days, including leading walks through Washington and even a trip to the Smithsonian's National Air and Space Museum. Yet homesickness and worry were constant companions inside the rooms they shared, two by two, at the Washington Plaza Hotel, especially for Kamala. She called Kritika at least once every day, first straight from the hotel phone, but later through store-bought calling cards after the hotel staff alerted the Nepalis to the potentially massive bill. The men were fascinated by the seemingly limitless options on the hotel's giant televisions, and inadvertently purchased almost every pay-per-view movie on offer without actually watching any of them, ringing up a string of room charges reaching into the thousands of dollars. The hotel's managers had a good laugh and forgave the charges.

If Kamala and the rest of the Nepalis were overwhelmed by their surroundings, Fryszman's own stress levels soared beyond what she had experienced in any other case, so much so that she could measure them on the bathroom scale at her home in leafy northwest Washington. Worry and stress had cost Fryszman fifteen pounds. Kamala would be the last of the Nepalis to sit for a deposition, and while she was under fire, Cohen Milstein would have just one week left to answer KBR's misconduct petition. The firm hired outside counsel to assist with its defense against the charges, and spent more than two hundred thousand dollars to try to quell the KBR offensive. When she assessed matters in a purely intellectual and dispassionate way, Fryszman knew she had little to fear. Judge Ellison was an inherently fair and careful jurist. She felt secure in the evidence she had amassed in the case, although, like all driven and slightly manic lawyers, she wanted more. She also knew it was outrageous for KBR to argue, essentially, that she had no evidence with which to sue the company. In some of her worst moments of doubt, she would seek reassurance from her husband, a prominent civil rights lawyer named Stuart Ishimaru. He helped her see through the fog of war, and the assurance of another experienced attorney that everything was going to be okay boosted Fryszman during her most difficult moments. Still, the nagging fear that her case and her career could be derailed by all this was, at a minimum, a slightly terrifying and ever-present possibility.

The depositions were taken about four blocks from the North Lawn of the White House, on the top floor of an eleven-story glass box of an office building, a floor occupied exclusively by Baker & Hostetler, KBR's law firm. The most prominent feature of the building was a ground-to-sky glass atrium dominated by a fifty-foot-long American flag hung through its center like a tapestry. There was so much glass on the outside of the building that it was hard to imagine there were any windowless rooms inside, but unforgiving bulbs provided the only light in the interior conference room where they met over the course of the ten-day period for the depositions. The effect was something like that of a casino floor, which is designed to be windowless in order to keep gamblers from marking the passage of time. Billy Donley, the KBR lawyer Fryszman had been bracing for, was nowhere in sight, with the questions coming instead from the more affable Michael Mengis, but DiCaprio had been so primed to be Fryszman's pit bull during the depositions that he fiercely fired objections at the questions Mengis asked. It got so bad at one point that Mengis had to request a break and took Fryszman aside. "Agnieszka, what is going on here?" he asked. She apologized, having all but forgotten that her strategy with DiCaprio had been targeted around Donley. *Oops, I brought the attack dog,* she thought to herself, and then asked DiCaprio to turn it down a notch or two.

There were no major stumbles or revelations throughout the opening days, as the Nepalese men testified about long-established facts of their loved ones' journeys. If KBR and Daoud were expecting to score any body blows, as they believed they had done with Buddi Gurung, they were disappointed.

On the afternoon of March 6, Kamala took her oath and first sat down for cross-examination. Fryszman wanted her to be the final witness. Joseph Sarles, the Los Angeles lawyer representing Daoud, took the lead ahead of Mengis, and he spent two hours picking away at the tiniest and seemingly most irrelevant details about Kamala's life: Who, exactly, had set her up with Jeet? How many hours a day did they work on their farm, and how many days per week? Did anyone else work on the farm with them? How much were her mother-in-law's pension payments from the British Army? What did Jeet pack for his trip to Jordan? How long was the bus ride to Kathmandu? Kamala did everything DiCaprio had asked of her, answering each question shortly and succinctly, volunteering nothing extra, and maintaining her steely posture throughout the afternoon. After nearly three hours of icy back-and-forth, they broke for the day.

When they resumed first thing the next morning, Sarles started with a couple of questions seeking the sort of details that the defense easily could have learned from written exchanges with Fryszman's office, such as Kamala's home address. After Kamala gave it, DiCaprio quietly interjected, gesturing toward Sarles, "If a guy looking like him shows up, don't answer the door." Within a few minutes, however, Sarles cut straight into a line of questioning that seemed designed to rile Kamala's emotions rather than elicit relevant information.

"How old was your daughter when Mr. Jeet left for the last time?" Sarles asked her.

"She was just twenty to twenty-two months old," she said.

"Before he left, did you ever talk with Mr. Jeet about what you were going to do when he returned?"

"We had," Kamala said, careful as always to volunteer nothing extra. Sarles wasn't letting go.

"What did you talk about with regard to that?" he asked.

"He had said, 'I will go and earn a lot of money,'" Kamala said, almost in a whisper. "'You take care of our daughter, and you take care of mother. I'll take good care of you when I come back.'" Her face tightened as she dropped her gaze, and then she gathered herself briefly and looked back up across the table. "'Then we can educate our daughter and give her the best.'" After speaking these words, Kamala took a deep breath, lifted her eyes toward the ceiling, and closed them. Then she buried her face in her scarf. They were only eight minutes into the day's questioning, and Sarles didn't break his stride. He asked Kamala how she had planned to be in touch with her husband after he left for Jordan, and DiCaprio cut him off as they all watched Kamala quietly crumple. "Would you ask the witness if she needs a moment?" DiCaprio interjected.

After crying into a paper napkin she had picked up off the center of the table, Kamala raised her head. "It's okay," she said. "Can you please repeat the question?"

"I had asked," Sarles said, "how Mr. Jeet had said he was going to contact you after he left." Kamala said that her husband had promised to write home, but no letters ever came. As Sarles started to zero in on her husband's kidnapping and murder, Kamala became more forthcoming, her emotions overtaking her preparations for the first time, perhaps by Sarles's design. He asked her about hearing the news of Jeet's abduction on the radio, without knowing that when it was broadcast, she had been plotting their winter vegetables on the terrace below the farmhouse in the village that cut through the clouds like a peninsula on the shores of the sky.

"I don't remember much, but the only thing I remember is they said his name, my husband's name, and his address, and then they said that he had been captured. And that's all I remember. I don't remember much," she said.

As it was clear that Kamala was both upset and opening up, DiCaprio became increasingly combative, arguing with Sarles about everything, from his questions to the coarseness of the napkins KBR's law firm had left on the table for Kamala to wipe away her tears. "We're just trying to get some tissue," DiCaprio said, "something that's not quite as rough as those things, a little softer than that."

Sarles continued focusing on all the news Kamala had heard or seen about Jeet's abduction and then his murder, and conversations she had had with other family members about it, asking her to burrow down in excruciating detail on the radio reports from almost a decade earlier. "Did the report say anything about how Mr. Jeet had been killed?" he asked, repeating the question as Kamala expressed bewilderment, until finally she asked for a short break.

Soon Sarles moved to the execution video, asking Kamala to state precisely when and where and how long ago she had watched it, and precisely what she saw on the small screen of her phone when she had finally mustered the courage to see for herself what had happened to her husband.

"I object to this line of questioning," DiCaprio said.

Although they were seared into her mind, Kamala found it impossible to recount the details. Sarles's motive for this line of questioning was unclear, but lawyers for both KBR and Daoud possessed written discovery from Fryszman in which she indicated that these were the very images that most deeply haunted Kamala during her darkest moments, when she sometimes felt that she, too, might walk down the footpath that her mother-in-law had tried to follow into the gloomy shade, wanting only to wander until she was lost.

With Sarles's questions about the video, Kamala retreated into a kind of shell, issuing a stream of "I don't know" and "I don't remember" and "I can't."

Sarles changed course, and after digging deeply into the minutiae of her finances, he asked Kamala about "any physical ailments" she had suffered as a result of her husband's death.

Kamala thought about the question for a long, silent moment, and then, nearly whispering, she replied, "I feel that I'm lonely. Doing all the work by myself is very difficult. I can't sleep at night." She paused again, and considered her reflection in the table, still crying silently. "I can't give the love to my daughter that she would have gotten from her father. I can't satisfy her needs, her emotional needs. When my daughter asks about her father, I just can't tell her what has happened to him. Whenever my daughter asks, I tell her that he's away in foreign countries, that he's abroad. And I know that her father is never going to come back. I know that I'm not ever going to bring her father to my daughter, but still it's very hard for me to tell her that her father lives no more, and that they have killed him." She covered her face again with her scarf.

"Would you like to take a break for a minute?" Sarles asked Kamala, before he was cut off by DiCaprio.

"In fact, the witness would prefer to finish this," DiCaprio said curtly.

Once this segment of Kamala's testimony had reached a natural break, the two sides paused for lunch so they could join by phone a previously scheduled status hearing with Judge Ellison. "I want to thank Your Honor for allowing us to delay a few minutes," Michael Mengis said into the speakerphone in his firm's Washington office and across the long-distance line connected to Ellison's courtroom in Houston.

"We were at a very emotional part in the testimony, and for the witness's sake, we didn't want to interrupt that and come back. And all the lawyers agreed that was the appropriate thing to do, and thank you for your patience."

In addition to the attorneys who were attending the depositions in Washington and joining in by speakerphone, Paul Hoffman, a noted human rights lawyer serving an increasingly important role as cocounsel with Fryszman, had dialed in from California. Billy Donley, the KBR defense lawyer, was in Ellison's courtroom in person, along with another lawyer from his firm, and an in-house attorney from KBR.

Almost as soon as he got a chance to speak, Donley began beating the drum that his client was the true victim in the case. He asked Ellison to hold a hearing and rule as soon as possible on the motion for summary judgment, which, if the judge granted it, would end the case in KBR's favor. Donley also pressed the judge about his petition on KBR's behalf leveling misconduct charges against Fryszman, Hoffman, and the rest of their team. "I can tell you, I've never filed one. I hate that I had to file one in this case," Donley said, with dubious sincerity. "But we've also filed that motion as well, and would like to have that set for a hearing."

By the time he got his crack, Hoffman was polite if somewhat incredulous. He said that Judge Ellison still had not ruled on important discovery disputes, as KBR had continued to refuse to provide more documents that were fundamental to the heart of the case, especially those related to its relationship with Daoud. At the same time, lawyers for the families had identified the most important people from KBR at Al Asad whom they needed to depose, but KBR had both refused to provide contact information and forbade the plaintiff's team from initiating any contact with them on their own without a ruling from Ellison. At the top of the list was Robert Gerlach, the KBR procurement manager who had executed the laundry contract under which the twelve were being delivered to work all the way from their villages in Nepal. "We're in a—we're in a catch-22, even with respect to depositions, where we're trying to arrange those depositions," Hoffman told the judge. "We have not been given their contact information, and we've been told not to contact them."

These issues were of paramount importance, Hoffman said, given that he and Fryszman, without KBR's help in discovery, had identified other KBR personnel from Al Asad who had said in sworn declarations "that the fact that these men were trafficked was widely known at the base, that it was impossible for KBR not to know about, [that] it was discussed openly. And we, in order to get to the bottom of that, we need to take the depositions of Mr. Gerlach and the other people who were responsible at KBR and establish the relationship between KBR and Daoud, what they knew, how they worked together . . . What we should be entitled to, based on what they [KBR] actually did file as a motion, is to be able to get into their documents to show that they had control over what Daoud did, that they knew what Daoud did, that it was widely known that these men were trafficked, [but] that they didn't do anything to deal with that. Those are the kinds of issues that we're entitled to get discovery of."

A defense lawyer for Daoud on the line from Los Angeles named Zachary Krug, who had not been present for the depositions unfolding in Washington, then claimed to the judge that new evidence had emerged from the testimony of the Nepalis that could exonerate the defendants. Fryszman practically exploded. "I would just like to say that Mr. Krug, who hasn't been present at any single one of the depositions, has completely mischaracterized what testimony we've received and completely misstated the evidence that's been obtained at the depositions and—"

"Slowly. Slowly," Judge Ellison told Fryszman, to little effect. Perhaps because of what had unfolded that morning with Kamala; or because of the weight of the somewhat existential challenges to her case and her career bearing down on her; or because of her having to listen to Donley once again launch into a soliloquy about the victimization of KBR through her alleged misdeeds—whatever the reason, Fryszman seemed unable to slow down as she rattled off, in her machine-gun style, what she saw as the mountain of evidence against the defendants. Ellison interjected three times to try to get her to compose herself. "I'm trying," she replied, before diving back in. Ellison repeatedly implored her with his refrain of "Slowly— slowly." Finally, even the judge who tolerated almost anything from lawyers in his courtroom felt he had to shut her down, albeit in his genteel Southern manner. "Well, Ms. Fryszman, maybe somebody else should make the argument. We just can't keep up with you. Mr. Hoffman?"

"I'll slow down," Fryszman implored him.

"Can you make the argument instead, Mr. Hoffman?" the judge said, cutting her off. Fryszman finally went silent, perhaps one of the few times Ellison had ever silenced a lawyer appearing before him.

The hearing ended with Ellison offering little satisfaction to Hoffman and Fryszman. Although KBR had been sitting on the ball for years when it came to discovery and would not cooperate in the plaintiffs' lawyers' effort to depose Gerlach and the others, Ellison was unwilling to allow for more time before deciding whether the case deserved, finally and fully, to go before a jury. He also did not indicate how he would rule on Donley's request to schedule a hearing on the misconduct charges.

"Is there anything further?" Ellison said.

"Nothing further, Your Honor," Hoffman replied.

"Thank you all very much," Ellison said, signaling that he was done. In succession, Donley, Mengis, and Krug each thanked the judge. Fryszman and Hoffman were silent.

Twenty-six minutes after they got off the phone with the judge, the lawyers from both sides assembled again in Baker & Hostetler's Washington conference room with Kamala. The break in the deposition had given Kamala a chance to compose herself, even if it had the opposite effect on Fryszman.

"Ms. Magar," Sarles began, addressing Kamala, "are you seeking any money from KBR and Daoud in this case?"

Kamala gently swiveled in the leather chair and took a long moment to consider her answer, before slightly raising her head, looking across the table, and saying quietly, "I need justice."

Sarles seemed taken aback, slightly stumbling as he repeated the question, but pausing between his words, staccato. "Are you asking for money to be paid to you as part of justice?"

"Out of this case, the most important thing that I need is justice, and if I get justice, that's enough," Kamala said.

Sarles then pressed her about any expenses she may have incurred because of Jeet's journey and murder, such as the loans the family had taken to buy Jeet's job in Jordan and the interest payments on top of them, which they had repaid to the lenders out of the charity payment they'd received from the Nepalese government in the wake of the riots. "Is one of the things that you're asking for from KBR and Daoud in this case that they pay you for the money you paid off the loans with?" Sarles asked.

"I want justice," she said again.

"Do you also want the money that you paid for the loans to be paid back to you?"

She paused once more and swiveled slightly. "I want justice," she repeated, unwavering.

Plaintiffs' lawyers have everything to lose when they put

their clients into depositions. Inevitably, something will go wrong when you subject even the best-prepared clients to days of cross-examination by world-class defense attorneys. Those realities are enshrined in a saying among practitioners: the value of your case starts dropping the minute you leave the room after a deposition, as when you drive a new car off a dealer's lot. The only question is: how *much* will it fall? As Fryszman and DiCaprio left Baker & Hostetler's offices that day, DiCaprio turned to Fryszman and said, "This is the only time in my career I've ever walked out of a deposition and watched the value of my case go *up*." The plaintiffs' lawyers had little doubt that even the most cynical jury would, in the face of such testimony, savage KBR, especially given that it carried the legacy of one of the most hated companies in America.

Kamala felt a sense of peace. When she sat at the conference table after her deposition and the room fell quiet, she thought about the exhibits on the table—photocopied pictures of her holding her baby daughter just after Jeet's death, a picture of Jeet posed outside the farmhouse, and even a photo of her mother-in-law. All reminded her of what she'd overcome to reach that moment, and to keep the promise that she'd made to Jeet in her prayers at the famous Manakamana temple, on the other side of the horseshoe ridge: *I swore I would do everything I possibly could to bring you justice. Now I've kept my sacred promise to you.* No matter what happened in the case, she told herself, she had done everything she could to try to set things right.

Fryszman drove Kamala to a store not far from her hotel, where they bought a stuffed panda bear and a gray teddy bear with a black nose for her to take back to Nepal for Kritika. Kamala had turned the tide.

15

Inside a dusty file room on the western edge of Kathmandu, Ganesh Gurung furiously combed through stack after stack and drawer after drawer stuffed with paper records. Agnieszka Fryszman had relentlessly driven the Nepalese academic to locate any other men who had been recruited to Jordan in the same group as Jeet and his eleven murdered compatriots. Evidence Fryszman had developed showed that the twelve were part of a bigger group of Nepalese men fed into Iraq through the same pipeline. The pressure Fryszman was under got passed on to Gurung over long-distance phone calls as she hammered him to come up with witnesses who had shared the twelve men's path to Iraq under KBR's contract with the U.S. military. Although he was among his nation's most respected public intellectuals, Gurung was not a trained or experienced investigator, and he'd exhausted nearly every possibility he could think of until, almost in desperation, he decided to physically comb through all the chaotically organized files at Nepal's Department of Foreign Employment. As he stared at the cabinets and stacks, he faced the almost paralyzing realization that more than one hundred thousand foreign labor permits had been issued each year since 2001. This was orders of magnitude beyond searching a haystack for a needle, but it was all he could do, and it would be worth doing even if he came up with nothing. At least then he could tell Fryszman that he had left no piece of paper unturned, and perhaps she would relent.

On his sixth day in the dust-filled room, and on the brink of giving up, Gurung looked down through his thick black-framed reading glasses and saw the words "Moon Light" on a file folder. Because the documents were organized roughly by the date when they had been submitted, he jumped to one of the last files in the group, which contained paperwork for dozens of men from across Nepal recruited and sent to Jordan in the same group as Jeet and the others. Gurung stared wide-eyed as he thumbed through the papers, which were not only for the twelve but for dozens of others: contracts promising jobs at Le Royal Hotel in Jordan, demand letters from Eyad Mansour, and the rest of the transnational deceptions used to get the men off their farms and into Iraq. Gurung copied the documents, scurried to another government office, one that issued passports, and within days came up with passport application records containing information he could use to start locating as many of these men as possible, so he could speak to them.

Alerted to Gurung's find, Anthony DiCaprio boarded a plane and rushed to Kathmandu.

In early April, just days ahead of the deadline for filing their final brief on KBR's motion for summary judgment, DiCaprio began meeting at Gurung's office with men who had been fed through the same pipeline as the twelve. In all, lawyers for the plaintiffs took sworn statements from seven men who had been delivered to the joint operations of Daoud and KBR at Al Asad and other U.S. military bases—including Fallujah, where they landed just before the bloody and infamous Second Battle of

Fallujah; the nearby Al Taqaddum Air Base, which served Fallujah; and the Kirkuk Air Base. Even beyond the airtight general evidence that thousands of foreign workers like the twelve had been brought to Iraq under conditions that U.S. investigators deemed human trafficking, Fryszman now had specific evidence showing a systematic and organized pipeline feeding Nepalese men to U.S. operations, a pipeline that began with Moon Light and ended with KBR. It was exactly the kind of evidence KBR's lawyers had hammered Fryszman for lacking since the first hearing.

DiCaprio met Biplav Bhatta, who had been just twenty-four years old in 2004 when he replied to Moon Light's ad for cooks to work at a hotel in Jordan. After buying his job the way everyone else did, Bhatta was put on a plane in July 2004, landed in Amman, and was met at the airport by men with a "Moon Light" sign. They took his passport and drove him to a compound, where he was ushered through a gate, down concrete stairs, and into a room with at least two dozen other Nepalese men inside. The door was locked behind him, from the outside. "We were all housed in two foul, overcrowded rooms without windows," Bhatta told DiCaprio. "The room where we had to cook our food, which was one of the two rooms, was also the bathroom. The toilet would clog and overflow with feces from overuse because there were so many people sharing one toilet." The Nepalis there included Jeet and at least three others from among the twelve that he could remember: Ramesh Khadka, Prakash Adhikari, and Mangal Limbu. Bhatta told DiCaprio that Arab men "would come to the compound once a day or so and throw food [in] from the outside," or, at other times, would order the Nepalis to keep quiet. He added that the Arab men would put their fingers to their lips in a shushing motion and then feign tearing up the Nepalis' passports or would even make throat-slitting gestures.

Because Bhatta could speak some English, he said that he tried to act as a sort of ambassador for the Nepalis, communicating with the Arab men who occasionally came to deliver food or menace them, asking the men specifically about the jobs the Nepalis had purchased. The men, he said, replied, "in broken English, that our papers and jobs were being processed." After five days in the foul and overcrowded rooms, the Nepalis were visited by two Arab men who entered and started calling out some of their names. They ordered Bhatta and a handful of others to gather their things, telling them they were headed "to our work site." Jeet and his compatriots "remained behind, since their names were not called," Bhatta remembered.

After a ten-hour car drive, Bhatta arrived at what he would later learn was "an American military base in Iraq called Camp Fallujah." He repeatedly told supervisors for Daoud and KBR that he and the others were supposed to be working in Jordan, not Iraq, but the men were told they had no choice. "I was frightened by the DP [Daoud and Partners] men and knew that we were trapped," he said, adding that he and the other Nepalis with him didn't have their passports, "and we were in the middle of a war zone." He also told DiCaprio, "From the moment I arrived at Fallujah, I told KBR people almost every day that my friends and I wanted to return to our families in Nepal, that we had been promised jobs in Jordan, had been brought to Iraq against our will, and that we wanted our passports back." KBR supervisors allegedly told the Nepalis that these issues were between them and Daoud, or they "would simply say I was there to work," Bhatta said. Angry over their plight, the men went on strike, refusing to work and demanding to be sent home immediately. Bhatta told DiCaprio that the strike ended "because KBR and DP refused to give us food until we went back to work," adding, "After about five days we were too hungry to continue our protest." DiCaprio interviewed others Ganesh Gurung had found, all of whom either traveled with the twelve or were held with them in Amman. Everyone was fed into the same human supply chain.

I met Bhatta myself in Kathmandu three years after DiCaprio. I showed him a photo array made up of random candid pictures of Arab men, some that I had copied from the Internet and others of friends of mine from the Middle East—along with a candid picture of Amin Mansour, the man first introduced to me as "Abdullah" so long ago in Amman. I turned my laptop toward Bhatta and asked him to identify anyone he recognized. Without hesitation, he laughed and pointed to my computer screen. "There's Amin," he said, scoffing at a photo of Amin Mansour smoking a cigarette. He also identified pictures of Mansour's property at No. 58 Malfuf Street in Amman as the place where he had been held for five days in two foul, overcrowded rooms, and where Jeet and the others remained for a total of nearly fifty days.

Sworn statements from Bhatta and the other men Ganesh Gurung had located landed in Washington moments before Fryszman ran up against her final deadline for answering KBR's motion to kill the case. Including the misconduct charges, the replies to KBR's attacks totaled 1,835 pages and were made without full discovery of KBR's records she had sought and without deposing a single witness. The federal antitrafficking law, which had been toughened specifically because of these

twelve men, imposed culpability on "whoever knowingly recruits, harbors, transports, provides, or obtains, by any means,
any person for labor or services" deemed to involve forced and
coerced labor, language that a federal appeals court had found
to criminalize a broad spectrum of conduct befitting the supply
chain nature of the crime itself. Fryszman's biggest hurdle in
keeping the families' case alive was to show Judge Ellison that
there was a genuine issue of material fact to present to a jury
about whether KBR's conduct was "knowing" in regard to human trafficking within its operations for the U.S. military in
Iraq. KBR's lawyers had never disputed that its executives knew
about trafficking allegations in their human supply chain; they
said only that it was impossible to pinpoint *when* they knew,
and whether they knew before Jeet and the others were massa-
cred. This is precisely why Fryszman had worked so hard to get
into the company's files, and perhaps why KBR had fought and
stalled for so long to keep her out.

Still, Fryszman and Hoffman believed they had gotten
enough to defeat KBR's summary judgment motion and get
a trial in front of a jury, including some internal KBR e-mails
and documents the company had handed over, and others between Daoud and KBR that they had received from Daoud.

Their case to Judge Ellison began in the main staging area for
the initial invasion of Iraq, at the logistical hub for KBR and the
entire invasion force, which was a base in Kuwait called Camp
Arifjan. On June 3, 2004, a captain in the U.S. Army's Central
Command gave a damning memo to KBR about the treatment
of foreign nationals being sent into the war zone from Arifjan,
just as the insurgency was seriously intensifying its attacks on
contractors. Given how vital these men were to the operation,
he cited "both a moral imperative and [a] self-interest to require

a minimum standard of care for the employees working for our contractors," not just in Kuwait but also across Iraq. His top concern in the three-page memo: "Drivers hired by brokers to work in Kuwait [are] being financially blackmailed to cross the border against their will." Military officials also told KBR that when the drivers purchased their jobs, they had been promised they would be in Kuwait, not Iraq, and that those who didn't want to risk their lives were fired with the debts they had still hanging over their heads. The memo also said that contractor deaths and injuries were not being reported for compensation. Army officials then called a meeting and wrote on the agenda, "Recruiting Practices and Free Will."

On July 1, 2004, Robert Gerlach, the KBR purchasing and procurement manager over Al Asad and the entire Anbar Province, the very same man Fryszman and Hoffman had been trying to depose, e-mailed a top Daoud executive. It was just three days before Jeet and some of his countrymen landed in Amman. Gerlach's subject line was "Now what?"

Without comment or question, Gerlach cut-and-pasted a BBC News report that he said KBR supervisors on the ground in Fallujah had raised with him. It alleged that Indian men who worked for Daoud had been recruited to work in Jordan but had now been held against their will in Fallujah for two months, and the company refused to send them home. Gerlach did not seek to investigate these allegations himself but merely wrote the Daoud executive to "give me feedback," and nothing more. She replied the next morning—"Dear Bob"—claiming the Indian men had "signed papers agreeing to work in Iraq," but promised that they would be immediately transported to Baghdad and then sent home. Gerlach does not appear to have looked into any of the claims, or initiated any kind of inquiry by anyone else, or tried to speak to any of the Indian workers himself, although he did forward the exchange to other KBR executives. Within days of those e-mails, Biplav Bhatta and his compatriots, too, would have been working under Daoud and KBR in Fallujah, where, they would later allege, they immediately started complaining to anyone they could find, including KBR supervisors, about their passports being taken, about being deceived, about being brought to Iraq against their will— all despite paperwork from Moon Light promising them hotel jobs in Jordan—allegations virtually identical to those contained in news reports regarding the Indian men. In fact, each of the men Gurung located for DiCaprio said in his own sworn statement that he had raised such issues with either Daoud or KBR, or both, *before* Daoud's broker in Amman organized the ill-fated convoy for Jeet and the others. Some of the twelve dead Nepalis had said the same when the terrorists filmed them giving their final statements before the black banner.

Fryszman also had found KBR workers who were posted at Al Asad in April, May, and June 2004 and gave sworn statements saying it was common knowledge among KBR employees that third-country nationals had been trafficked to the base. An employee named Terri Hobbs said in a sworn statement that the treatment she observed was "offensive to me as an American" and was of an ilk "no American company should permit to occur." Mistreatment and human trafficking "were spoken of so often and in so many contexts by so many people, including the American KBR workers, that no person working with or near foreign workers, including KBR managers, could have remained ignorant of these claims and concerns," she said. Another KBR employee, Rebecca Durham, said there "was a culture of fear among KBR employees, and it was generally understood that employees should not discuss the mistreatment of TCNs." Hobbs named the KBR supervisor who she said had told her "she should shut up" about the issue because anyone reporting it to the military "would be fired."

Three weeks after the twelve were killed, the KBR LOGCAP project manager for Iraq, a man named Robert Hill, fired off an e-mail to KBR executives saying he had found out that the Naval Criminal Investigative Service, or NCIS, was going to investigate KBR's human supply chain, based on the concerns of a Marine lieutenant colonel on the base named Jay Huston. The First Marine Expeditionary Force held operational control of the base, and Hill wanted to shut down their investigation fast. "It has come to my attention that NCIS has been asked to conduct an investigation of our subcontractors' hiring practices. LTC Huston has decided that D&P has slave labor working for them. I need your input ASAP, please get [another Marine commander] involved. We need to squash this immediately. He has no business in our operations." Another e-mail a few weeks later, this one from the KBR regional security chief, warned of the same thing, repeating that a senior U.S. Marine commander believed that Daoud was "running slave labor camps" for KBR at Al Asad.

Duane Banks, a contractor hired to audit KBR's bookkeeping practices, arrived at the base in August 2004. In his own sworn statement, he told Fryszman that "shortly after arriving at Al Asad, many people approached me to tell me about the abuse and mistreatment of TCNs at Al Asad that they had witnessed," including that workers had been held against their will and passports had been confiscated. He said that many of his sources were KBR or Daoud employees, and they often "appeared at my quarters, uninvited, at night, explaining that they feared KBR or DP would retaliate against them for making such disclosures to me." Although he had no background in human trafficking or forced and coerced labor, Banks was so outraged that he wrote a long, damning e-mail summarizing these issues about six weeks into his work on the base. His e-mail quickly ricocheted up the food chain at KBR, eventually landing in the in-box of a senior executive named Thomas Quigley, the man in charge of the overall LOGCAP operation in Iraq. Quigley and other KBR executives turned to their top procurement man in Anbar Province to respond to Banks's concerns: Robert Gerlach.

Gerlach wrote a scathing attack on Banks for his bosses, and called for Banks to be removed from the base. "You may read into this what you choose, but this is nothing but social editorial rhetoric unworthy of response. Tom [Quigley], as you have seen from my earlier email I want this guy removed . . . he is out of his lane so far," Gerlach wrote. Banks said in his sworn statement that Gerlach then "came to my quarters, uninvited, agitated, and angry. Mr. Gerlach asked me, 'What the hell is going on?'" Banks said he informed Gerlach that KBR employees had visited him after hours to make these allegations, and had levied allegations about Gerlach himself. "Mr. Gerlach responded by saying that he wanted me out of Iraq." Banks almost immediately was flown to Dubai, where he was fired.

"Duane is being pulled," a KBR executive said in an e-mail to Gerlach, copying Quigley. "I gave instructions this morning." The e-mail also proposed sending someone to Al Asad to speak with Gerlach, so he could personally "walk them through all your research so this [controversy about TCNs] can be closed once and for all. Can we do that?" It also said, "As you know,

Bob, this isn't the first time the issue of TCN treatment has come up. You get it from various sources. It also seems to come up every so often in the media"—he added that several e-mail chains about the issues raised by journalists were being circulated within KBR. Gerlach replied that he was happy with the proposal to guide someone through why he believed TCNs were well treated, adding that it was important for them to be treated with respect. In the very same sentence, however, he also said that "these kinds of allegations really need to be put to bed in such a manner that we do not revisit them each time a 'social crusader' comes on the scene."

Fryszman packed all this and more into the case she made to Judge Ellison that KBR had had enough evidence of what was happening for him to find that its conduct was "knowing" or perhaps willfully blind. Still, there were significant allegations she did not know about inside KBR's records regarding the man whom senior executives had turned to repeatedly to deal with allegations about Daoud and trafficked workers, the man who proposed putting any and all questions to bed, once and for all. It was the same man KBR had first identified as a key potential witness in the case when it was trying to get the lawsuit moved from California to Texas, and the same man it would not let Fryszman and Hoffman speak with: Robert Gerlach.

In 2005, a former KBR subcontracts administrator who worked at Al Asad named Harry "Hap" Barko Jr. filed a sealed federal lawsuit against KBR and Daoud under a law called the False Claims Act. The law penalizes companies that defraud the government and allows whistleblowers bringing evidence of such fraud to get a portion of any awards, ranging from about 15 to 25 percent. Barko's lawsuit, which was unsealed in 2009, alleged that the KBR contracting environment in Anbar Province was rife with fraud, collusion, and other anticompetitive activity, and it accused KBR of submitting false claims to taxpayers by rigging bids, inflating costs, and otherwise engaging in improper procurement practices involving Daoud, all while KBR employees were accepting kickbacks. The suit covered the laundry contract, the overall labor agreement for foreign workers, and other aspects of KBR's work. Barko's lawyers eventually obtained, through discovery, a long list of allegations about corruption at Al Asad that KBR executives had received through their "Code of Business Conduct" program, including some that came via a telephone hotline. Robert Gerlach was at the center of the allegations.

Between June 2004 and July 2005 alone, records filed in the case show that KBR employees reported to the company that "political ties between KBR and Daoud and Partners" made it impossible to enforce contract terms; that Gerlach had allegedly "pressured people to manipulate the system so that Daoud would be awarded contracts whether they were the low bidders or not"; that Gerlach had allegedly "abused his authority [by] leak[ing] information from other bids received, giving favored vendor [Daoud] leverage to lower his bid in order to gain contracts"; that Gerlach "has too close a relationship with the D&P subcontractor"; that Gerlach is "in bed with D&P—they are practically married"; that Gerlach allegedly was engaging in unethical conduct; that Gerlach and a handful of other KBR executives in Anbar dealing with Daoud had "received kickbacks from D&P." Finally, an employee specifically reported seeing another senior KBR manager at Al Asad pocket a large stack of U.S. bills, topped by a one-hundred-dollar note, while standing with a Daoud manager in the Jordanian company's on-base office, and then, after noticing he had been seen, the KBR manager hastily claimed that the Daoud manager had just been "making change."

In addition to these allegations, e-mails uncovered by Barko's lawyers showed that a senior KBR executive had visited Anbar in December 2004 to check out the reports and had concluded in her own report to her supervisors that Daoud was getting the majority of the work "not because they are the best subcontractor," and that other companies were "begging to conduct business with KBR" but "they are not invited to bid" on work. That same KBR executive who had visited Anbar to personally check out the reports also had received allegations that Gerlach was engaging in "unethical practices," including "the exchange of money and suppression of competition, [and] receipt of gifts." Based on her report, the company forced Gerlach to resign the next month, according to internal e-mails. A human resources executive said in one e-mail with the subject line "Bob Gerlach" that there were "enough issues raised to warrant his being sent home. We would prefer to address it from a 'things have changed here and it is time for a change for you, it is time for you to move on, and we want to give you the opportunity to resign' approach."

According to testimony in the case from one of KBR's in-house lawyers, KBR's internal personnel had conducted three investigations of Gerlach and the Al Asad corruption allegations based on these reports and others like them, but the company had refused to hand over any of the investigative files to Barko in the lawsuit, claiming that doing so would violate attorney-client privilege; KBR's in-house lawyers had participated in the probes.

Barko's lawyers also discovered that every employee interviewed about the corruption allegations by KBR's internal investigators was made to sign a nondisclosure agreement when his or her interview was done, and faced potential firing for violating it. Barko's lawyers suggested that this was a cover-up.

The federal judge on the case in Washington, U.S. District Court judge James S. Gwin, agreed with Barko's attorneys that KBR's internal investigations were not privileged and had to be handed over. Before he made his ruling, Gwin examined the internal investigations for himself, and then he cheekily dribbled out some of the details in his opinion, writing that the internal reports "are eye-openers. KBR's investigator found Daoud 'received preferential treatment.' The reports include both direct and circumstantial evidence that Daoud paid off KBR employees and KBR employees steered business to Daoud."

KBR launched what is now considered to be, in American corporate legal circles, a precedent-setting, epic fight to keep the records under wraps, taking Judge Gwin to a federal appeals court twice in order to keep privileged the in-house investigations. The company ultimately won, and the Supreme Court declined to intervene on Barko's behalf. Without access to the internal investigation files, Barko lost a critical motion for summary judgment in his case in the spring of 2017—after twelve long years. The only sanction against KBR: the Securities and Exchange Commission independently filed an unprecedented complaint against the company, alleging that it had violated whistleblower protections through its use of the nondisclosure agreements during the investigation, and KBR settled by paying a fine and agreeing to change the language of the agreements. The company and Gerlach had denied the corruption allegations throughout.

In the case brought by the families of the twelve dead Nepalis, KBR's lawyers never revealed any of the assertions that the company had collected internally about Gerlach's alleged unethical relationship with Daoud; nor did they reveal the existence of their internal investigations of him, nor that he had been forced to resign because of those allegations less than four months after the twelve were killed. All the while, they threatened to have Fryszman and Hoffman censured if they tried to approach Gerlach for a deposition, in addition to actually filing a petition for misconduct sanctions against them for, among other things, allegedly withholding important evidence. It's unclear whether Fryszman's initial requests for discovery had been broad enough to cover evidence of the alleged corruption at Al Asad involving Gerlach and other KBR personnel critical to her case, or whether the company's defense team simply frustrated her out of ever getting that far.

Even without any of the evidence regarding alleged corruption, the sworn statements from the workers whom Ganesh Gurung had found contained powerful allegations. Yet the plaintiffs' team had to put them together so quickly to meet judge Ellison's final deadline that Fryszman filed some of them without proper signatures or dates. The statements went to Ellison's clerk just two days before his scheduled hearing on KBR's motion to kill the lawsuit, and the company's lawyers tried to get the judge to throw them all out, on substantive grounds and for far less; they even argued that they should be thrown out because the interpreters Fryszman had used hadn't presented appropriate credentials, although one worked for the same translation firm that KBR's own lawyers had used in the case.

KBR also asked Judge Ellison to strike the statement from fired auditor Duane Banks, along with those from the former KBR employees whom Fryszman had located on her own after she realized KBR wasn't going to budge on discovery.

When the day arrived for the hearing on KBR's motion for summary judgment in the case, April 11, 2013, Judge Ellison seemed perturbed before the assembled lawyers. His very first question was "What do we do with this new evidence? I mean, I don't know why these witnesses were not identified ahead of time, and I don't know what badges of reliability they have." He also said he was uncomfortable with the legal arguments Fryszman had made in support of the new witnesses. Paul Hoffman, the human rights lawyer working with Fryszman, jumped in right away. "We have been looking for the men," he told the judge. "One of the reasons that we switched to presenting our evidence to defeat summary judgment in the way that we have is that we have not had access to KBR's documents of the crucial people, and we—and we decided we had to present our case through declarations. And, so, we have—we've had people in Nepal finding these men, and they were found, and we have their declarations. It was a difficult, laborious task, but we got them."

KBR lawyer Billy Donley told Ellison that even if the judge allowed the men's statements into the case, it wouldn't be enough. "For human trafficking, as well as forced labor, plaintiffs have to prove that KBR had knowledge," he said. "None of these declarations prove that KBR had knowledge of anything in particular with regard to *these* plaintiffs"—that is to say, KBR's specific knowledge that *these* twelve dead men themselves were being trafficked. Donley then also reverted to the "dead men tell no tales" defense raised throughout the saga's history: "KBR would have had no knowledge of where they came from or what their story might have been, because those individuals simply never made it inside of the base."

Paul Hoffman then made an impassioned case that Donley's years-long drumbeat of "they have no evidence" about KBR's knowledge of what had happened simply did not survive the weight of the evidence the plaintiffs' lawyers had amassed. He also told Ellison that those lawyers had presented page upon page of evidence that there was no distinction between the operations of Daoud and KBR at Al Asad—that the two were one and the same in all but name. Calling Daoud an "independent contractor" wasn't enough to make its actions truly independent. The real relationship "doesn't depend on labels," Hoffman said; "it doesn't depend on"—Ellison interjected with a kind of amen: "No, it doesn't"—and Hoffman kept running: "It doesn't depend on what you call it."

Judge Ellison concluded by asking Hoffman to clean up the statements of the Nepalese workers and to correct the defects that KBR's lawyers had cited to try to strike them from the record. "Give us the dates, give us certificates of a translator," the judge said, before saying he would take the arguments under advisement and adjourning the hearing. If he sided with KBR, it would be the final hearing in the case. If he sided with Hoffman, Kamala and the other families could finally get their trial.

As Ellison weighed the evidence in Houston, the Supreme Court of the United States released its long-awaited decision in the case of Esther Kiobel, the Nigerian woman whose husband had been killed for opposing oil exploration and production in their ancestral homelands in the Niger Delta. KBR's lawyers had believed the case offered a chance for them to pull the rug out from beneath Fryszman and Hoffman. The suit alleged that Royal Dutch Shell had been complicit in a government campaign against drilling opponents that involved attacking villages; beating, raping, killing, and arresting residents; and destroying or looting their property. The victims and their families had used a 1789 law to sue the oil company, the same law invoked in Kamala's lawsuit.

Human rights lawyers had first started using that law in the 1970s to sue foreign torturers and dictators, including Ferdinand Marcos of the Philippines. At the time, the courts gave such cases a warm reception, seemingly happy, even proud, to let American values be evidenced to the world through America's courts. It was perhaps the peak of the human rights era in the United States. But the mood in some courts significantly and noticeably shifted decades later, after Paul Hoffman and others had started using the same law to attack international human rights abuses allegedly perpetrated, or aided and abetted, by some of the nation's largest and most valuable corporations, including the likes of Exxon, Union Carbide, and Chiquita. By 2013, *Kiobel v. Royal Dutch Petroleum* and other cases like it also fell squarely in the center of the most significant ideological debates playing out in the highly polarized U.S. Supreme Court—debates over the fundamental role of the courts, the role of international law in the United States, and how corporations can be considered legal "persons" when they want protection from the law, as in giving unlimited campaign contributions to politicians, but can avoid the same when they want to escape potential liabilities.

As Kiobel was en route to the Supreme Court, a federal appeals court had ruled that only foreign governments and individuals could be sued under the law, not corporations, even though the lawyers in the case had never raised that argument. The Supreme Court justices, however, didn't rule on that issue when the case got to them. Instead, they sent it back to the lawyers and asked them to completely rebrief and reargue it on another issue, one that had barely been raised during the case's existence, or during the more than two-century history of the law. The justices focused on concern that *Kiobel* was a "foreign-cubed" lawsuit, which is to say that the plaintiffs were foreign citizens when the alleged atrocities occurred, the defendant was a foreign company, and the allegations involved events that had transpired overseas. Was it enough to justify a lawsuit in an American court that Royal Dutch Shell did business through American banks— virtually everyone does, whether they know it or not—and on the New York Stock Exchange?

Supreme Court decisions often are like the modern-day equivalent of pronouncements from oracles, leaving lower courts for years to sort out how they should be interpreted, and this case was no exception. Just after arguments had been wrapped up before Judge Ellison in Kamala's case, the Supreme Court justices appeared to be unanimous in ruling that foreign-cubed cases had no place in American courts, but they were divided on other key issues covered in separate sections of the opinion that could have a bearing in Houston and beyond. They left open the possibility that some lawsuits in which alleged abuses had occurred overseas could be brought in American courts if the defendants were U.S. citizens or U.S. companies. Cryptically, the justices appeared to leave open this possibility in cases where the events at issue "touch and concern the territory of the United States . . . with sufficient force," but they didn't offer any guidance about what they meant. The court had also ruled that no American law could be read to apply internationally unless Congress had explicitly said so.

Word traveled fast to Fryszman, given that Paul Hoffman, her partner on the case for Kamala and the other Nepalis, was the lead lawyer for Esther Kiobel and had argued the case before the Supreme Court. (The justices had cut him off about eleven seconds into his presentation at oral arguments.) Fryszman didn't panic, however, because she believed her lawsuit could stand on the main claim she had brought under the antitrafficking law. Word also traveled fast to the lawyers working for KBR and Daoud. KBR had hoped all along that a Supreme Court decision would give the company refuge from Kamala's lawsuit. "The Supreme Court's ruling in *Kiobel v. Royal Dutch Petroleum Co.* transformed the law governing this case," KBR's lawyers said in a new filing rapidly fired off to Judge Ellison, adding, "*Kiobel* is a watershed." Judge Ellison would mull the fate of Kamala's case for several more months, with the Supreme Court's decision and subsequent arguments about its meaning complicating the issues before him. In addition to weighing the evidence, he had to sort out what the oracles' sudden new pronouncements meant.

On August 21, 2013, nine years and two days after Jeet and the others were driven into Iraq on the Highway Through Hell, Ellison issued a twenty-three-page decision and order. It represented KBR's worst imaginable defeat.

He had heeded the Supreme Court's *Kiobel* decision and dismissed the part of the case that relied on the 1789 law, but that part of the lawsuit had always been redundant, serving as a sort of safety net, which Ellison and the plaintiffs' lawyers believed meant it could be shed without damage. Ellison let stand the main claim brought under the U.S. antitrafficking statute, dismissing each of KBR's arguments, and hence ordering the company to face Kamala and the other families at a trial in his courtroom. He allowed into evidence the statements of the Nepalese workers found at the last minute by Ganesh Gurung, along with the statements of the former KBR workers, all of which the company's lawyers had tried to strike. And he dismissed the separately pending misconduct allegations against Fryszman and her team, past and present, in just twenty-five words, refusing even to dignify them with a separate opinion. "This is a complicated and fact intensive case. Emotions understandably run high when human lives have been lost. However, sanctions are not—even remotely—justified." With that, all the pain and stress that had long been hanging over the plaintiffs' lawyers' heads was eliminated.

Perhaps to soften the blow of such a crushing defeat, Ellison decided to grant a request from KBR's lawyers that he black out roughly two hundred fifty words from the publicly available copy of his decision—the entire section in which he recited his summation of the evidence alleging that KBR knew about human trafficking, including the e-mail saying that the Marines were building a file against the company and were alleging, among other things, that there were "slave labor camps" at Al Asad, and concluding, "We need to squash this immediately."

Some other damage to the lawsuit, however, had been done by the Supreme Court's *Kiobel* decision. Ellison found he had no choice other than to dismiss the case against Daoud in its entirety, given that he saw it as "foreign cubed" because Daoud was a Jordanian company run through a shell in the British

Virgin Islands and operating exclusively in Iraq, and the victims were all from Nepal. Rather than risk an appeal, Daoud decided to offer Kamala and the other families a modest settlement, which Fryszman counseled them to accept.

KBR's lawyers from Baker & Hostetler had some last-ditch efforts pending to try to help them in the event of a trial, including an effort to name the U.S. government as a "responsible third party" in the lawsuit, arguing that "decisions made by the U.S. military in this wartime environment caused or contributed to the alleged injuries for which the plaintiffs seek recovery." For example, they said that the ill-fated convoy into Iraq had "proceeded without military escort, despite the fact that the military was aware that TCN convoys traveling without military escort were targeted by insurgents and that unrest and violence had grown in 2004 . . . But for these and other military decisions, this case would not exist." Arguments such as these smacked of desperation.

In the wake of Ellison's ruling against virtually every KBR assault on the case, the company fired Billy Donley, David Rivkin, Michael Mengis, and the rest of the defense team from Baker & Hostetler. It's not clear whether KBR fired them because the aggressive tactics they had employed in the case quite possibly worsened the company's fortunes with the judge, or whether KBR fired them because it believed those tactics weren't aggressive enough, or for some other reason, but Fryszman and Hoffman were not sad to see them go.

Fryszman and her case had survived so many assaults, but finally Kamala and the other families were going to get to tell their stories to a jury, an outcome that KBR had fought so tenaciously to avoid for so many years, and one Fryszman and Hoffman now relished.

• • •

At about eleven on the morning of Saturday April 25, 2015, Kamala unlocked and rolled up the steel door to the dress shop on the ground floor of her building with Kritika by her side. Kritika's cousin, a boy named Mishon, had come for a visit and was with them. Beginning at 11:56 a.m., and with absolutely no warning, the earth beneath Kamala's building buckled and shook wildly, the walls rattling all around her, the ceiling shaking above her head—for forty terrifying seconds. An earthquake reaching a staggering 7.8 on the Richter scale had ripped across Nepal, instantly leveling thousands of ancient structures and new ones fashioned from kiln-fired bricks or concrete blocks, such as Kamala's. Because they were on the ground floor, Kamala and the two children did not feel the building sway as violently as others did who were higher up, but the terrified trio ran from inside the shop into the street. Almost as soon as they were out, the shop's steel shutter door slammed down on its own behind them. Confused, Kamala ran up and down the street, having no idea about the safest place to plant herself and the children. The boy Mishon headed toward an open space on the other side of the street from Kamala's building, where there was an outdoor basketball court, and Kamala grabbed Kritika and ran for the same spot. In just forty seconds, thousands were dead, and rubble had trapped thousands more who were still alive. Hundreds of thousands, if not millions, instantly became homeless, exposed to the ravages of cholera and other diseases that soon would descend. The quake was felt across the Ganges River Basin in India, in China, and even as far away as Bangladesh, but its epicenter was deep beneath the heart of Gorkha, less than thirty miles from Kamala's childhood home on the horseshoe ridge, and communications across the nation were down.

As the aftershocks continued, Kamala remained terrified, but she kept her emotions in check so her daughter would not worry, cradling Kritika each time the earth buckled beneath them. With Kamala's elderly uncle, they moved down the road from her house and into an open space where people had assembled to camp. Virtually an entire nation had gathered under the sky, as people feared to remain inside structures. Near nightfall, Kamala walked back up the hill toward her building to see if it was still standing, and there she saw Surya Bhujel, from her neighboring village on the horseshoe ridge, the man who had set up a shuttle service, the man she had thought she might marry, sitting on the ground outside her building, waiting for her to return. Bhujel had been in his microbus, parked at a terminus on the edge of Kathmandu, when the earthquake hit. Worried about what had become of Kamala and Kritika, he had abandoned his vehicle and started walking the roughly five miles through the chaos to reach Kamala's house, crossing over and around the rubble spread across the devastated city to get to her. Upon seeing him waiting outside her home, Kamala felt an overwhelming sense of relief, even joy.

They all camped outside together those first several nights, and Kamala felt, for both herself and Kritika, a kind of security that would not have existed without Bhujel's presence, given that everyone was out in the open and such tragedies can sometimes bring out the worst in people. She realized how much worse this all would have been without Bhujel, as now she was without Jeet, alone with their daughter.

The aftershocks that continued terrifying people across the country became something of a new normal in everyone's life.

One week after the initial earthquake, Kamala, Kritika, and Bhujel made their way back to his microbus, and then began the long journey into the hills toward Gorkha, back to the horseshoe ridge.

After Ellison ordered KBR to trial, the company hired a new defense team headed by Houston's Geoffrey Harrison. Harrison was something of a gunslinger, representing both defendants and plaintiffs in his practice. He had for years been fighting claims by dozens of Oregon Army National Guard members who alleged that KBR Halliburton had negligently exposed them to highly toxic, cancer-causing chemicals at a water treatment facility in Iraq. The first twelve soldiers to go to a federal jury trial in Portland won an eighty-five-million-dollar verdict against the company, the vast majority of which resulted from a punitive damages finding. Jurors found that KBR had acted with "reckless and outrageous indifference to a highly unreasonable risk of harm" and had shown "conscious indifference to the health, safety and welfare" of the soldiers. In significant part, that verdict had served to bolster Fryszman's and Hoffman's view that KBR was destined to look bad in front of a jury made up of virtually anyone other than KBR employees.

Although Harrison lost the Oregon trial, he was fighting an impressive battle through the federal appeals court, and it looked likely he would get the verdict thrown out on procedural grounds; he argued that Portland was the wrong venue for the trial and that the judge had erred in not moving the case to Houston. The Portland defense also could tap into a nearly bottomless treasury to pay Harrison and the rest of the company's lawyers—as in the *U.S. Treasury*. The work in Iraq that had led to the lawsuit was carried out under a controversial multibillion-dollar contract KBR Halliburton had been awarded to "Restore Iraq Oil," known as RIO for short, a contract it got without facing competition. The deal contained a provision that indemnified the company from resulting litigation, meaning that taxpayers could reimburse KBR for its costs in defending the lawsuit.

Harrison went back into court in Houston for KBR to try to convince Judge Ellison that he had made a mistake in how he had interpreted the oracles in the wake of the Supreme Court's *Kiobel* decision. At a minimum, Harrison was laying the groundwork to take the case to the U.S. Court of Appeals, as he was doing in Portland, and trying to give himself the strongest possible hand. The legal leg that Agnieszka Fryszman, Kamala, and the other families were still standing on was the antitrafficking law. The trouble was, when the twelve men were killed, the law enacted by Congress did not include language showing that it expressly applied overseas; that wasn't specified in the statute until 2008—an amendment made, at least in part, because the case of the twelve had brought the oversight to light.

Judge Ellison had dealt with this issue from the start of the case, previously ruling that the lack of specificity in the law when the men were killed was meaningless because Congress, in 2008, had clarified that the intent all along was that the law be applied internationally. After all, it was absurd to believe that the inherently transnational crime of human trafficking could be addressed by a law that could be applied only to acts committed exclusively within the borders of the United States. He had ruled that the entire thrust of the antitrafficking law "would be severely undermined" if he were to find that "defendants who gained a commercial advantage in this country through engaging in illegal human trafficking were free from liability, so long as the trafficking acts themselves took place outside of American borders." He also had told KBR rather bluntly, "The defendants do not now, nor did they in 2004, have the right to traffic human beings at home or abroad." But Harrison and KBR believed that Ellison had been wrong all along, and his error had become glaring in the light of *Kiobel* and another, separate case.

As the dust began to settle in courtrooms across the country following the Supreme Court decision, Harrison argued that the high court had clearly ruled that no statute passed by Congress could be construed to have an international application unless it was expressly stated in the statute; and that meant an amendment later extending the law's reach could not be applied retroactively. It seemed Judge Ellison had no room left.

Unlike the contentious and occasionally rough tactics deployed by KBR's first defense team, Harrison's approach was more dispassionate. He limited his arguments to questions of the law, which, thanks to the Supreme Court, now seemed squarely in KBR's favor. He also radiated confidence. After walking into Ellison's courtroom, Harrison parsed the judge's own words on slides he displayed on a big screen, juxtaposing them with excerpts from the Supreme Court's more recent, and seemingly contradictory, instructions. In the glare of these disparities, Harrison and KBR made clear to Ellison that the fate of the entire case rested on the narrow questions opened up by the high court. They also made clear that they would push quickly and forcefully for the Fifth U.S. Circuit Court of

Appeals to reverse the judge if he did not reverse himself. Both Fryszman and Hoffman realized they were now up against a far more skilled litigator, one of the best attorneys KBR's money could buy. By the end of Harrison's slide show, it seemed obvious that Ellison had little choice but to reconsider his decision to send the case to trial.

Outside the courtroom, Ellison told confidants how the case had shocked his conscience. He compared the execution video's gruesome images to the historic photographs of young Emmett Till's mutilated corpse, which sixty years earlier had shocked the world and helped open its eyes, including Ellison's, to the long and brutal history of injustice faced by black Americans. Till, a fourteen-year-old black boy from Chicago, was visiting his family in segregationist Mississippi in the summer of 1955 when he was kidnapped, savagely beaten, and shot to death by a group of white men after he supposedly flirted with a white woman in a store. Despite the national and international attention that the case drew, his killers escaped justice after being acquitted by an all-white jury. Ellison was a child of the South when Till was murdered, and the photos of the boy's body remained seared in his consciousness. They now were joined in his psyche by images from a massacre perpetrated fifty years later and seven thousand miles away, a crime of violence that also revealed a wider injustice.

Before he became a judge, Ellison had spent twenty years in private practice as a corporate defense lawyer, working for some of the world's biggest multinationals, including Exxon, Chase Manhattan, and American Airlines. Representing such clients is not what he had dreamed of when he first discovered his passion for the law. Instead, his lifelong dream was to become a federal judge, a goal that dated to the same era in which he had first seen the photos of Till's body. As a ten-year-old boy in New Orleans, Ellison had adopted Judge J. Skelly Wright as his hero after Wright kept the city's public schools open despite the strong commitment of many white parents and local public officials to shut them down rather than yield to desegregation. Although Wright displayed great courage in breaking segregation in New Orleans, his power ultimately flowed from the fact that the Supreme Court was on his side, and with it, the powers of the federal government. Sixty years later, it did not appear there was any room for Ellison to argue the same in a case that weighed on him unlike almost any other throughout his nearly four-decade legal career.

Republican senators had questioned Ellison's potential fidelity to Supreme Court precedent during his 1996 confirmation, as they did with many nominees put forward by Democratic presidents. Would he adhere to Supreme Court rulings even if he profoundly disagreed with them, or would he become a "judicial activist," a label carrying the power of a smear in the post–civil rights era. "With respect to any case that I am called upon to decide, if I am fortunate enough to be confirmed, I will not allow any of my own opinions to keep me from applying the law objectively and dispassionately," Ellison said in response to written questions from then-senator Jeff Sessions, the Alabama Republican. "As I stated in my testimony to the Senate Judiciary Committee, any federal judge who cannot apply the law independent of his personal feelings should resign." At this critical moment in the case, perhaps lessons Ellison had learned from the second judge he clerked for, U.S. Supreme Court justice Harry Blackmun, might have been the most formative. Blackmun was known as someone who was unyield-ingly fair to all who appeared before him, but who also, in the words of another former clerk, "allowed his views of the law to develop carefully, step-by-step, with respect for the Constitu-tion and the laws he was sworn to uphold, and attention to the ever-changing factual patterns presented by a complex world."

Ellison lived up to the promises he made to the Senate, al-though it clearly wasn't easy. Rather than wait for the Fifth U.S. Circuit Court of Appeals to reverse him, he reversed himself in 2014, agreeing with Harrison and KBR and dealing a mortal blow to the case brought by Kamala and the other families. Even so, his unhappiness with how the Supreme Court had shifted the ground beneath a case that had been playing out for years in his courtroom remained evident to attorneys on both sides; he entertained arguments from Fryszman and Hoffman that he was, once again, wrong, and he kept those arguments open on the case's docket for more than a year. With them came countless more pages of written arguments, all of which KBR and Harrison countered at every step. In allowing the debate to go on for another year, Ellison seemed to be buying time in the hope that other courts across the country, also re-acting to the changes wrought by the Supreme Court in *Kiobel*, might add more persuasive arguments to the record that could help keep the case alive. Yet no such relief came, and there was no escaping the fact that the Supreme Court's ruling meant that it simply wasn't against U.S. law for KBR, or any other American company, to be involved in or benefit from *interna-tional* human trafficking abroad *until* 2008—more than four years after Jeet and the others had been sent to their deaths.

On March 24, 2015, Ellison issued his final, somewhat pained ruling, in which he dispatched the lawsuit. "Indeed," he wrote, "part of the delay in issuing this decision has been to see if new decisional authority might bolster Plaintiffs' legal position." In the concluding paragraph, he used the kind of language one rarely sees from a federal judge. "The Court again notes its profound regret at the outcome of this action. The crimes that are at the core of this litigation are more vile than anything the Court has previously confronted. Moreover, the herculean efforts of Plaintiffs' counsel have been in the highest traditions of the bar. No lawyer or group of lawyers could have done more or done better." But because he had no jurisdiction to extend the case internationally on the date the men were killed, "the perpetrators of the subject crimes are not before the Court, and the relief that the Plaintiffs seek is not appropriate as to those who are before the Court."

When they arrived on the horseshoe ridge after the earthquake, Kamala and Kritika came first upon Jeet's family farmhouse, the place where Kritika had been born into the arms of her grandmother. The entire upper floor of the house had collapsed. No one had been killed, and Jeet's mother and his eldest brother's family were now living in a storage building behind the house, although many in the village on the ledge were still sleeping outdoors. When Kamala saw the farmhouse, she felt a strange numbness. She had such warm memories of her first couple of years there, but her feelings had been soured by what had transpired within the four walls after Jeet's death, and so she wasn't necessarily sad to see those walls reduced to rubble and fallen timbers.

In the coming days, as she and Kritika helped friends and family in the village on the ledge and across the horseshoe ridge, Kamala realized that so many important people in her life now understood something of her suffering of more than a decade earlier, when the same thing had happened to her on the same lush mountainside—when everything she'd come to love (except for Kritika), her sense of security and home and family, all had vanished without warning and without cause. Kamala knew from her own experience that these villagers, her friends and former family members, would find their way with loved ones who had survived the quake, that they now shared a special bond of loss with all their neighbors the same way she had with the women in the ashram with whom she'd found bravery and emotional courage after her own loss. She saw pettiness disappear and a deeper kindness and generosity take root. Kamala also decided she would use some of the compensation money she had left to help friends and family rebuild, including Jeet's family.

The settlement money from Daoud arrived in Nepal just as everyone was rebuilding. The families agreed among themselves to divide it thus: those who had gotten nothing in the original compensation case because they had lost brothers were given the largest share; the parents, who had gotten the smallest payouts the first time, got the second-largest slice; and Kamala and the other widows, who originally had gotten the most, took the smallest cut. Kamala would use her money to rebuild the high wall ringing her property, which had fallen in the quake.

After a few weeks of helping loved ones and other victims of the earthquake on the horseshoe ridge, Kamala took Kritika's hand and they headed along the same path they had walked down a decade earlier, when Kamala was just a child herself, a girl on her way to Kathmandu carrying in her arms all she had left. When they arrived back in the city this time, she stood with Kritika on the basketball court across the street from her four-story building. At first, she eyed the building carefully, up and down, searching for damage or subtle weaknesses wrought by the earthquake. She didn't see any, but soon she found herself lost in the view, feeling a sense of pride and security, and realizing that she and her daughter were finally home.

EPILOGUE

On January 3, 2017, a divided panel of the Fifth U.S. Circuit Court of Appeals in New Orleans upheld Judge Ellison's dismissal of the case following the Supreme Court's decision in *Kiobel*. Kamala and the other families had relied on a more-than-two-hundred-year-old law called the Alien Tort Statute, which gave foreigners a right to sue in U.S. courts for exceptionally heinous crimes considered to be "*hostis humani generis*, enemy of all mankind," and in violation of the law of nations. Such crimes included the likes of international piracy and slavery. In the face of a growing number of lawsuits targeting multinational corporations for participating in alleged human rights abuses abroad, the high court justices had decided to limit that law's application dramatically. In the case brought by Kamala and the other families, the appeals court vote was 2 to 1.

Fifth U.S. Circuit Court of Appeals judge James E. Graves Jr. not only voted against the majority, but also wrote an impassioned eighteen-page dissent in favor of Kamala and the other plaintiffs. He seized on something in the divided Supreme Court's wording in its *Kiobel* decision that potentially left the door open for suits if the alleged abuses overseas "touch and concern the territory of the United States . . . with sufficient force." The high court did not define precisely what that meant, as is nearly always its way, but many read the phrase to cover cases in which the issues at stake involved significant U.S. policy interests and in which a significant amount of the overseas conduct had been controlled from American soil, such as a corporate headquarters. In his dissent, Judge Graves argued that there was enough evidence for both in the plaintiffs' case. The lawsuit touched and concerned the United States with force because it alleged that a *U.S. company* under a *U.S. government contract* to provide labor on a *U.S. military base* had participated in human trafficking. Also, Graves wrote, the issue represented an important U.S. policy concern given that the government had signed and ratified an international treaty requiring it to hold U.S. citizens accountable for international trafficking. Graves also listed much of the evidence that Agnieszka Fryszman had marshaled alleging that KBR executives back in Houston knew about abuses. He said that a fair reading of those allegations in the plaintiffs' favor meant that a jury could conclude that the company's U.S. employees had "failed to properly investigate accusations of human rights abuses by KBR overseas, and either willfully ignored evidence of such abuses or actively sought to cover up the misconduct." The company had also continued wiring money from the United States to Daoud and Partners after learning of the allegations, Graves wrote, adding that paying for trafficked labor could easily be construed as "an action critical to the operation of a global trafficking scheme. This is domestic conduct relevant to the alleged law of nations violation."* What may never be known is

---

*All three members of the panel agreed that at the time when Jeet and the other men were recruited, moved across the globe, and murdered in 2004, it simply had not been illegal under the antitrafficking law alone for Americans to engage in trafficking outside the United States. The panel further said that changes to the trafficking law by Congress in 2008 were not clearly put forward as "clarifications," and therefore represented a new law altogether, meaning that KBR could not be held accountable retroactively without invoking another law, like the Alien Tort Statute.

how much weight might have been added to their "touch and concern" argument had Agnieszka Fryszman and Paul Hoffman had the evidence that allegations of corruption involving Robert Gerlach and other KBR managers had reached and caused serious concern in Houston. Even so, Graves's strongly worded dissent gave Kamala and the other families a fighting chance to have their case heard by the Supreme Court. Fryszman even entertained some such hope when President Barack Obama nominated Merrick Garland to replace the late conservative icon Antonin Scalia, but after Republicans in the Senate refused to hold hearings on Garland's nomination, and Donald Trump won the White House, she feared the worst. Trump then appointed the conservative Neil Gorsuch to replace Scalia. On September 25, 2017, the justices sat for their last conference of the summer, and Kamala's case was among those they weighed. It was not, however, among the tiny fraction they agreed to hear. Only about 1 percent of all such appeals are ever granted by the high court. That decision effectively ended the lawsuit against KBR.

On November 30, 2017, Judge Ellison took up the case for one final matter. He ordered KBR to reimburse the plaintiffs' side more than two hundred thousand dollars it had spent fighting KBR's frivolous misconduct allegations against Fryszman, Hoffman, Matthew Handley, and Molly McOwen. He suggested KBR simply had been out to bully Kamala's lawyers, adding that its actions raised "the inference of improper motive" given that it filed what he called baseless and onerous charges "at a time when the intensity of the litigation was at its peak."

At the end of 2017, a separate lawsuit Fryszman had filed on behalf of Biplav Bhatta and some of the other workers whom

Ganesh Gurung had found in Nepal as the deadline expired in Kamala's case was still pending before Judge Ellison. She had put forward a slightly different legal theory in that lawsuit by alleging, not that KBR had outright trafficked, but that it had aided and abetted trafficking. KBR is currently fighting the case and denies the allegations.

Efforts to bring criminal prosecutions met a similar fate. In January 2014, an investigator from the U.S. State Department who had been assigned to the Justice Department's human trafficking unit made a special trip to London, where I live, to brainstorm about how the federal government might conceivably bring war trafficking prosecutions, but he wasn't optimistic. The statute of limitations in the case of the twelve was close to expiring, as it would be for many of the war's worst abuses, and he had only recently been assigned to take up the inquiry. We spent an intellectually stimulating day inside a cluttered office used for storage in the bowels of the U.S. embassy in London, where we ran through investigative strategies, but nothing came of it. Soon, he was back at the State Department and reassigned overseas.

Matthew Handley, working with Fryszman, had represented the families of a group of Iraqi interpreters who had been slain while helping train police recruits. The Iraqis were ambushed and shot execution-style to send a message to anyone else working with the Americans. When Handley fought to get compensation for their relatives, as he had for Kamala and the other Nepalese families, he discovered that the insurance company had withheld from the government information in company files about the very existence of the victims' dependents. The judge in the case was so angered that he told the U.S. Labor Department to investigate whether the company should face criminal charges called for within the compensation statute. Richard Robilotti, the labor official who had overseen Kamala's compensation case, recommended that the Justice Department bring charges, but it never did.

Molly McOwen today works in Washington as an enforcement attorney in the Consumer Financial Protection Bureau, a federal agency set up as a sort of watchdog in the aftermath of the financial crisis. She recently gave birth to a son, Cuinn McOwen Cook.

Fryszman continues to serve as the chair of the human rights practice group at Cohen Milstein. In June 2017 she filed a federal lawsuit in California against U.S. and Thai companies alleging human trafficking and forced labor in the global seafood industry. Paul Hoffman and Anthony DiCaprio are cocounsel in the case.

Handley remarried and now has two children. He continues to serve as the director of litigation for the Washington Lawyers' Committee for Civil Rights and Urban Affairs. Handley underwent surgery in 2017 for a form of kidney cancer and the operation was deemed a success.

Kritika Magar is now a teenager and lives with her mother in Kathmandu. She is the equivalent of a freshman in high school and has attended some of the country's best private schools, where she has become fluent in English.

Kamala continues to run her dress shop and continues to weigh the marriage proposal she received long ago from Surya Bhujel, the driver who trekked across the broken city to find her on the day of the devastating earthquake. She also worries constantly about whether Kritika is spending enough time studying. The pair recently changed apartments inside Kamala's building because Kritika insisted on having her own bedroom. Kamala has not yet shared her experiences with Kritika, but plans to do so by having Kritika read this book aloud to her in Nepali.

Following fascism's defeat during World War II, the United States pushed for the acceptance of "universal human rights" for people around the world. In many ways, this was the global extension of some of the same forces that had spurred the push for civil rights inside the country, including desegregation in New Orleans and other cities. By 2016, the presence of "human rights" in the American civic dialogue had become, in the words of scholar Mark Philip Bradley, almost prosaic, even if the application wasn't always uniform. "Some American fifth graders now spend as much time studying the Universal Declaration of Human Rights as they do Mark Twain's *Tom Sawyer*," Bradley wrote in a 2016 treatise on the subject. Yet such basic assumptions appear upended following Trump's election and the rise of populist movements across the globe. Ironically, the strong political sentiments against globalization that helped propel Trump into the White House now threaten to diminish many of the protections that evolved to keep some of globalization's worst excesses in check, including human trafficking. In line with his "America First" slogan, it seems clear that Trump has little interest in pursuing or expanding international legal strictures and treaties, especially those designed to provide protections for the weak against the powerful. Even before Trump's election, however, the idea of using American laws and courts as a check on the conduct of global players, especially border-crossing corporations, was in significant retreat.

At the very same time, the power and reach of multinationals were greater than ever.

Beyond the courts or international treaties, there was one significant exception to this trend, and that was in the area of unilateral U.S. government action against international human trafficking. President Obama in 2012 signed an executive order with potentially far-reaching implications. It banned government contractors, subcontractors, and their employees from engaging in the kinds of practices that Jeet and the other Nepalis were subjected to, and it required contractors to take responsibility for every link in their human supply chains. Spurred by continuing concerns over the conduct of contractors in Iraq and Afghanistan, the order included barring any "recruitment," or broker, fees for foreign migrant workers, as forcing workers to borrow vast sums to buy their jobs creates conditions that can easily lead to debt bondage and human trafficking.

Obama went further, recognizing the power of collective consumer action by U.S. taxpayers to impact human trafficking beyond military service providers. With the federal government spending more than $460 billion on goods and services each year, his order reached into procurement for everything from building supplies to computers and mobile phones. That, in turn, appears to have influenced some of the world's largest companies (especially those already under public pressure, including Apple) to ban fees for workers in their supply chains and take similar actions designed to prevent trafficking. (Apple's action followed a 2013 exposé in *Bloomberg Businessweek* magazine.) The global electronics industry has been a major source of human trafficking, given that factories in some of its most important Asian hubs, including Malaysia, Singapore, and Taiwan, rely heavily on foreign migrant workers from Nepal and other poor countries. The problem has been especially severe in Malaysia, where most of the world's top electronics brands turn for components—including Apple, which sourced from twenty-eight different Malaysian plants when Obama signed his order. Given the scale of the problem, and because many of the most recognizable consumer electronics brands in the world "source components of their products from Malaysia, this means that virtually every device on the market today may have come in contact with modern-day slavery," according to a 2013 study paid for by the U.S. Department of Labor. Congress wrote many of Obama's reforms into law for defense contractors, but his broader changes came only through executive order, and these could be in jeopardy. Trump has pledged to repeal every one of Obama's executive orders. Even if the protections remain in place, though, it's unclear whether Trump's Labor Department will seek to enforce them.

The State Department and the United Nations' International Labour Organization estimate that a large swath of the world's more than 230 million international migrants are at risk each year for forced or coerced labor. Increased domestic legal protections are important in nations that are key suppliers of cheap global labor, such as Nepal, but these governments tend to be weak and corrupt, and to lack the resources for meaningful enforcement, hence one major reason their citizens are so often exploited. Protections in the wealthier countries the workers are headed for have far more potential to effect change, because those at the end of the supply chain have the most power to look back, retrace every step, and correct abuses—unless they choose a path of exploitation or willful blindness. And indeed, actions in destination countries remain wanting. Beyond companies themselves taking more direct responsibility for their supply chains, global consumer pressure remains the most powerful force for change, whether it's Apple banning fees for foreign migrants working at its suppliers or global soccer fans threatening a boycott over the stream of laborers returning to Nepal in caskets from construction sites in Qatar ahead of the 2022 World Cup. The calculation is not the same for companies such as KBR, however, which rely on political clout rather than consumer sentiment.

People commonly ask how often things work out for men and women who, unlike Jeet, ultimately make it home to their families. To be sure, foreign migrants tend to be a brave and self-selecting bunch, choosing to leave loved ones for unknown lands with the sole intention of improving life for their families. Many often make the best of even the worst abuses that come their way. In any case, the question is a variation on one that has been posed for centuries to justify exploitation, from slavery in America to modern-day slavery around the world: Aren't they better off? The trouble is, this is and always has been the wrong question.

The only question that matters: Are they truly free?

NOTE ON SOURCES

The narrative in this book is drawn from interviews with more than eighty people over the course of twelve years, more than thirty thousand pages of documents, my own observations during a decade of reporting, and a visual record from hundreds of photographs and videos.

An appendix listing of many of those whom I interviewed follows this note. Those who played the most significant roles were interviewed multiple times, and the most significant of these was Kamala Thapa Magar. Cumulatively, we spent about one month together, and we visited virtually every location from her life referenced. Interviews with her were conducted in 2005, 2013, 2014, and 2016, in Kathmandu and Gorkha, and follow-ups, including videoconferences, took place in 2016 and 2017. I also interviewed her family members, whose names are listed in the appendix.

Documents include a large trove gathered in the first stage of my investigation, as well as those amassed in the decade-long record of the two cases that resulted. The largest cache of documents relates to the federal human trafficking lawsuit brought on behalf of Kamala and the other family members of the murdered Nepalese men. The case is *Adhikari et al. v. Daoud & Partners et al.*, Civil Action No. H-09-cv-1237, U.S. District Court for the Southern District of Texas. The public record alone from the District Court proceedings exceeds twenty-six thousand pages, but I also drew on thousands of pages beyond the public record, including hearing transcripts and depositions. Records from other cases involving KBR Halliburton also were useful, including *Barko v. Halliburton et al.*, No. 1:05-cv-01276, U.S. District Court for the District of Columbia; *United States of America v. Albert Jackson Stanley*, No. 4:08-cr-597, U.S. District Court for the Southern District of Texas; *Jamie Leigh Jones v. Halliburton et al.*, Civil Action No. 4:07-cv-2719, U.S. District Court for the Southern District of Texas; and *Bixby et al. v. KBR et al.*, Civil Action No. 3:09-cv-632PK, U.S. District Court for the District of Oregon. Also useful were briefs and opinions from appellate court and U.S. Supreme Court proceedings in the *Kiobel* case.

For the opening chapter of the book and part 3, which encompass the litigation, I have eschewed litigation-style citations from case dockets. I do not believe case citations would serve or please anyone other than the most litigious reader. Suffice it to say that direct quotations are drawn from official transcripts or video recordings of the proceedings, or from written positions put forward on the record by the parties. For Nepalese speakers, including Kamala, a few direct quotations deviate slightly from the official court transcripts because those transcripts were made from real-time interpretations that were sometimes imprecise.

I am deeply indebted to several authors and journalists for their own work on some of the issues covered in this book, especially for the history of KBR Halliburton contained in chapter 7. Most notable is the incomparable Robert A. Caro. Others are T. Christian Miller, David Phinney, Dan Briody, P. W. Singer, David S. Rohde, Ariana Eunjung Cha, Sarah

Stillman, and the historians Joseph A. Pratt and Christopher J. Castañeda. I am also indebted to filmmaker Jon Shenk, who generously provided me with transcripts of the interviews he and Pete Nicks conducted for *Blame Somebody Else*, their 2006 Emmy Award–winning documentary.

I also relied on hundreds of photographs and videos for many of the descriptions in the narrative. These include those that I took myself, but also hundreds taken by the incredible José Moré, whose work for the *Chicago Tribune* in 2005 yielded a visual diary of my investigation in Nepal and the Middle East.

APPENDIX: INTERVIEW SUBJECTS

Kamala Thapa Magar

Associates and Family of Kamala Thapa Magar

Shakuntala Basnet, tailoring and sewing teacher, Tulsi Meher Ashram

Bhadra Kumari Ghale, Gandhian activist, writer, and former chairman of the Tulsi Meher Trust, Kathmandu, Nepal

Bijay Bahadur Khadka, former chief executive of Tulsi Meher Ashram, Kathmandu, Nepal

Ganga Bahadur Thapa Magar

Bhakti Maya Thapa Magar

Budhi Thapa Magar

Dhan Maya Thapa Magar

Duku Maya Thapa Magar

Fauda Singh Thapa Magar

Maya Thapa Magar

Dwarika Manandhar, textile instructor, Tulsi Meher Ashram

Sunna Shrestha, staff member, Tulsi Meher Ashram

Uday Thapa, primary school teacher, Gorkha District, Nepal

Family Members of the Other Victims in Nepal

Devaka Adhikari

Mahendra Adhikari

Ramchandra Adhikari

Yubaraj Adhikari

Bishnu Khadka

Jeet Bahadur Khadka

Rhadika Khadka

Sudarshan Khadka

Bhagwat Koiri

Bindeshore Singh Koiri

Iswar Singh Koiri

Pukari Devi Koiri

Satya Narayan Shah

Renuka Karki Shrestha

Tara Shrestha

Ram Dulari Sudi

Jitini Devi Thakur

Ram Kumar Thakur

Ram Naryan Thakur

Samundri Devi Thakur

Bhim Bahadur Thapa

Bishnu Maya Thapa

Krishna Maya Thapa

Kul Prasad Thapa

Others

Nepal

Biplav Bhatta, former worker in Iraq

Prabin Bhetwal, former worker in Iraq

Shamser Bahadur Karki, Nepal Foreign Employment Manpower Council

Yubaraj Ghmire, journalist and former editor of *Samay* magazine, Nepal

Prahlad Giri, Moon Light Consultant Pvt. Ltd., Kathmandu, Nepal

Ganesh Gurung, Nepal Institute of Development Studies

Reena Gurung, attorney, Nepal Institute of Development Studies

Members of the Kumar family, Taksar, Nepal

Gana Magar, New Bamboo Cottage, Kathmandu, Nepal

Prakash Mahat, former Nepalese foreign minister

Indra Tamang, former worker in Iraq

Govind Prasad Thapa

Kumar Thapa, subagent in Kathmandu, Nepal

Lok Bahadur Thapa, former Nepalese ambassador to Saudi Arabia

Middle East

Wadih al-Absi, First Kuwaiti Trading and Contracting

Ricardo Endaya, former chargé d'affaires of the Philippines in Baghdad (interviewed by Aamer Madhani)

Amin Mansour, Bisharat and Partners, labor broker for Daoud and Partners, Amman, Jordan

Eyad Mansour, Morning Star for Recruitment and Manpower Supply, Amman, Jordan

Ali Kamel al-Nadi, Bisharat and Partners, labor broker for Daoud and Partners, Amman, Jordan

Officials of the Indian government

Nader Rabadi, journalist, Amman, Jordan

Haitham Shwarham, Daoud and Partners

United States

Laurel Calkins, journalist, Houston, Texas

Craig Cook, husband of Molly McOwen

Marie de Young, KBR whistleblower

Rebecca Durham, former KBR worker, Iraq

Hon. Keith P. Ellison, U.S. District Court judge, Southern District of Texas, Houston

Agnieszka Fryszman, partner at Cohen Milstein Hausfeld and Toll

Matthew Handley, former partner, Cohen Milstein Hausfeld and Toll

Geoffrey Harrison, partner at Susman Godfrey

Michael Hausfeld, former chairman and partner at Cohen Milstein Hausfeld and Toll

Paul Hoffman, partner at Schonbrun Seplow Harris and Hoffman

Stuart Ishimaru, civil rights lawyer, husband of Agnieszka Fryszman

Michael D. Kohn, partner, Kohn, Kohn and Colapinto, LLP

Michael Land, former KBR worker, Iraq

Aamer Madhani, former reporter, *Chicago Tribune,* currently at *USA Today* (interview transcript provided by Jon Shenk)

Molly McOwen, former plaintiffs' lawyer, Cohen Milstein Hausfeld and Toll

Michael Mengis, partner at BakerHostetler

John R. Miller, U.S. ambassador at large and former head of the State Department's Office to Monitor and Combat Trafficking in Persons (died in October 2017)

Melissa Norcross, KBR Halliburton former spokeswoman

Sara K. Payne, senior vice president, Rutherfoord International

Richard V. Robilotti, former district director, U.S. Department of Labor Office of Workers' Compensation Programs

U.S. Representative Chris Smith, author and key proponent of several human trafficking laws

Mark B. Taylor, former senior coordinator for reports and political affairs, U.S. State Department Office to Monitor and Combat Trafficking in Persons

Martina E. Vandenberg, attorney, and founder and president of the Human Trafficking Pro Bono Legal Center, Washington, DC

Angela Keel-Welsh, U.S. Army

NOTES

Chapter 1

8 She had hoped for a quicker resolution: Sarah McGovern and Timothy J. Dowding, "Sustainable Cotton and Gap Inc.: A Case Study," University of Connecticut Stamford, 2017, http://global.business.uconn.edu/wp-content /uploads/sites/1931/2017/01/Sustainable-Cotton-Gap-Inc.pdf; Cam Simpson, "Tech's Tragic Secret: The World's Most Sophisticated Smartphones and Tablets Start in the Tin Mines of Bangka Island," *Bloomberg Businessweek*, Aug. 27–Sept. 2, 2012, pp. 48–57; and "A Collective Approach to Achieving a Sustainable Indonesian Tin Sector: Legacy Report of the Tin Working Group," April 2017, https://www.idhsustainabletrade.com/uploaded /2017/06/Aidenenvironment_TWG-Legacy-Report_final_Website.pdf.

Chapter 2

18 This reality is captured in a sacred Hindu text: "The Laws of Manu," chap. 5, verses 156–61, Dharmashastras (sacred Hindu texts).

18 In 2015, when Nepal's president, a widow herself: Hari Kumar Shrestha, "UDMF 'Cleanses' Janaki Temple After Worship by 'Widow Prez,'" *Nepal Mountain News*, Dec. 19, 2015, http://www.nepalmountainnews.com/cms /2015/12/19/udmf-cleansesjanaki-temple-after-worship-by-widow-prez/.

19 At the start of the school day: Uday Thapa, interview with the author, Gorkha District, Nepal, 2016.

20 a norm meant to silence women and keep them from participating in any public conversation: Sylvia D. Hoffert, *When Hens Crow: The Woman's Rights Movement in Antebellum America* (Bloomington: Indiana University Press, 1995).

34 The tiny Persian Gulf state of Qatar: "UN Special Rapporteur on the Human Rights of Migrants Concludes Country Visit to Qatar," Office of the United Nations High Commissioner for Human Rights, Nov. 10, 2013, http://www .europarl.europa.eu/meetdocs/2009_2014/documents/droi/dv/1307_unsr rightsofmigrants_/1307_unsrrightsofmigrants_en.pdf.

34 But the global shift under way: "International Migration Report 2013," United Nations Department of Economic and Social Affairs, Population Division (2013),

http://www.un.org/en/development/desa/population/publications/pdf
/migration/migrationreport2013/Full_Document_final.pdf.

34 Although relatively small, Nepal rose rapidly: Ibid., table II.2.

34 Because there were no income-earning opportunities: Ganesh Gurung and Jaganath Adhikari, "Nepal: The Prospects and Problems of Foreign Labour Migration," in Pong-Suhl Ahn, ed., *Migrant Workers and Human Rights: Out-Migration from South Asia* (New Delhi and Geneva: International Labor Organization 2004).

35 By 1999, the money these men sent home . . . would become their nation's top export: Jaganath Adhikari and Mary Hobley, "Everyone Is Leaving—Who Will Sow Our Fields? The Effects of Migration from Khotang District to the Gulf and Malaysia," Swiss Agency for Development and Cooperation (SDC), Kathmandu, December 2011.

35 The English- and Nepali-language brochures: Promotional materials from brokers collected by the author in Kathmandu, 2005.

35 The licensed brokers: Gurung and Adhikari, "Nepal: The Prospects and Problems"; and interviews by the author in Nepal, 2005, 2013.

36 International airlines: Records obtained by the author from the Civil Aviation Authority of Nepal, Air Transportation and Regulation Directorate, Kathmandu, 2004.

36 To squeeze more workers onto every flight: Gulf Air promotional literature on its fleet, obtained by the author from the airline in 2005. The company named each of its economy-only 767s the "Gulf Traveller," a moniker it used on billboards and other signs in Kathmandu.

36 During takeoff, they heaved: Author's personal observations on a B767 "Gulf Traveller" flight, Kathmandu to Manama, Sept. 15, 2005.

37 The two-century history: Keiko Yamanaka, "Nepalese Labour Migration to Japan: From Global Warriors to Global Workers," *Ethnic and Racial Studies* 23, no. 1 (2000): 62–93.

37 Overseas workers had to pay massive fees: Adhikari and Hobley, "Everyone Is Leaving"; Gurung and Adhikari, "Nepal: The Prospects and Problems"; and interviews by the author in Nepal, 2005, 2013.

38 the job would pay in the range: "Report of the Commission of Inquiry, Established by Decree of the Council of Ministers of His Majesty's Government [of Nepal], Sept. 6, 2004, Chairman Top Bahadur Singh, former Justice of the Supreme Court of Nepal, obtained by the author in Kathmandu, 2005.

39 On June 9, 2004: Ibid.; Le Royal details obtained from Emporis, a private provider of data on building and construction projects, http://www.emporis.com/buildings/131261/le-royal-hotel-amman-jordan.

39 A Jordanian labor broker . . . "room boys": "Report of the Commission of Inquiry"; and copy of the advertisement obtained by the author from the offices of *Kantipur Daily*, Kathmandu, 2005.

Chapter 3

43 A bulletin cut into the afternoon music: BBC Monitoring translation report of Radio Nepal broadcast, obtained by the author, 2004.

43 The terrorists . . . something called "Bisharat": "Report of the Commission of Inquiry"; and numerous news reports, including "Islamist Group Says It Has Abducted 12 Nepalese in Iraq," Agence France Presse, Aug. 20, 2004, 5:39 p.m., GMT, dateline Dubai.

45 Less than one-half of 1 percent: Google Public Data, "World Development Indicators, Infrastructure, Fixed Broadband Internet Subscribers: India, Nepal, Pakistan," accessed by the author, https://www.google.co.uk/public data/explore?ds=d5bncppjof8f9_&met_y=it_net_user_p2&idim=country: NPL:IND:PAK&hl=en&dl=en#!ctype=l&strail=false&bcs=d&nselm=h&met _y=it_net_bbnd&scale_y=lin&ind_y=false&rdim=region&idim=country: NPL:IND:PAK&ifdim=region&hl=en_US&dl=en&ind=false.

46 It was among the first . . . would eventually become ISIS: Aki Peritz, "I Watched All the Terrorist Beheadings for the U.S. Government, and Here's What I Learned," *PostEverything* (blog), *Washington Post*, 2014, https://www .washingtonpost.com/posteverything/wp/2014/07/02/i-watched-all-the -terrorist-beheadings-for-the-u-s-government-and-heres-what-i-learned /?utm_term=.4ff0f50b576c.

47 On October 1, 1999 . . . a wedding ground and public space: Interviews of witnesses by the author in Nepal, 2016; and *Nepal: A Spiralling Human Rights Crisis* (London: Amnesty International, 2002).

47 Maoists also kidnapped hundreds: Ibid.

48 The Ministry of Foreign Affairs had mobilized . . . Arabic-language radio and television: "Report of the Commission of Inquiry."

52 The violence had started in full: Thomas E. Ricks, *Fiasco: The American Military Adventure in Iraq* (New York: Penguin Group, 2006).

52 Nearly one hundred contractors: Contractor casualty data collected by the author in 2005; similar data available at icasualties.org, "Iraqi Coalition Casualties: Contractors—A Partial List," http://icasualties.org/Iraq/Contractors.aspx.

55 Within just one day: "Report of the Commission of Inquiry."

55 They spontaneously and simultaneously attacked . . . that lasted four days: Ibid.

57 The meaning of loss . . . into the effigy: Sthaneshwar Timalsina, "Ritual, Reality, and Meaning: The Vedic Ritual of Cremating a Surrogate Body," *Zeitschrift der Deutschen Morgenländischen Gesellschaft* 159, no. 1 (January 2009): 45–69.

Chapter 4

62 Five-star hotels clad in white stone . . . the country's GDP: Ibrahim Saif and David M. DeBartolo, "The Iraq War's Impact on Growth and Inflation in

Jordan," research paper of the Center for Strategic Studies, University of Jordan, 2008, http://iraqslogger.powweb.com/downloads/cssjordan_report .pdf. For troop levels, see Amy Belasco, "Troop Levels in the Afghan and Iraq Wars, FY2001–FY2012: Cost and Other Potential Issues," Congressional Research Service, Washington, DC, 2009, https://fas.org/sgp/crs/natsec /R40682.pdf.

64 Mansour had told the wire service: Ravi Nessman, "Militant Website Reports That 12 Nepalese Hostages Slain in Iraq," Associated Press International wire, Aug. 31, 2004.

64 Mansour made a brief appearance: Shafika Mattar, "Jordan-Based Firm Trying to Determine Fate of 12 Kidnapped Nepalese Workers Sent to Iraq," Associated Press International wire, Aug. 23, 2004.

64 In fact, the kidnappers themselves: "Islamist Group Says It Has Abducted 12 Nepalese in Iraq."

65 After Israel and Jordan officially ended their status as enemies: Mary Jane Bolle, Alfred B. Prados, and Jeremy M. Sharp, "Qualifying Industrial Zones in Jordan and Egypt," Congressional Research Service report, Washington, DC, 2006.

65 Those workers accounted for almost half: Ibid.

66 That wasn't the case for other, wealthier Middle Eastern nations: Among many such reports, see Ahn, *Migrant Workers and Human Rights.*

66 Workers routinely were lured abroad . . . a report by the United Nations' International Labour Organization: Gurung and Adhikari, "Nepal: The Prospects and Problems."

66 Many endured conditions akin to slavery: Romina Halabi, "Contract Enslavement of Female Migrant Domestic Workers in Saudi Arabia and the United Arab Emirates," in *Human Rights and Human Welfare* (online journal), https://www.du.edu/korbel/hrhw/researchdigest/slavery/fmd.pdf.

66 Employers or labor brokers in the destination countries . . . no legal representation: Pong-Suhl Ahn and Virginia N. Sherry, "Bad Dreams: Exploitation and Abuse of Migrant Workers in Saudi Arabia," in W. Brown and J. Saunders, eds., Human Rights Watch report, 2004, https://www.hrw.org /reports/2004/saudi0704/saudi0704.pdf; and Anh Nga Longva, "Keeping Migrant Workers in Check: The Kafala System in the Gulf," *Middle East Research* 211 (1999).

67 The ILO expert in Bangladesh . . . for importing workers: Tasneem Siddiqui, "Bangladesh: The Complexities and Management of Out-Migration," in Ahn, *Migrant Workers and Human Rights.*

68 Brokers and other business owners knew: Cam Simpson and Aamer Madhani, "U.S. Cash Fuels Human Trade," *Chicago Tribune*, Oct. 9, 2005.

68 wage rates plummeted by more than half: Siddiqui, "Bangladesh."

69 Officials across the U.S. government knew . . . could no longer be ignored: Simpson and Madhani, "U.S. Cash Fuels Human Trade."

72 Each Nepalese man carried with him a sealed envelope: Interviews with former workers by the author in Nepal, 2005 and 2016; and sworn declara-

tion of Biplav Bhatta, dated April 16, 2013, filed in *Adhikari et al. v. Daoud & Partners et al.*, Civil Action No. H-09-CV-1237, U.S. District Court for the Southern District of Texas.

73 Al-Nadi ran what Iraq War contractors called "body shops": See David Phinney, "They Forcibly Brought Me to Iraq," *CorpWatch*, Oct. 17, 2006, http://www.corpwatch.org/article.php?id=14178.

73 These small apartments sometimes housed: Interviews by the author in Jordan and Washington, DC, 2005; and unpublished U.S. government documents, including "SUBJECT: Contractor Personnel Authorized to Accompany the U.S. Armed Forces," Oct. 3, 2005, Instruction Number 3020.41, Department of Defense.

75 Daoud and Partners' presence, at least on paper: "Company Profile Report, Daoud & Partners Co. Ltd.," International Business Company Formation, Inc., unpublished subscription service report obtained by the author, generated April 2005.

75 That seemed beneath a pittance: Anna Fifield, "Contractors Reap $138bn from Iraq War," *Financial Times*, March 18, 2013.

81 A story appearing in the *Manila Standard*: Joyce Pangco Pañares, "Turkey Backs RP Ban on Deployment to Iraq," *Manila Standard*, Dec. 13, 2004.

82 Within a week of my meeting with al-Nadi: Nikko Dizon, "Filipino Worker Killed in Baghdad," *Philippine Daily Inquirer*, April 19, 2005; see also Joyce Pangco Pañares, "Government to Blacklist Firm That Recruited Ambushed OFW," *Manila Standard*, April 20, 2005; and Eloisa I. Calderon and Beverly T. Natividad, "RP Mulls Blacklisting Employer of Five OFWs Ambushed in Iraq," *Business World*, April 20, 2005.

Chapter 5

83 Only a widow dresses in a white sari: Punam Yadav, "The White Sari: Transforming Widowhood in Nepal," *Journal of Gender, Technology and Development* 20, no. 1 (2016): 2; see also Mukulika Banerjee and Daniel Miller, *The Sari* (London: Bloomsbury Academic, 2003).

95 In the early years of her marriage: Elisabeth Bumiller, *May You Be the Mother of a Hundred Sons: A Journey Among the Women of India* (New York: Random House, 1990).

Chapter 6

117 Bandits plagued the Amman-to-Baghdad highway: Author interviews, Amman, Jordan, and Washington, DC, 2005; and David Filipov, "Rebuilding Iraq, Letter from Iraq: Jordan-to-Baghdad Highway Fraught with Sticking Points," *Boston Globe*, Sept. 14, 2003; also Charlie Mayer, "The Road from Amman to Baghdad: An Online Report from Charlie Mayer, on Assignment in Iraq," *Beyond the War in Iraq* (blog), NPR.org, July 15, 2003, http://www.npr.org/news/specials/iraq2003/mayer_030715.html; and Michael Hastings, *I Lost My Love in Baghdad: A Modern War Story* (New York: Scribner, 2008).

117 Even though human cargo from Amman became more limited: Todd Pitman, "As Highway Violence Grows, Foreign Truckers Begin to Flee," Associated Press, July 28, 2004; Debra Amos, "Jordan, One of Iraq's Neighbors," *All Things Considered*, National Public Radio, Oct. 19, 2004.

118 By June 2004, the danger had so intensified . . . more essential than others': "Jordanian Truckers to Receive Iraqi Police Protection on Border Roads— Iraqi Minister," IPR Strategic Business Information Database, July 1, 2004; and Pitman, "As Highway Violence Grows."

118 American civilian personnel were flown: Interviews conducted by the author, Washington, DC, and Amman, Jordan, 2005; and Cam Simpson, "Pipeline to Peril: Desperate for Work, Lured into Danger," *Chicago Tribune*, Oct. 9–10, 2005.

118 On July 26, 2004: Author interviews in Amman, Jordan, 2005; and Pitman, "As Highway Violence Grows."

119 Still, flying the men to Baghdad was out of the question: E-mail exchange obtained by the author between Daoud and Partners and KBR, dated Aug. 31, 2003.

120 Word went out to Daoud and KBR executives: Interviews by the author in Amman, Jordan, 2005; and an internal KBR site status report for Aug. 20–21, 2004, obtained by the author, which states that "12 more hostages were taken last night. Nepalese coming to work the laundry."

Chapter 7

133 Richard B. Cheney wanted to run for president: Tara Trower, "Cheney to Take Charge at Halliburton; Former Defense Secretary Named Chairman, CEO," *Dallas Morning News*, Aug. 11, 1995.

134 his former company was the war's largest private partner: Fifield, "Contractors Reap $138bn from Iraq War."

134 Damage to Halliburton endured: Harris Insights and Analytics, "The Harris Poll Releases Annual Reputation Rankings for the 100 Most Visible Companies in the U.S.," Feb. 18, 2016, http://www.theharrispoll.com/business/Rep utation-Rankings-Most-Visible-Companies.html.

134 The outrage, however, has been somewhat misdirected: Dan Briody, *The Halliburton Agenda: The Politics of Oil and Money* (New York: Wiley, 2006), p. 153.

134 Herman Brown, the son of a grocer: Robert A. Caro, *The Path to Power: The Years of Lyndon Johnson* (New York: Vintage Books, Kindle ed., 1983), chap. 20.

134 When his men weren't in county jails: Ibid.

134 These weren't painted highways: Briody, *The Halliburton Agenda*, p. 20.

134 Brown started with four mules: Caro, *Path to Power*, chap. 20.

135 Road building was a tough business . . . the right Texas politicians: Ibid.

135 Someone inscribed George's high school yearbook: Briody, *The Halliburton Agenda*, p. 24.

135 Dan Root, who was married to the Brown brothers' sister: Ibid., pp. 25–26; and KBR's online company history, at https://www.kbr.com/about/our-com pany/history.

135 Although contemporaries considered George more genial: Robert A. Caro, *Means of Ascent: The Years of Lyndon Johnson* (New York: Vintage Books, 1991), p. 15.

135 They were racists: Caro, *Path to Power*, chap. 24.

135 Herman Brown also made a tidy sum: Ibid.

136 Brown and Root's lawyer and chief fixer . . . it also was a boondoggle: Briody, *The Halliburton Agenda*, pp. 47–48 and 56.

136 Johnson went to work . . . reportedly told one of his aides: Caro, *Path to Power*, chap. 24.

136 Their thanks were so great: Ibid.

137 Johnson and the Brown brothers entwined their fortunes: Ibid., introduction.

137 And the cash wasn't just for Johnson's own races: Caro, *Path to Power*, chaps. 31 and 32.

137 If Johnson's mammoth ambition . . . "the next plateau": Ibid., chap. 24.

137 As the 1930s drew to a close: Ibid., chap. 30.

138 Brown and Root wasn't qualified: Ibid.

138 The Browns quickly found another way . . . campaign cash: Ibid.

138 The Navy Department suddenly learned: Ibid.

139 The company's first experience . . . on time: Briody, *The Halliburton Agenda*, pp. 81–85.

139 The Browns could apply such lessons: David Hunn, "Brown & Root Helped Pave Way for Houston's Growth," *Houston Chronicle*, July 12, 2016.

139 "Now Lyndon,": Briody, *The Halliburton Agenda*, p. 160.

140 Brown and Root became part of a private joint venture . . . cost-plus contract: Ibid., p. 164.

140 Antiwar protesters: Ibid., pp. 166–67.

140 None of this hindered Brown and Root's fortunes: Ibid., p. 168.

141 Before he retired: Harry Hurt, "The Most Powerful Texans," *Texas Monthly*, April 1976, p. 73.

141 After the rapid success of the Gulf War . . . let alone a private company: Briody, *The Halliburton Agenda*, p. 184; and P. W. Singer, *Corporate Warriors: The Rise of Privatized Military Industry* (Ithaca, NY: Cornell University Press, Kindle ed., 2007).

142 A national contractors' lobbying group would call it: Anthony Bianco and Stephanie Anderson Forest, "Outsourcing War: An Inside Look at Brown & Root, the Kingpin of America's New Military-Industrial Complex," *Business-Week*, Sept. 15, 2003.

142 Brown and Root's workers increasingly deployed . . . piece of the LOGCAP business: "War and Piecework," *The Economist*, U.S. ed., July 10, 1999; and Greg Schneider and Tom Ricks, "Profits in 'Overused' Army; Cheney Slams Deployments That Benefit His Former Firm," *Washington Post*, Sept. 9, 2000.

143 Before long, though, government auditors raised . . . over five years: Briody, *The Halliburton Agenda*, p. 202.

143 By 2000 . . . Balkans extension: Ibid., p. 186; and Schneider and Ricks, "Profits in 'Overused' Army."

144 The LOGCAP contract neared its expiration . . . December 17, 2001, press release: Halliburton press release, as distributed by PR Newswire; and prepared testimony of Alfred V. Neffgen, CEO, KBR Government Operations, submitted to the Committee on Government Reform, U.S. House of Representatives, Washington, DC, July 22, 2004.

144 Secretary of Defense Donald Rumsfeld beamed . . . "ways to destabilize the Iraqi leader were under way": David E. Sanger, "A Nation Challenged: Policy—'On a Roll, but Where?'" *New York Times*, Dec. 17, 2001.

146 The base PX: T. Christian Miller, *Blood Money: Wasted Billions, Lost Lives, and Corporate Greed in Iraq* (New York: Little, Brown and Company, Kindle ed., 2006).

146 Contractors at war . . . would outnumber U.S. forces: Office of the Special Inspector General for Iraq Reconstruction, *Hard Lessons: The Iraq Reconstruction Experience*, U.S. Independent Agencies and Commissions, Washington, DC, 2009, p. 38 of publicly released draft, https://usiraq.procon.org/sourcefiles /hard_lessons12–08.pdf.

146 Yet security contractors made up only 16 percent: Sarah Stillman, "The Invisible Army," *The New Yorker*, June 6, 2011.

147 Madhani's reporting drew praise: William Langewiesche, "Welcome to the Green Zone: The American Bubble in Baghdad," *The Atlantic*, November 2004.

147 KBR called a large segment of the forty-eight-thousand . . . was growing fast: Author interviews, Amman, Jordan, and Washington, DC, 2004–2005; and Simpson and Madhani, "U.S. Cash Fuels Human Trade."

149 Subcontracting bosses routinely took and held these documents: *Trafficking in Persons Report*, U.S. Department of State, June 2005, p. 37, and MNF-I FRAGO 06–188 [Trafficking in Persons], General George W. Casey (April 4, 2006), order obtained by the author.

151 We gave Halliburton sixty detailed . . . "expected to follow in every aspect of their work": Written correspondence between the author and Melissa Norcross, Halliburton public relations, Aug. 12 and 18, 2005.

152 The U.S. Army, which had oversight for the contract . . . "not Army issues": Simpson and Madhani, "U.S. Cash Fuels Human Trade."

153 And prominent figures had publicly raised . . . absolved itself of any related responsibility: Correspondence between members of the U.S. Helsinki Commission and the Honorable Richard L. Armitage, deputy secretary of state, May 5, 2003, obtained by the author; and correspondence between the Honorable Christopher H. Smith, congressman from New Jersey and chairman of the U.S. Helsinki Commission, and Joseph E. Schmitz, Office of the Inspector General, Department of Defense, Aug. 25, 2005, also obtained by the author.

154 In meetings with senior U.S. military officials: Correspondence between Smith and Schmitz.

154 Defense Secretary Donald Rumsfeld . . . remains unknown: Donald Rumsfeld, "Combatting Trafficking in Persons," Memorandum No. OSD11599–04, Sept. 16, 2004, contained in the case record for *Adhikari v. Daoud*.

156 Cheney got a deferred salary and bonuses: David E. Rosenbaum, "A Closer Look at Cheney and Halliburton," *New York Times*, Sept. 28, 2004.

156 GAO auditors . . . "purchasing system controls": James Cox, "Halliburton Under Pressure from Many Angles," *USA Today*, July 22, 2004.

156 These were among the earliest signs . . . $700 million for dining facility services: Commission on Wartime Contracting in Iraq and Afghanistan, "Final Report to Congress: Transforming Wartime Contracting; Controlling Costs, Reducing Risks," Washington, DC, 2011, pp. 75–85.

156 One day after the release of a 2004 GAO report: Prepared testimony of Alfred V. Neffgen, CEO, KBR Government Operations, submitted to the Committee on Government Reform, U.S. House of Representatives, Washington, DC, July 22, 2004.

Chapter 8

161 Even within ethnic groups and regions where *sati* wasn't practiced: Yadav, "The White Sari."

162 In 2005, the same year Kamala joined the ashram: Ibid.

Chapter 9

174 This side of the firm's practice . . . Department of Justice: Author interviews, Washington and London, 2016; and Robert D. McFadden, "Jerry S. Cohen, 70, Labor and Class-Action Lawyer, Is Dead," *New York Times*, Jan. 1, 1996.

175 Like his mentor: Kurt Eichenwald, "Texaco to Make Record Payout in Bias Lawsuit," *New York Times*, Nov. 16, 1996.

175 He spent the firm's vast resources . . . off the backs of concentration camp slaves: Author interviews, Washington and London, 2016; and Michael J. Bazyler, *Holocaust Justice: The Battle for Restitution in America's Courts* (New York: NYU Press, Kindle ed., 2003).

179 She had taken on the lead litigation role: Steve Coll, *Private Empire: Exxon-Mobil and American Power* (New York: Penguin Press, 2012), p. 405.

180 The theory behind the World War II–era law . . . Department of Labor: See the ProPublica series, "Disposable Army: Civilian Contractors in Iraq and Afghanistan," https://www.propublica.org/series/disposable-army.

191 Just weeks before the *Tribune* stories: See p. 2 of Francis T. Miko and the Congressional Research Service, "Trafficking in Persons: The U.S. and International Response," Library of Congress, Washington, DC, Jan. 19, 2006, https://pdfs .semanticscholar.org/eb12/f56c8b855d8445e0dba222edb7f83659390c.pdf.

193 The resulting memorandum verified the *Tribune* investigation . . . "U.S. persons or U.S. contractors": Thomas F. Gimble, principal deputy of Department of Defense Office of Inspector General, "Memorandum for Under Secretary of Defense (Personnel and Readiness): Alleged Trafficking in Persons Practices by Department of Defense Contractors in Iraq," April 14, 2006, obtained by the author and also filed in the case record of *Adhikari v. Daoud*.

Chapter 10

215 On the second wave of Holocaust cases: Bazyler, *Holocaust Justice*.

Chapter 12

245 In so doing, Wright waged a one-man battle . . . hung in the White House during Obama's presidency: Prepared remarks of Judge Keith P. Ellison on the occasion of Black History Month, February 2006; and Jack Bass, *Unlikely Heroes* (New York: Simon and Schuster, 1981).

246 One day, the young clerk made a reference to their shared experience: Ellison, prepared remarks on the occasion of Black History Month.

247 Wright once borrowed from the children's author Theodor Geisel: Speech by Ruth Bader Ginsburg, "Judge Robert A. Ainsworth Jr. Memorial Lecture: Four Louisiana Giants in the Law," Loyola University New Orleans, School of Law, February 4, 2002, http://www.supremecourt.gov/publicinfo/speeches /sp_02–04–02.html.

247 After Ellison clerked for Wright: *Confirmation Hearings on Federal Appointments, Hearing Before the Committee on the Judiciary, United States Senate,* 106th Cong. (June 13, July 29, Sept. 14, Oct. 7, and Nov. 10, 1999), Part 1A, Serial No. J-106–33 (Washington, DC: U.S. Government Printing Office, 2005).

Chapter 13

278 In the end, members of the jury didn't buy her story: Paul Oldenburgh, *6 Days in Baghdad: Jamie Leigh Jones and Her Story of Sexual Assault as Told at Trial in Houston* (Houston, TX: self-published, 2012); Stephanie Mencimer, "Why Jamie Leigh Jones Lost Her KBR Rape Case; Her Story of a Brutal Attack in Iraq Sparked a National Outcry—but the Jury Didn't Buy It," *Mother Jones,* July 7, 2011; and Stephanie Mencimer, "The War of Rape: What Happened to Jamie Leigh Jones in Iraq?" *Washington Monthly,* Nov./Dec. 2013.

278 the company's lawyers had asked . . . "That Doesn't Mean Most Women Do": "Key Events in the Story of Jamie Leigh Jones," *Houston Chronicle,* Oct. 2, 2011; and Mike Tolson, "Court Costs Awarded to KBR Lawyers in Rape Case; Claimant Lost Suit, Ordered to Pay $145,000," *Houston Chronicle,* Sept. 28, 2011.

Chapter 15

333 Before he became a judge . . . "should resign": *Confirmation Hearings: Hearing Before the Committee on the Judiciary.*

335 Blackmun was known as someone who was unyieldingly fair: Diane P. Wood, "Justice Harry A. Blackmun and the Virtues of Independence," 71 *North Dakota Law Review* 25 (1995), available at http://chicagounbound.uchicago .edu/cgi/viewcontent.cgi?article=3043&context=journal_articles.

SELECTED BIBLIOGRAPHY

Although not all of these are cited in the "Note on Sources," I found them all useful in the writing of this book.

Banerjee, Mukulika, and Daniel Miller. *The Sari*. London: Bloomsbury Academic, 2003.

Bass, Jack. *Unlikely Heroes*. New York: Simon and Schuster, 1981.

Bazyler, Michael J. *Holocaust Justice: The Battle for Restitution in America's Courts*. New York: NYU Press, 2003.

Bradley, Mark Philip. *The World Reimagined; Americans and Human Rights in the Twentieth Century*. Cambridge, UK: Cambridge University Press, 2016.

Bravin, Jess. *The Terror Courts: Rough Justice at Guantanamo Bay*. New Haven, CT: Yale University Press, 2013.

Breyer, Stephen. *The Court and the World: American Law and the New Global Realities*. New York: Knopf Doubleday, 2015.

Briody, Dan. *The Halliburton Agenda: The Politics of Oil and Money*. New York: Wiley, 2006.

Cameron, Mary M. *On the Edge of the Auspicious: Gender and Caste in Nepal*. Urbana and Chicago: University of Illinois Press, and Kathmandu: Mandala Publications, 1998 and 2005.

Caro, Robert A. *Means of Ascent: The Years of Lyndon Johnson*. New York: Vintage Books, 1991.

Caro, Robert A. *The Path to Power: The Years of Lyndon Johnson*. New York: Vintage Books, 1983.

Coll, Steve. *Private Empire: ExxonMobil and American Power*. New York: Penguin Press, 2012.

Fallows, James. *Blind into Baghdad: America's War in Iraq*. New York: Knopf Doubleday, 2009.

Kipp, Eva. *Bending Bamboo, Changing Winds: Nepali Women Tell Their Life Stories*. Delhi and Kathmandu: Book Faith India and Pilgrims Publishing, 1995 and 2006.

Miller, T. Christian. *Blood Money: Wasted Billions, Lost Lives, and Corporate Greed in Iraq*. New York: Little, Brown and Company, 2006.

Oldenburgh, Paul. *6 Days in Baghdad: Jamie Leigh Jones and Her Story of Sexual Assault as Told at Trial in Houston*. Houston, TX: self-published on Amazon by a juror in the trial, 2012.

Olds, Sally Wendkos. *A Balcony in Nepal: Glimpses of a Himalayan Village*. Delhi: Ardash Books, 2004.

Pandey, Sita. *Fever*. New Delhi: Nirala Publications, 2004.

Parijat, *Under the Sleepless Mountain*. Varanasi, India: Pilgrims Publishing, 2007.

Pratt, Joseph A., and Christopher J. Castañeda. *Builders: Herman and George R. Brown*. College Station: Texas A&M University Press, 1999.

Ricks, Thomas E. *Fiasco: The American Military Adventure in Iraq*. New York: Penguin Group, 2006.

Singer, P. W. *Corporate Warriors: The Rise of Privatized Military Industry*. Ithaca, NY: Cornell University Press, 2007.

Stephenson, Joanne. *Rawa Dolu: The Story of a Mountain Village*. Pittsburgh and Kathmandu: Dorrance Publishing and Pilgrims Book House, 1996.

Thapa, Deepak, and Bandita Sijapati. *A Kingdom Under Siege: Nepal's Maoist Insurgency, 1996 to 2004*. Kathmandu: Printhouse, 2004.

Thapa, Manjushree. *Forget Kathmandu: An Elegy for Democracy*. London and New Delhi: Penguin Books, 2005.

Upadhyaya, Eda, ed. *Hulaki: A Collection of Short Stories from Nepal*. Kathmandu: Institute of Advanced Communication and Research, 2013.

INDEX

ABOUT THE AUTHOR

CAM SIMPSON is an international investigations editor and writer for *Bloomberg Businessweek* magazine and Bloomberg News, where he has worked since 2010. Previously, he was a Middle East correspondent and Washington correspondent for the *Wall Street Journal*, and worked in Chicago, in Washington, and overseas for the *Chicago Tribune*. Among the honors he's received during three decades of reporting are two George Polk Awards, three awards from the Overseas Press Club of America, the Robert F. Kennedy Journalism Award for international reporting, and the Gerald Loeb Award for magazine writing. He lives in London. Visit camsimpson.com to learn more.